The New Politics of Unemployment

Since 1980 average unemployment in the European Union has never dropped below 8 per cent. Mass unemployment has been a feature of Western Europe ever since the mid 1970s. Even countries such as Sweden, Austria and Switzerland, which previously kept unemployment under control, now have levels comparable to the rest of Europe. Orthodox policies designed to fight unemployment have clearly failed: alternatives are needed.

In this innovative study radical unemployment policies from Germany, France, Italy, Britain, Spain, Denmark, Norway, Switzerland and the EU are laid out and evaluated with respect to their political acceptability in order to determine under what conditions they would receive a sufficient level of support to be accepted as government policy and implemented on a large scale. In order to make systematic comparison possible, all the contributions use a common definition of 'radical unemployment policy', a common chapter format, and provide especially detailed analyses of a particular common policy – work-sharing. The final chapter builds on this by using a comparative perspective to test a number of current theories about policy innovation.

The New Politics of Unemployment is a valuable contribution to the study of public policy in Europe and will be a vital resource for students of European politics as well as public policy.

Hugh Compston teaches politics at the School of European Studies, University of Wales, Cardiff.

European Political Science Series
Edited by Hans Keman
Vrije University, Amsterdam, on behalf of the European Consortium for Political Research

The European Political Science Series is published in Association with the European Consortium for Political Research – the leading organisation concerned with the growth and development of political science in Europe. The series will present high-quality edited volumes on topics at the leading edge of current interest in political science and related fields, with contributions from European scholars and others who have presented work at ECPR workshops or research groups.

Sex Equality Policy in Western Europe
Edited by Frances Gardiner

Democracy and Green Political Thought
Sustainability, rights and citizenship
Edited by Brian Doherty and Marius de Geus

Citizenship, Democracy and Justice in the New Europe
Edited by Percy Lehning and Albert Weale

The New Politics of Unemployment

Radical policy initiatives in
Western Europe

Edited by Hugh Compston

London and New York

First published 1997
by Routledge
11 New Fetter Lane, London EC4P 4EE

Simultaneously published in the USA and Canada
by Routledge
29 West 35th Street, New York, NY 10001

© 1997 Hugh Compston, selection and editorial matter;
individual chapters, the contributors

Typeset in Times Ten by Florencetype Ltd, Stoodleigh, Devon

Printed and bound in Great Britain by
Mackays of Chatham PLC, Chatham, Kent

British Library Cataloguing in Publication Data
A catalogue record for this book is available from the British Library

Library of Congress Cataloging in Publication Data
The new politics of unemployment: radical policy initiatives
   in Western Europe / edited by Hugh Compston.
      Includes bibliographical references and index.
      1. Full employment policies – Europe – Case studies.
      2. Unemployment – Europe – Case studies.   I. Compston, Hugh, 1955–
HD5764.A6N48   1996
331.13.794 – dc20   96–26288

ISBN   0–415–15054–X (hbk)
ISBN   0–415–15055–8 (pbk)

Contents

Series editor's preface   vii
List of figures   ix
List of tables   x
List of contributors   xi

Introduction   1

1 **The European Union**   6
  Hugh Compston

2 **Germany**   21
  Ulrich Widmaier and Susanne Blancke

3 **France**   47
  Susan Milner and René Mouriaux

4 **Italy**   68
  Elisabetta Gualmini

5 **Britain**   87
  Jonathan Tonge

6 **Spain**   103
  Martin Rhodes

7 **Denmark**   123
  Jørn Loftager and Per Kongshøj Madsen

8 **Norway**   146
  Thore K. Karlsen

9 **Switzerland**   168
  Kermit Blank

10 **Comparisons and conclusions**   188
  Hugh Compston

Index   215

Series editor's preface

Levels of unemployment have been increasing in Europe over a long period, and they remain high notwithstanding recent signs of economic recovery and some growth of the world economy. Western European countries have been strongly affected by the economic recession, part of what has been called the 'stagflation crisis' existing since the mid 1970s. Many studies have been published on the effects of the crisis in terms of widespread and enduring unemployment – especially as this relates to the opportunities for lower skilled and younger people on the one hand, and for the re-entry to the workforce of women and older workers on the other. In short, we are confronted with deepseated public concern in Europe, and a political problem to which there appears no easy solution by means of public policy formation.

The problem of unemployment is a particularly urgent one for the European Union, whose unemployment levels are high compared to other OECD countries. It cries out for an analysis of the relationship between the policy capacities of the EU – especially after the creation of a Single Market and the signing of the Maastricht Treaty in 1991 – and policy initiatives at the national level. There are two compelling reasons for this, apart from the unemployment problem *per se*: first, the Single Market stimulates freedom of movement of labour within the EU and thus affects national employment policies; second, the EU as a political body has declared the struggle against unemployment a common concern for all member states, and one which ought to be coordinated – as far as 'subsidiarity' allows – in policy efforts. It is now questionable whether the EU member states are capable of coping with these problems at a national level by means of public regulation and related domestic policymaking.

It is thus an appropriate moment for the European Political Science Series to publish a volume on the relationship between national policies and policy efforts at the EU level. Addressing this topic and related issues from the perspective of political economy is clearly a task for political scientists. Thorough comparative analysis and a concern for the unemployed that transcends national or even parochial interests is to be welcomed when economic arguments, however valuable they may seem,

have offered few practical solutions in terms of policy proposals successful in reducing levels of unemployment.

This volume represents another example of what the European Political
Science Series, a collaboration between the European Consortium of
Political Research and Routledge, is trying to achieve. Here we have
a political science which not only deals with issues and topics that are
of special contemporary relevance, but which offers an approach based
on thorough analysis informed by the latest theoretical insights and
supported by convincing arguments and evidence.

The contributors to this second volume in the series go beyond
existing domestic practices of employment policy. The shared idea and
common focus underlying each chapter is an exploration of 'radical'
initiatives, whether these be at an EU or national level. The strength and
attractiveness of the approach adopted throughout this volume is that the
contributors do not attempt to present clear-cut answers nor to come up
with idealistic solutions. Rather, they discuss the various initiatives and
related policy proposals in great detail for the countries under review as
well as in relation to developments at the EU level.

Each chapter focuses on alternative policy programmes to reduce
unemployment by means of the creation and redistribution of work:
time-sharing and job-sharing are carefully discussed in the light of possible
political and economic objections; political obstacles to accepting new
policies and institutional constraints to their implementation are taken into
account; finally, the possibility and viability of radical initiatives are assessed
within the context of domestic politics and types of policy concentration,
both at the (sub)national and transnational levels of democratic decision-
making. The concluding chapter highlights not only the analytical results of
the country studies, but also attempts to re-establish the comparative
insights gained and the commonalities underlying radical policy initiatives
in the West European countries under review in relation to recent developments in the European Union.

To be sure, there are no final answers to be found in this book. It is
precisely the recognition of this, together with the contributors' thoughtful
consideration of the range of possible answers, which makes this collection
of essays essential reading, not only for political scientists and social
economists, but for all those concerned about the creation of a sustainable
and acceptable level of employment in Western Europe.

Professor Hans Keman
Wassenaar, July 1996

Figures

1.1 Unemployment in the EU   7
2.1 Unemployment in Germany, 1972–1994   22
2.2 Four potential arenas to conduct unemployment policies
    in Germany   37
3.1 Unemployment in France, 1972–1995   51
4.1 Unemployment in Italy, 1972–1995   69
5.1 Unemployment in Britain, 1972–1995   88
6.1 Unemployment in Spain, 1972–1995   104
7.1 Unemployment in Denmark, 1950–1995   124
7.2 Expenditure on labour market policy in the EU, 1990,
    1991 or 1992   125
7.3 Number of paid leaves granted in first three quarters of
    1994 in Denmark   129
8.1 Unemployment in Norway, 1972–1995   147
8.2 Trade union membership in Norway, 1988–1993   163
9.1 Unemployment in Switzerland, 1972–1995   169
9.2 Total Swiss labour force, 1975–1994   175
9.3 Foreign labour force adjustment in Switzerland (by category)   177
9.4 Use of short-time workers in Switzerland, 1975–1994   178
9.5 Contribution of short-time work to employment in
    Switzerland, 1975–1994   179
10.1 Deregulation initiatives and union strength   197
10.2 Part-time work initiatives and union strength   198
10.3 Private sector solidarity agreements and union strength   199
10.4 Solidarity agreements and industrial action   200
10.5 Solidarity agreements and Catholic trade union confederations 201
10.6 Deregulation and left/right governments   205
10.7 Part-time work initiatives and left/right governments   205
10.8 Firm-level work-sharing and left/right governments   206
10.9 Solidarity agreements and Catholicism   207

Tables

1.1 Radical unemployment policies at the EU level 8
2.1 Radical unemployment policies in Germany 25
3.1 Trends in 'precarious' forms of employment in France, 1993–1994 52
3.2 Radical unemployment policies in France 54
3.3 Guy Aznar's 1993 proposals on work-sharing 61
3.4 Estimated job creation potential of work-sharing proposals in France 62
4.1 Mainstream labour policies at the end of the 1980s in Italy 71
4.2 Radical unemployment policies in Italy 74
5.1 Mainstream unemployment policies in Britain, 1995 89
5.2 Radical unemployment policies in Britain, 1995 91
5.3 Constraints upon the development of radical unemployment policies in Britain 97
6.1 Radical unemployment policies in Spain 107
7.1 Danish paid leave arrangements, 1994 127
7.2 Costs and benefits of paid leave arrangements in Denmark 132
7.3 Attitudes towards paid leave arrangements in Denmark 141
8.1 Radical unemployment policies in Norway 155
9.1 Radical unemployment policies in Switzerland 176
9.2 Recent Swiss initiatives on reducing working time 185
10.1 Radical unemployment policies in Western Europe, 1990–1995 190

Contributors

Susanne Blancke is Assistant to the Chair of Political Science, Comparative Politics and Public Policy at the Ruhr-Universität Bochum, and has published on issues relating to labour relations and trade unions.

Kermit Blank is a doctoral researcher at the University of North Carolina, Chapel Hill, and is currently doing research at the Institut für Politik-wissenschaft at the University of Bern for his dissertation *Globalisation and the Political Economy of Unemployment*.

Hugh Compston lectures in the School of European Studies, University of Wales, Cardiff. His main research interest is the politics of unemployment in Western Europe. Recent publications include statistical studies of trade union participation in economic policymaking and its impact on unemployment.

Elisabetta Gualmini is a doctoral researcher at the Centre for Public Policy Analysis at the University of Political Science in Bologna. Her main research interests are policy analysis and organisational theory.

Thore K. Karlsen is a researcher at the Institute for Applied Social Science in Oslo.

Jørn Loftager is Associate Professor in the Department of Political Science, University of Aarhus. His main research interests are social and political theory and labour market policy. Among recent publications is 'Citizens' income – a new welfare state strategy?', in *The Rationality of the Welfare State*, E.O. Eriksen and J. Loftager (eds) (forthcoming).

Per Kongshøj Madsen is Associate Professor at the Institute of Political Science, University of Copenhagen. His main research interests are economic policy, the political aspects of economic planning and macro-economic modelling, and labour market and industrial economics.

Susan Milner is Senior Lecturer in European Studies at the University of Bath. Among her recent publications are *The Dilemmas of Inter-nationalism: the French Syndicalist Movement and the International Trade Union Movement* (1990), plus articles and chapters on the French labour movement and on vocational training as an issue in European labour relations.

René Mouriaux is Professor at the Centre d'études de la vie politique francaise, Fondation Nationale des Sciences Politiques, Paris.

Martin Rhodes is currently on secondment from the Department of Government, University of Manchester, to the Robert Schuman Centre at the European University Institute, Florence. Among his recent publications are *The Regions and the New Europe* (ed.), (1995) plus articles and chapters on European industrial relations, social policy and political economy.

Jonathan Tonge is Lecturer in Politics in the Department of Politics and Contemporary History, European Studies Research Institute, University of Salford. Among his recent publications are several articles on the role of Training and Enterprise Councils in combating unemployment in Britain.

Ulrich Widmaier is Professor of Political Science, Comparative Politics and Public Policy at the Ruhr-Universität Bochum, and director of a large-scale panel study on the efforts of the German mechanical engineering industry to cope with increased international competition. He has published widely in the fields of comparative politics, political economy, research methodology and the labour market.

Introduction

Hugh Compston

For we who live in the mid 1990s, mass unemployment is a fixed feature of the economic, social and political landscape. The precise level fluctuates, but since 1980 average unemployment in European Union countries has never dropped below 8 per cent and each peak – and trough – has been higher than the last. Various policies have been tried to stem this rising tide, but even the previously successful low-unemployment regimes of Sweden, Austria and Switzerland, which resisted the general trend until the early 1990s, resist no longer: mass unemployment is now endemic.

In policy terms this means that the unemployment policies being practised today have failed. Policies designed to keep unemployment low coexist with high levels of unemployment. It may be that no conceivable policy could have prevented the emergence and persistence of mass unemployment, but it is nevertheless quite clear that the ones that have been tried have failed.

It follows from this that if mass unemployment is to be beaten – a big 'if' – then new policies will have to be devised and put into practice, policies which depart from the failed orthodoxies of the present: radical unemployment policies. From the point of view of reducing unemployment it is pointless simply staying with the status quo: the possibility cannot be excluded that current policies will start to bring unemployment down if they are persevered with, but past experience suggests that this is unlikely. Thus new policies must be tried to supplement – or replace – the policies that have manifestly failed. In the end these new policies may not work either, but if we don't try them we will never know.

If one accepts that new policies need to be sought, the next question may well be, which new policies? One purpose of this book is to put together a menu of possible candidates from a number of West European countries. This has not been done before.

Subsequently attention may well move on to the economic merits or otherwise of specific policies: if implemented, would they really reduce unemployment? This is an important issue, and we do deal with it in the course of our analyses, but it is not the main focus of the book.

Instead we address a related issue that is just as important, but political rather than economic. In evaluating radical unemployment policies an answer to the economic question is not enough: even if a new policy would work in theory, it would still not be a solution to unemployment unless it were in practice politically possible to introduce it and have it accepted and implemented in a large-scale manner. Economic soundness by itself may not necessarily be sufficient to ensure this.

It is therefore the aim of this book to analyse the political dynamics of a number of recent radical unemployment policies and policy proposals in Western Europe – the new politics of unemployment – with a view to identifying at least some of the conditions under which they might break through to become standard components of national and EU strategies to bring down unemployment. A belief among policymakers that such policies are economically efficacious is one such condition, but there are also other more overtly political factors, such as individual and institutional financial self-interest, that may influence whether particular policies are accepted or rejected. Thus we consider the influence of economic beliefs as a political factor, as distinct from analysing their economic worth, but only as one such factor among others: it is the range of political factors as a whole that interests us.

No-one has ever analysed the political dynamics of radical unemployment policies in this way before. This is not to say that no-one has ever analysed the politics of particular radical policies – that would be absurd – but no-one has ever sought to gather together a host of such policies and subject them to systematic political analysis for the purpose of shedding light on their future chances of implementation. Ours is therefore an exploratory study rather than a definitive one, but in being exploratory it has the considerable advantage of opening up a lot of new terrain to our view.

The method we have used to investigate the politics of radical unemployment policies is to examine the political dynamics at both European Union level and national level. We then compare the findings of the resulting case studies in order to draw some general conclusions about the politics of these policies and the conditions under which they might be adopted as part of the armoury of unemployment policies in Western Europe.

Our study covers eight West European industrial democracies: all five of the biggest – Germany, France, Italy, Britain and Spain – plus three of the smaller countries: Denmark, Norway and Switzerland. We also include a chapter on the European Union, at which level economic policies have changed significantly since 1992. Although it would have been preferable to obtain analyses of all OECD countries, which as economically-advanced Western democracies might be considered the relevant population of polities, our nine cases are sufficient to enable at least some meaningful comparisons to be made.

Investigating the politics of radical unemployment policies even in just eight countries, plus the EU, reveals a whole new world of innovative ideas and practices, far too many for all of them to be analysed in detail in a book of this size. In order to make systematic comparison possible over all eight countries and the EU for at least one type of policy, all contributors provide especially detailed analyses of a particular common policy: work-sharing. We might equally well have chosen something else to concentrate on, but work-sharing is appropriate as the policy focus because it is an unorthodox policy that has been on the recent political agenda (at least) of almost all the countries covered.

Comparison is also facilitated by all contributors using a common definition of 'radical unemployment policy', and a common chapter format, as follows.

DEFINITION OF 'RADICAL UNEMPLOYMENT POLICY'

Conceptually, the term 'radical unemployment policy' is defined as a policy or policy proposal directed at significantly reducing unemployment that is new at the European level and/or the national level. By 'new' is meant both policies officially accepted and implemented since 1990 and policy proposals that have yet to be officially accepted or implemented.

Operationally, the common definition of 'radical unemployment policy' has two specific criteria.

First, that a policy is plausibly asserted by proponents as being capable of significantly reducing unemployment. By 'plausibly asserted' is meant that it finds at least some support among recognised experts. This stipulation is designed to exclude crackpot ideas and to focus attention on the more important initiatives and innovations. Note that we do not foreclose options by making prior judgements as to the actual economic efficacy of new policies: plausibility is enough at this stage.

The second criterion is that a policy is either qualitatively innovative and new in the 1990s at the national level or outside the mainstream of West European economic policy as defined by the economic policy agreed at the EU level by all member states. This means that radical policies include not only those that are new at both EU and national levels, but also policies that are new at the national level but not the EU level, and policies that are new at the EU level but not at the national level. While this 'either/or' criterion yields a more diverse collection of policies than a more singular criterion would generate, it has the merit of enabling a wide range of non-mainstream policies to be collected for analysis.

The exact definition of what is new at the national level must perforce be left to each national specialist, but the specific indicator chosen for economic orthodoxy at the EU level is common to all: the Council Resolution of 21 December 1992 on the Need to Tackle the Serious and Deteriorating Situation Concerning Unemployment in the Community.

The reason for choosing this particular document is that it expresses agreed policy just before the extensive policy changes that started with the Edinburgh Growth Initiative of December 1992 – despite the fact that this Resolution was not formally passed by Council until ten days after the Edinburgh European Council.

In brief, the Resolution asserts that reduction of unemployment depends upon non-inflationary, lasting, environmentally sustainable and employment-creating economic growth, which in turn depends on productive investment, improving the competitiveness of enterprises, and sound conditions of economic demand. Achieving this was held to be essentially a matter for member states, but a role was also seen for coordinated supporting action at EU level, as well as for the participation of both sides of industry in searching for solutions. Four specific lines of approach were recommended:

1 Changes in work practices in order to take full advantage of changes in technology and markets.
2 Greater economic integration – that is, completion of the Single Market, closer economic convergence, and improved economic and social cohesion.
3 Improvements in the competitiveness of enterprises by (a) increasing the efficiency and adaptability of productive systems (for example by adopting new technologies); (b) providing support for new enterprises (especially small and medium enterprises); and (c) avoiding the imposition of new rigidities.
4 The adoption of appropriate labour market policies, in particular (a) high quality services for the unemployed and prospective employers (for example information, counselling, training, work experience, ready access for employers to suitable job applicants, and improved labour mobility); and (b) well-organised patterns of work that reflect the needs of enterprises and workers. Job-sharing was also listed here, but must be discounted in view of its utter rejection by member states in Council and the European Council in 1993: job-sharing is not, and never has been, a mainstream EU economic policy.

To sum up, radical unemployment policies are defined as those which are both economically plausible and either new at the national level or outside the categories of EU orthodox policy listed above.

CHAPTER FORMAT

To further facilitate comparisons, all case studies are organised under the same five headings:

1 *Introduction* – to give an idea of what is to follow.
2 *Context* – a short description of historical context, recent economic developments, institutional framework, and present mainstream policies.

3 *Radical unemployment policies* – short descriptions of the main radical unemployment policies current during the 1990s, including a fairly detailed description of work-sharing policies (if any).
4 *Political dynamics* – discussion and explanation of the political dynamics of (a) work-sharing proposals/programmes and (b) in some chapters, one or more of the other radical unemployment policies identified in the previous section.
5 *Outlook* – short discussions of the political outlook for the policies discussed in the previous section, with special attention to identifying conditions under which these might break through to become major mainstream policies.

We begin our study by looking at radical unemployment policies at the EU level. This is followed by eight national case studies, and the book concludes with a chapter in which the findings of the previous chapters are summarised and compared.

REFERENCE

Council Resolution of 21 December 1992 on the Need to Tackle the Serious and Deteriorating Situation Concerning Unemployment in the Community (93/C 49/02) *Social Europe* 2(93): pp.168–170.

ACKNOWLEDGEMENTS

This book is the initial result of a research project that began as a Workshop at the 1995 Joint Sessions of the European Consortium for Political Research in Bordeaux and continued under the aegis of the Employment Policy Innovation Research Network (EPIRN), a grouping of political scientists and political economists with members in almost all the countries of Western Europe. Research continues along the lines opened up so far, and we are hoping to extend our membership to encompass like-minded researchers in all the affluent industrial European democracies in due course. I would like to thank the members of EPIRN who contributed to this book, namely Susanne Blancke, Kermit Blank, Elisabetta Gualmini, Thore K. Karlsen, Jorn Løftager, Per Kongshøj Madsen, Susan Milner, René Mouriaux, Martin Rhodes, Jonathan Tonge, and Ulrich Widmaier. It has been a pleasure working with them. I would also like to thank David Hanley and David Jackson of the School of European Studies, University of Wales, who gave the project a push at the beginning; the European Consortium for Political Research, for bringing us all together at Bordeaux in May 1995; and Heikki Paloheimo, who contributed to the discussions there but was unable to contribute a chapter. I would also like to thank Ulrich Widmaier and Susanne Blancke for organising a second meeting in Bochum in September 1995 to finalise this manuscript.

1 The European Union

Hugh Compston

INTRODUCTION

With the increasing pace of European economic integration over the past ten years or so, one might expect that the European Union would take the lead in trying to find new ways of controlling unemployment. To a considerable extent this is indeed the case, especially with the 1993 Commission White Paper on Growth, Competitiveness and Employment. In this chapter, proposals from the White Paper and elsewhere for radical innovations in unemployment policy are set out and discussed, before work-sharing in particular is singled out for further analysis.[1]

CONTEXT

To some degree the European Union has always been designed to minimise unemployment. Even though 'a high level of employment' was not included as an official objective in the Treaty of Rome until its amendment at Maastricht in 1991 (Article 2), it was implicit in the Community's general strategy of facilitating economic growth by max-imising intra-Union trade through measures such as the Customs Union, the Single Market, and economic and monetary union. In addition, there are specific measures, such as the European Social Fund, that have been targeted on specific types of unemployment. Most major decisions on employment policy are taken using the consultation procedure, under which legislation is proposed by the Commission, often on the basis of unanimous agreements reached at the European Council level, then sent to the European Parliament for a non-binding Opinion before being sub-mitted to the Council of Ministers, where it requires unanimous approval to be passed. This means that the main players are the Commission and the member states: the European Parliament has a real say only on those relatively few occasions when legislation is considered using the cooper-ation procedure, under which legislation can be passed by Council by a qualified majority if Parliament approves the draft.

During the 1960s European integration was associated with high growth and low unemployment, but since then the economic strategy

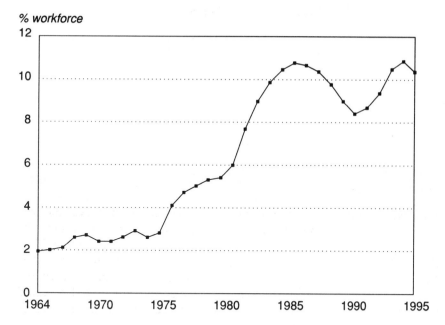

Figure 1.1 Unemployment in the European Union (12 member states)
Source: European Economy 59 (1995):193

of the EU has not worked very well: unemployment began to grow in 1974, and since 1980 average EU unemployment has never dropped below 8 per cent. Nevertheless, as the EU entered the 1990s its insti- tutions appeared confident that economic health and prosperity could be obtained by following a strategy of promoting non-inflationary growth and improved international competitiveness by completing the Single Market, controlling national budget deficits, keeping interest rates high, limiting wage growth below the rate of productivity growth, promoting closer economic convergence between member states, increasing labour market flexibility, supporting structural adjustment, encouraging small and medium enterprises, improving education and training, and facili- tating research and development (CEC 1990, 1991). Since the signing of the Maastricht Treaty this strategy has been complemented by moves towards economic and monetary union, including the adoption of economic policy guidelines for member states (*Bull. EC* 12-1993:7–11, Council 1994).

As the recession worsened in 1992, however, doubts began to creep in as to whether this approach was adequate, and unemployment moved to centre stage in the policy debate at the EU level (CEC 1993a). It was at this time that proposals for new approaches to unemployment policy

Table 1.1 Radical unemployment policies at the EU level

Strategy	Measures
Investment in infrastructure	Trans-European networks
Cuts in statutory charges on labour	(Implementation left to member states)
New areas of work	(Implementation left to member states)
Europe-wide Social Pact	(Not implemented)
Reductions in working time	(Not implemented)

began to receive a more sympathetic hearing, especially in the Commission, which produced its White Paper on Growth, Competitiveness and Employment in December 1993 (CEC 1993e).

RADICAL UNEMPLOYMENT POLICIES

The radical unemployment policies put forward at the EU level since 1992 can be divided into five main groups: as shown in Table 1.1.

Investment in infrastructure

This was the first new policy to be decided, in the form of the Edinburgh Growth Initiative of December 1992. It sought to provide 450,000 new jobs over two years by switching national public expenditure towards investment and increasing lending at the EU level for infrastructure (*Bull. EC* 12-1992:20–2, 4-1993:19, CEC 1993b). Although the use of public works to create jobs is a standard move at national level, at the EU level the idea is a new one. Its main focus is the programme for Trans-European Networks in the fields of transportation, telecommunications and energy.

Since 1992 the Commission and the European Parliament have been partly successful in persuading member states gradually to expand the EU lending facility for infrastructure programmes (CEC 1993e, EP 1995:63–5, Ecofin 16 March 1995, European Council 1993, 1994b). The reason for this success appears to be that member states view the Trans-European Networks not only as a direct job-creation measure but also as a means of improving the general functioning of the European economy.

However, a number of more ambitious loans proposals have been blocked, including a Commission proposal in 1992 for an economic stimulus equivalent to 1 per cent of Community GDP, blocked by Germany; a proposal in 1993 to double the size of the Edinburgh Growth Initiative, blocked by Britain, Germany, Denmark and the Netherlands; and a more recent French proposal to issue EU bonds up to a value of ECU 100 billion, blocked by Germany, Spain and Britain. The main reasons for resistance appear to be rejection of Keynesian ideas of stimulating the economy, and wariness of incurring debt at the EU level at a time when efforts were being made at the national level to reduce borrowing (*Financial Times* 1992:20; *Guardian* 26 October 1993:12, 6 December 1993:12; *European* 8 December 1993:1, 15 April 1994:1, 15 April 1994:1; *Independent* 29 November 1993:24; ER 1993:1).

In addition, implementation of the EU investment programme has been slow (European Council 1993, 1994, 1994a, 1995), and so far there does not appear to be any evidence to suggest that it has yet had any appreciable impact on unemployment.

Cuts in statutory charges on labour

Although the idea of pricing people into jobs by reducing employers' non-wage labour costs via cutting statutory charges on labour is not a new one at the national level, it did not become prominent at the EU level until 1993, when it emerged as one of the chief recommendations of the Commission White Paper. In Chapter 9 of the White Paper it is argued that a reduction in social security contributions equivalent to 1 per cent of GDP could lead to a reduction in unemployment of as much as 2.5 percentage points over four years if targeted on low-skilled workers (CEC 1993e:140). This proposal is perhaps the most popular of the radical unemployment policies discussed here, at least in principle, enjoying as it does the strong and continuing support not only of the Commission but also of the Parliament and the governments of all member states (EP 1994:64, Council 1994a:7, European Council 1993, 1994, 1994a, 1995).

The problem arises when it comes to deciding on compensation for the loss of revenue that such cuts in labour charges would cause. The Commission would prefer to introduce a resources tax for this purpose, but although France, Germany, the Netherlands and Denmark are broadly in favour of an EU resources tax – although not necessarily as a means of financing cuts in statutory charges on labour – the Southern European countries are doubtful and the British government is unequivocally opposed. For the moment at least the Commission has given up on the idea, and is devising guidelines to enable individual member states to introduce a CO_2 energy tax on a non-compulsory basis (CEC 1993d:24, CEC 1992, Guardian 7 June 1993:12, European Council 1994a:4). Member states have also rejected the alternative of introducing a tax on financial capital (CEC 1993d:24), and agreement has still not been reached on the other main possibility, which is to finance revenue shortfalls by coordinated rises in VAT.

As a consequence of the cost problem, implementation of the agreed policy of reducing statutory charges on labour is being left up to individual member states: at the EU level it is in effect blocked, due to the unwillingness of certain member states to agree to the institution of European-wide taxes to finance it.

New areas of work

This White Paper proposal aims at providing new jobs by mobilising regional and local initiatives to meet currently unmet needs in areas such as home help for the elderly, childcare, provision of leisure and cultural facilities, renovation of old housing, development of local public transport, maintenance of public areas, clean-up of pollution, and provision of energy-saving equipment. According to the White Paper these needs are not met by the market, due to the inability of beneficiaries to pay and the often degrading nature of the work involved, such as cleaning and personal service (CEC 1993e:19–20). However no action – such as funding – was proposed at the EU level to encourage such initiatives apart from the provision of information and advice, so that although this proposal was approved by the European Parliament and officially accepted by the December 1993 Brussels European Council, in effect action was left to the discretion of individual member states (CEC 1994a, CEC 1995, European Council 1993:9). It is unclear whether member states have done any more in this area as a result of EU exhortation than they would have anyway. In short, words but not deeds.

A Europe-wide social pact

In 1993 the government of Belgium proposed that member states, EU institutions, employers and trade unions should negotiate a corporatist-style agreement designed to promote economic recovery, along the lines of agreements concluded by a number of member states at national level. This was mentioned in passing in the White Paper, and has been raised occasionally by the European Parliament, but has made no progress at all at the Council or European Council level (CEC 1993f:17–18, CEC 1993e:15, EP 1995:64).

Reductions in working time

The idea of tackling unemployment by sharing out the available work among more people has been around at the EU level for some time, but it remained a relatively minor issue until 1992, when it came under active consideration by EU institutions as they searched for new ways to curb unemployment (e.g. Council 1993:170). One reason for this new interest was the realisation that forecast rates of economic growth did not appear to be sufficient to significantly reduce EU unemployment, which meant that if unemployment was to be significantly cut, then the employment intensity of growth had to be increased (CEC 1993e:123). As the Commission pointed out, the employment density of economic growth:

> is determined, not only by the relative use of capital and labour, which determines the volume of employment for a given volume of output,

but also by the way in which a given volume of employment is divided up between numbers of jobs and hours of work.

(CEC 1993c:100)

For this reason the issue of reduced working time was considered within the Commission as part of the process of drafting its White Paper for the European Council in Brussels in December 1993. As evidence that unemployment can in fact be reduced by reducing working hours, the Commission argued that about half of the 30 per cent rise in employment in the Netherlands between 1983 and 1991 could be attributed to a 13 per cent cut in average working hours per person per week over the same period (*Financial Times* 23 November 1993:2, CEC 1993e:126). Most of the drafting in the area of work-sharing was done by DGV (Employment, Industrial Relations and Social Affairs), although the Forward Studies Unit and the cabinet of Delors were also involved. By contrast, DGII (Economic and Financial Affairs), which prepared much of the rest of the White Paper, does not appear to have participated to any great degree. DGV Commissioner Flynn took the public relations initiative, for example suggesting the possibility of restructuring government income support in order to allow partial income support to be combined with income from work. Although this was not explicitly connected with the idea of work-sharing, it is clear that such a move would increase the financial attractiveness of part-time work, and in this way encourage work-sharing (Flynn 1993c).

Despite some generalised support for reducing working time from various EU policy actors, there does not appear to have been any concerted push from any quarter but the Commission. The European Parliament did express vague general support for the idea from time to time, but it was clearly not a high priority (EP 1992a:53, 1992b:592, 1993a:4–5, 1993b:8, *Bull. EU* 3-1994:11). One reason for this was a split between Left and Right: the Socialists explicitly recommended a general reduction in working time via agreement between employers and trade unions, provided that unit labour costs were not increased, but the conservative European Peoples Party was rather less enthusiastic (PES 1993:12, PPE 1993:3).

Employers and trade unions were also split on the issue. The European Trade Union Confederation (ETUC) has long favoured the idea of shorter hours without loss of pay, but its constituent national union confederations are somewhat divided, and the issue does not appear to be a major union priority. Employer groups were, and remain, implacably opposed to the idea of cutting working hours without proportionate cuts in pay, so it is not surprising that none of the EU forums in which both sides of industry were involved – the Economic and Social Committee, the Standing Committee on Employment, and the Social Dialogue – took a position on the issue (ETUC 1981:21, *Guardian* 15 May 1993:37, *Financial Times* 19 November 1993:2, ETUI 1988:46, ETUC 1994, Bastian 1994:305).

By late 1993 it was clear that drafts of the White Paper contained recommendations concerning shorter working time (*Guardian* 29 October 1993:10), and the penultimate draft, a twenty-five page paper prepared by the Commission for Ecofin in November 1993, explicitly argued that new jobs could be created 'by making increased use of part-time working, or by reducing working time by one means or another', provided that such reductions were consistent with maintaining or improving competitiveness and were applied at a decentralised company or administration level rather than being made mandatory by legislation (CEC 1993d:22). The draft then went on to say:

> This is such a novel move, though, that a flanking and incentive operation will be needed on the part of the authorities. The incentive aspect should be by reference to medium-term global objectives, to ensure that there are enough bold innovators to take the plunge; the flanking measures must concentrate on social protection facilities and reducing the negative effects of the lower level of income resulting from a reduction in individual average working hours.

(CEC 1993d:22)

This represents quite a radical step. The formulation is rather vague, with no specific measures being set out – although newspaper reports suggest that one thing the Commission had in mind was the gradual introduction of a four-day week (*European* 12 November 1993:2) – but it is clear that the Commission did envisage a general reduction in working hours, with proportionate wage reductions combined with measures on the part of authorities to offset the effects of these reductions on employees' living standards. This implies the use of policy instruments such as adjustments to employment law, wage subsidies and/or adjustments in taxes and social contributions of employers and/or employees.

When the draft White Paper was considered by Ecofin on 22 November 1993, however, its approach to reducing working time was categorically rejected by member states. According to press reports the result wasn't even close: the overwhelming majority of member states were opposed – ten out of twelve, according to British Chancellor Kenneth Clarke (*Financial Times* 23 November 1993:2; *Guardian* 23 November 1993:1). The unwillingness of member states to reveal the positions they take in Council meetings makes it difficult to ascertain these accurately, but it appears that the only two member states to support the idea were France and Belgium, both of which were making moves in this direction at the national level – and even France thought the Commission was going too far. The leading critics were Germany, Britain and Luxembourg, while the Spanish switched from support to opposition (*Financial Times* 10 November 1993:2; CEC 1993f:16; Bastian 1994:303, 306; ER 1903 24 November 1993:9; *Financial Times* 12 November 1993:2, 24 November 1993:2, 21; *Independent* 28 November 1993:15).

Shortly afterwards Commission President Jacques Delors seemed to subscribe to the majority view in Ecofin when he told a press conference that reducing working hours to share out employment was a Malthusian solution that would lead to despair: 'I refuse to recommend either an overall initiative, or regulations regarding work-sharing' (*Guardian* 4 December 1993:12). This was somewhat surprising from someone who had apparently backed the idea, but is consistent with reports that other policy actors, such as Commissioner Flynn and DGV, were the real motive forces within the Commission pushing the idea of shorter working time (Delors 1993, *Financial Times* 6 December 1993:2).

As a consequence of its rejection by Ecofin, the issue of reducing working time was de-emphasised in the final version of the White Paper, being relegated from one page in a twenty-five-page paper to one page in a 151-page book, and from a section entitled 'The question of work sharing' to one entitled 'Flexibility and job creation', in which the Commission recommended that member states should (1) encourage a reduction in the working week and/or annualised hours, in the context of increasing utilisation of capital equipment; (2) ensure that those who work shorter hours do not suffer loss of social protection or poorer working conditions; (3) minimise artificial financial incentives for those of above-average incomes to work overtime; (4) facilitate early retirement; (5) encourage job rotation by filling new jobs from the unemployed register; and (6) introduce or extend career, parental and sabbatical leave.

This represents a significant backdown on the part of the Commission: the new section failed to propose either incentives for the reduction of working hours or any specific action to implement its other recommendations relating to working time (CEC 1993e:124, 131).

While the vague working time recommendations of the final version of the White Paper were accepted by the Brussels European Council of 10–11 December 1993 in the context of its acceptance of the White Paper as a whole, at the same time the heads of government of member states delivered the coup de grace for the previous more ambitious proposals when they specified that measures to reorganise work 'must not be directed towards a general redistribution of work' (European Council 1993:9).

Since then progress has been minimal: efforts to remove obstacles to part-time work, the only form of shorter working time mentioned by either the Council or the European Council since then, have been blocked by Britain. Otherwise, when working hours are mentioned in the context of employment the emphasis is on flexibility, not reduction (*Financial Times* 7 December 1994:2). By late 1995 only outsiders continued to argue for stronger action at the EU level to control unemployment by encouraging generalised work-sharing (e.g. Holland 1995).

POLITICAL DYNAMICS

Why did EU member states reject the idea of concerted action on work-sharing? In particular, why did they reject the Commission's idea of instituting a system of incentives and 'flanking measures' to encourage agreements between employers and employees to save and/or create jobs by shortening working hours? After all, the Commission's proposal was rather cleverly crafted from a political point of view: no EU legislation was suggested, to defuse nationalist objections; agreements between employers and employees were to be entirely voluntary, to defuse the objections of those who dislike state interference in collective bargaining; wages as well as hours were to be cut, to ensure that competitiveness was not harmed, while at the same time steps were to be taken to offset the effects of these cuts on living standards, to defuse objections from workers, especially low-paid workers, and their defenders.

Drawing upon documentary sources, and interviews in Brussels, it appears that there were a number of reasons why member states still resolutely opposed the Commission's scheme.

First of all there was the argument that unit labour costs would rise even if cuts in working hours were accompanied by proportionate wage cuts. The Confederation of British Industry, for example, maintained that more people doing the same work would mean increased costs for recruitment and training, and furthermore would require additional equipment to produce the same output (*Financial Times* 19 November 1993:2). In opposition to this, the Commission argued that average productivity per hour tends to be higher for employees who work shorter hours, which implies improved competitiveness, and that the problem of less efficient equipment utilisation could be solved by introducing more flexible working hours in order to extend equipment operating times (CEC 1994a:7; Bosch 1994:21, 12–19; CEC 1995b:119–20). For these reasons this objection does not seem by itself to be fatal.

Second, the White Paper itself raised the problem that it might not be possible to find enough skilled new employees to do the work no longer being done by those going on shorter time, which would mean that shorter hours would lead to production cuts (CEC 1993e:9). Such labour shortages could also lead to wage inflation. However this argument does not preclude moves to encourage agreements on shorter hours in sectors where labour shortages are not a problem, or in the area of unskilled or semi-skilled work, and furthermore leaves open the possibility that work-sharing could be extended if the provision of training was improved.

This labour shortage objection is related to a third, more general economic argument centred on the idea that there is a certain rate of unemployment below which inflation tends to accelerate: the so-called Non-Accelerating Inflation Rate of Unemployment (NAIRU) (e.g. Layard *et al* 1991:502–8). This means that if the present rate of unemployment is at or below the NAIRU, then job-sharing through shorter hours would be counter-productive because any resulting short-term reduction in unemployment would lead to higher inflation and thence to restrictive economic measures that would push unemployment back up to, or past, the NAIRU. The only difference would be that production would now be lower, because those still in work would be working shorter hours. Even if one accepts this argument, however, it seems implausible that current rates of unemployment are below the NAIRU at present. In addition, the Commission argues that 'empirical estimation of the NAIRU is so fragile and unstable that the concept becomes unusable operationally' (DGII 1995:129).

A fourth objection to the Commission's scheme was cost: measures to offset the impact of wage cuts on living standards, such as wage subsidies or adjustments in taxes and social contributions of employers and/or employees, would lead to higher state spending and/or lower state revenues, which in turn would tend to increase budget deficits at a time when they were already high. This is a powerful argument, and might be considered conclusive were it not for the fact that anxiety about budget deficits did not prevent member states agreeing to cut statutory charges on labour taxes as part of the initiative to reduce labour costs. This suggests that cost, while an important consideration, was not by itself an overriding argument.

The final main objection raised is more basic, and in a way more emotional. In denouncing work-sharing, what politicians and officials seemed to object to most vehemently was the idea that unemployment had to be fought by redistributing presently existing jobs, as opposed to creating new jobs in the sense of increasing the total volume of work being done. Thus Delors objected to a 'Malthusian' policy that, in its suggestion that the amount of work was limited, would lead to despair, and the Brussels European Council expressly forbade measures leading to 'a general redistribution of work' (*Guardian* 4 December 1993:12, European Council 1993:9). The obvious answer to this objection is that the two approaches are not incompatible, and that it would make sense to pursue both at once, but this view did not appear to be acceptable.

If we look at all these arguments together, two points emerge. First, they are quite numerous, if we include the arguments that the Commission proposal was designed to meet as well as the five mentioned above. Second, none of them are by themselves conclusive.

This in turn suggests two possible conclusions. The first is that my analysis has failed to discover the real reason, due to Council secretiveness. Such a reason might be a particular line of economic argument, for example, or some political consideration relating to trade-offs among member states on different issues.

The second possibility is that the rejection of the Commission's November 1993 scheme by member states was due to a combination of objections, none of which were conclusive by themselves but which together formed a formidable corpus of related arguments most of which originate in the liberal free market approach to economic analysis and prescription. In other words, even though work-sharing can be fitted into an orthodox liberal economic policy framework, it nevertheless runs against the grain. This suggests that the rejection of work-sharing by the governments of member states was due not so much to expert arguments as such as to their general adherence to a gestalt, an economic paradigm, with which work-sharing feels inconsistent even if it isn't technically inconsistent.

Consider the following. First, as mentioned earlier, member states were prepared, at least in principle, to spend money on cutting statutory charges on labour but not on providing incentives and 'flanking measures' to encourage work-sharing. Why? One possibility is that the cost of creating employment by compensating a shorter working week would be much greater than the cost of creating the same number of jobs by cutting labour taxes. Whether this is true is impossible to judge at present due to lack of empirical evidence. However another possibility is that the judgement of member state governments can be explained by the treatment of competitiveness in the rival schemes, given that a strong belief in competitiveness is arguably one of the defining characteristics of current liberal economic orthodoxy. This is because while cutting labour taxes without reducing working hours reduces hourly labour costs, compensating employees for a shorter working week merely keeps hourly labour costs constant. That is, from the point of view of competitiveness, in the first case public money is being used to create a 'good' (improved competitiveness), while in the second it is merely being used to compensate a 'bad' (weakened competitiveness).

The idea that rejection of work-sharing was due to its perceived incompatibility with the liberal economic paradigm is also consistent with the observed salience of the left-right divide: both the Socialists in the European Parliament and the ETUC were, and remain, generally in favour of reducing working time, and at the national level trade unions are the only organisations that, in some cases at least, have pushed hard for a shorter working week (e.g. the French CFDT). By contrast, both the conservative European Peoples Party in the European Parliament and the peak European employer group UNICE were, and remain, vehemently opposed to working time reductions without proportionate wage reductions, and are lukewarm at best towards working time reductions even when such wage cuts are proposed. Although the modern left subscribes to economic liberalism to a considerable extent, its commitment is less unconditional than that of the right, so one would expect that it would be more open to ideas that do not fit the paradigm.

Finally, the paradigm explanation is consistent with the member states' acceptance of the watered-down working time proposals contained in the final version of the White Paper: these did not threaten competitiveness in any way, and made no specific claims on government taxation or expenditure.

OUTLOOK

It is difficult to see how a new work-sharing initiative at the EU level could be successful in the near future. The Commission's November 1993 proposal was cleverly put together to disarm the obvious objections to work-sharing at a time when new policies were actively being sought by West European governments to counter rapidly rising unemployment, but it still failed.

Nevertheless, it is possible to identify a number of factors that, had they been existent at the end of 1993, might have improved the proposal's chances of success. These relate both to the policy environment and to the specific contents of the proposal.

First, the passage of work-sharing proposals through Council might have been easier had qualified majority voting applied to employment policy, although in fact the result in Ecofin in November 1993 would not have gone the other way, given that ten out of twelve member states were opposed. In addition, most of the major decisions are taken at the European Council level, where unanimity remains, and is likely to continue to remain, the rule. Furthermore, the extension of qualified majority voting to employment policy, for instance by the 1996 Inter-Governmental Conference, appears unlikely, as there is no move in this direction on the part of any major EU policy actor.

Second, official acceptance might have been more likely if more member state governments had been dominated by the left rather than by the right, given that the left is generally less opposed to work-sharing than the right.

Third, the idea of fighting unemployment by reducing working time would have been more credible had there been empirical evidence available which proved beyond reasonable doubt that cutting working hours was a particularly effective way of creating jobs. At present this sort of really compelling evidence does not seem to exist.

Although the Commission's proposal was well-designed from a political point of view, it is possible that its chances of acceptance might have been higher had its contents been slightly modified.

First, it would have helped to have had a good reason why the EU needed to be involved at all, especially since it can be argued that differences between member states concerning employment law would make it difficult for any EU measure in this area to be implemented effectively. One possible rationale might be that coordinating working time reduction at the EU level would have the advantage of allowing member states to retain competitiveness *vis-a-vis* each other if reducing working time turned out to mean higher labour costs, although clearly competitiveness would still be lost in relation to countries outside the EU, and it is hard to imagine EU member states deliberately sacrificing competitiveness at all.

Second, the objection on the grounds of cost could have been met by proposing a redistribution of taxes and social contributions of employers and employees from employees on shorter hours to those working longer hours (Rigaudiat 1993). Thus employers would be rewarded for employing people on shorter hours and penalised for employing people on longer hours in a way that would avoid the increases in public spending that measures such as wage subsidies would entail.

Finally, the Commission could have proposed that the introduction of more flexible working hours, a long-standing demand of employers, be made conditional on employers making significant reductions in employee working time without loss of pay. Such reductions would be possible due to additional productivity gained by longer operating hours for equipment (Rigaudiat 1993). For instance, employers would have to yield shorter working hours in return for annualising working hours, and give employees extra time off for overtime and working unsocial hours (nights, weekends) instead of extra payment (Bosch 1994:19). In summary, shorter hours but at less convenient times.

In conclusion, it seems clear that there are conditions under which work-sharing schemes such as that proposed by the Commission could become more acceptable to the governments of member states, but in the short term the chances of work-sharing being adopted at the EU level as a major anti-unemployment policy are slim. It may be only in the longer term, as the economic paradigm slowly changes – or snaps – that work-sharing schemes may have their day. In the meantime we must look to individual West European nation states for any progress in this area.

NOTES

1   Where not specifically referenced, the information used in this chapter is drawn from interviews in Brussels with Niels Bartholdy (Danish Representation), Daniel Brennan (Commission DGV), Andrew Chapman (Commission DGV), Reinhart Eisenberg (Council Secretariat), David Foden (ETUC), Marjorie Jouen (Commission Forward Studies Unit), Rudolf Lepers (German Representation), Manuel Martinez (Commission DGXI), Stefan Pfitzner (European Peoples Party), Derek Reed (Party of European Socialists), Ludwig Schubert (Commission DGII), F. Schumacher (Dutch Representation), and Ottorino Zanini (Italian Representation), to all of whom I would like to extend my thanks. I would also like to acknowledge the assistance of Nikolaus Adami (Commission DGII), John Carvel (Guardian), Robert Court (British Representation), Wayne David MEP, David Goodhart (Financial Times), Stuart Holland, Andrew Marshall (Independent), Barbara Nolan (Spokeswoman, Commissioner Flynn), Paul Ormerod, Lucy Walker (European), and Rory Watson (European).

REFERENCES

Bastian, Jens (1994), 'Work sharing: the reappearance of a timely idea', *Political Quarterly* 65(3):302–12.

Bosch, Gerhard (1994), *Flexibility and Work Organisation: Report of Expert Working Group* (follow-up to White Paper) (Brussels, European Commission Directorate-General for Employment, Industrial Relations and Social Affairs).

Bull. EC (Bulletin of the European Communities).

Bull. EU (Bulletin of the European Union).

CEC (Commission of the European Communities) (1990), 'Annual Economic Report 1990–91', *European Economy* 46.

—— (1991), 'Annual Economic Report 1991–92', *European Economy* 50.

—— (1992), *Proposition for a Council Directive Introducing a Tax on Carbon Dioxide Emissions and on Energy* COM(92) 226 final/2 (30 June 1992).

—— (1993a), 'Annual Economic Report 1993', *European Economy* 54.

—— (1993b), *Report to Ecofin on Actions Taken to Implement the Edinburgh Growth Initiative (at Community level)*, COM(93) 164 final (Brussels, 22 April 1993).

——(1993c), 'Community-wide framework for employment', *Social Europe* 2/93.

—— (1993d), *Growth, Competitiveness, Employment: Note for the Council of Ministers (Economy/Finance) on the Economic Elements of the White Paper* SEC(93)1855 final (Brussels, 24 November 1993). Although this is dated two days after the Ecofin meeting to which it refers, it is in fact the paper considered on 22 November.

—— (1993e), 'Growth, Competitiveness, Employment: The Challenges and Ways Forward into the 21st Century', *Bulletin of the European Communities* Supplement 6/93.

—— (1993f), *Growth, Competitiveness, Employment: The Challenges and Ways Forward into the 21st Century*, White Paper Part C (Luxembourg).

—— (1994a), *Seminar of Social Partners on Competitiveness, Productivity and Employment, Brussels, 12–13 April 1994*: Note from the Commission Services II/230/94 – EN (Brussels: DGII).

—— (1994b), *European Social Policy – A Way Forward for the Union (White Paper) Part B* COM(94) 333 final/2 (Brussels).

—— (1994c), 'New departures in job creation – local measures: results and prospects', *European Report* No. 2000 (10 December).

—— (1995), *Local Development and Employment Initiatives* (Brussels).

—— (1995a), *Annual Economic Report for 1995* (Brussels).

—— (1995b), 'Competitiveness, productivity and employment', *European Economy* 59.

Council of the European Communities (1993), 'Resolution of 21 December 1992 on the Need to Tackle the Serious and Deteriorating Situation Concerning Unemployment in the Community', *Official Journal of the European Communities* C 49.

—— (1994), 'Council Recommendation of 22 December 1993 on the broad guidelines of the economic policies of the member states and of the Community', *Official Journal of the European Communities* L 7:9–12.

—— (1994a), 'Council Recommendation of 1 June 1994 for the broad guidelines of the economic policies of the member states and of the Community', *European Economy* 58.

Delors, Jacques (1993), 'Some ideas on European employment policy', 12 November 1993 (Commission Press Release 93/131).

DGII (Directorate-General for Economic and Financial Affairs) (1995), 'The composition of unemployment from an economic point of view', *European Economy* 59.

Ecofin (1995), Press Release PRES/95/74 (16 March 1995).

EP (European Parliament)(1992a), 'Resolution on the European labour market after 1992', *Official Journal of the European Communities* C 241.

—— (1992b), 'Resolution on economic and unemployment policies', *Official Journal of the European Communities* C 305.

—— (1993a), *Draft Report by the Committee on Economic and Monetary Affairs on the Commission White Paper: Growth, Competitiveness and Employment* DOC_EN\PR\245\245474.

—— (1993b), *Report by the Committee on Economic and Monetary Affairs and Industrial Policy on the Commission's Annual Economic Report for 1993* DOC_EN\RR\222\222833.

—— (1995), 'Resolution on the Programme for 1995', *Bulletin of the European Union* Supplement 1/95.

ER (European Report) (1993) No. 1903, 24 November.

ETUC (European Trade Union Confederation) (1981), *Stop Unemployment: ETUC Manifesto for Employment and Economic Recovery* (Brussels).

ETUC (European Trade Union Confederation) (1994), *Statement to Corfu European Council, June 1994* (Brussels).

ETUI (European Trade Union Institute) (1988), *The Social Dimension of the Single Market: Employment* (Brussels).

The European.

European Council (1993), 'Brussels European Council, 10–11 December 1993: Conclusions of the Presidency', *Bulletin of the European Communities* 12–93.

—— (1994), *European Council at Corfu 24–25 June 1994: Presidency Conclusions* (Commission: Spokesman's Service DOC/94/1).

—— (1994a), *European Council, Essen, 9–10 December 1994: Presidency Conclusions* (Commission: Spokesman's Service).

—— (1995), *Presidency Conclusions – Cannes, 26 and 27 June 1995* (Team Europe).

European Economy.

European Report.

Financial Times.

Flynn, Padraig (1993b), 'Speech to CBI Conference on the future direction of social policy, 14 October 1993' (Commission Press Release 93/115).

Flynn, Padraig (1993c), 'Speech at the Employment in Europe Conference and Exhibition, 19 October 1993' (Commission Press Release 93/118).

The Guardian.

Holland, Stuart (1995), 'Negotiating a New Deal for Europe and its People', *European* 2 June 1995:18.

Independent.

La Croix.

Layard, Richard, Nickell, Stephen and Jackman, Richard (1991), *Unemployment: Macroeconomic Performance and the Labour Market*, Oxford, Oxford University Press.

OJ (Official Journal of the European Communities).

PES (Party of European Socialists) (1993), *Put Europe To Work* (Brussels).

PPE (European Peoples Party)(1993), *Growth, Competitiveness and Employment: Promoting Economic Renewal in Europe – Policy Statement by the PPE Group* (Brussels, 12 October).

Rigaudiat, Jacques (1993), 'Réduction du temps de travail: le retour', *Le Monde* 24 November 1993, Initiatives 5.

TEU (Treaty on European Union) (Luxembourg, 1992).

2 Germany

Ulrich Widmaier and Susanne Blancke

INTRODUCTION

As Germany slowly recovers from the recession of the early 1990s, economic signs indicate an upswing and most economists are generally optimistic about its sustainability. But the dark side of the picture shows a persistence of high unemployment rates, rising long-term unemployment and tremendous labour market problems in the East – full employment is far from being in sight. When faced with these divergent developments it is essential to study the causes. For political scientists it is of special importance to ask why existing policies are obviously unable to cope with the problem of rising mass unemployment in a satisfactory manner.

Within this context it is our general hypothesis that the German labour market institutions have preserved their structural characteristics and thus failed to adapt to the changes in the employment system. This has led to the increasing inefficiency of institutional arrangements, which no longer provide adequate policy instruments. This situation can only be changed either by replacing existing institutional arrangements or by implementing new policies which are conducted in other (new) policy arenas. Both strategies have to be considered 'radical' in the sense that they deviate from institutionally defined routines and 'standard operating procedures' (March and Olsen 1989). The latter strategy, however, offers a much better chance of leading to widely accepted policies because it is embedded in existing institutional settings and is therefore more likely to be considered as a legitimate offspring born under specific circumstances and applied in different political contexts (policy arenas).

The first section of this chapter contains a short description of the current situation and the specific problems of the German labour market, briefly describing the labour market institutions, policy actors and conventional labour market policies. Only in light of this can the initiatives, ideas and proposals for reform which dominate the present debate on labour market policy be examined and understood. The second section deals with the radical unemployment policies that have been on the agenda since the beginning of the 1990s. In the third section we discuss the arenas

% workforce/
unemployment

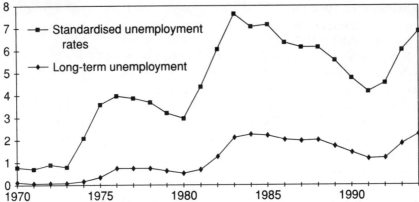

Figure 2.1 Unemployment in Germany, 1972–1994

Source: OECD *Employment Outlook*, annual volumes

in which these policies are conducted, and in the final section point briefly to feasible strategies for reform and transformation.

CONTEXT

Facts and trends

As in many other European countries German labour market policy is confronted with the problem of mass unemployment which has developed since the late 1960s in a cyclical and cumulative pattern (Figure 2.1). The unemployment rate of 0.8 per cent in 1970 rose up to 4.0 per cent in 1976 when the first oil crisis caused an economic depression after 1973. In spite of the economic recovery in the second half of the 1970s the unemployment rate did not fall to its old level. The same pattern emerged after the second oil crisis in 1979: the rate rose through the first half of the 1980s but did not decrease accordingly during the following economic upswing, although the number of persons employed increased considerably. In 1994 the rate of unemployment was 6.9 per cent in the West and 14.2 per cent in the East.

As the unemployment rate increased, so did the share of long-term unemployment (i.e. being unemployed for more than one year), from 8.8 per cent of those unemployed in 1970 to 20.3 per cent in 1978 and 31 per cent in 1993 (Figure 2.1).

These alarming numbers are attended by a high level of hidden unemployment – short-time employment, job creation measures (Arbeitsbeschaffungsmaßnahmen – ABM), participation in early retirement schemes (Vorruhestand) etc. – which amounted to around two million individuals in 1994 (ANBA 1994). Last but not least there is a 'silent reserve' of about two million people looking for a job who are not officially registered (ANBA 1994:23).

Faced with these numbers, facts and trends (especially the alarmingly high share of long-term unemployment) it becomes increasingly obvious that the traditional instruments of labour market policy in Germany are under pressure, and accordingly political pressure to search for new solutions is building up. The policy suggestions which we will describe in greater detail in the next section are the most prominent ones and are discussed, to a greater or lesser extent, by all important actors involved in labour market policy. Before we turn to these new and 'radical' policy suggestions, we will briefly introduce the central actors in the labour market as well as the institutional setting that constitutes the 'feasible set' for their political strategies.

Actors and institutions

German labour market policy is mainly conducted by five actors: the Federal Government, the Federal Labour Office (Bundesanstalt für Arbeit – BA), employer associations, trade unions and (more recently) municipal administrations. They mainly act in two institutional settings: the public labour market administration and the system of collective bargaining.

In the centre of German labour administration is the Federal Ministry of Labour. The BA, a statutory authority which implements most of the Federal labour market programmes, is governed by a president, a board of directors and a tripartite administrative board, and has subdivisions on the state and regional/local level. Although it is in principal a self-governing organisation, it is subject to control by the Federal Government through the right of the latter to reject its budget. A central political role is also played by the Federal Ministry of Finance, which has to allocate funds in the national budget to cover the chronic financial deficit of the BA.

The labour market policies of the BA are in the first place based on a compulsory state insurance system to which contributions are made equally by employers and employees and which has to be subsidised in case of a deficit by the Federal Government. Social benefits for the registered unemployed (Arbeitslosenhilfe), which have been directly financed out of the Federal budget since 1981, are granted after unemployment benefits are no longer paid, providing that the income of other family members does not exceed a certain level. In principle it is granted for an unlimited period at a level of up to 53 per cent of the last wage or salary (§136,2 AFG). The basic and residual levels of financial support for the unemployed are social welfare benefits, which are paid by municipalities (communes) to those who are no longer considered as being on the labour market.

The legal basis for the active labour market policy of the BA is defined by the Labour Promotion Act (AFG) of 1969. It came into being at a time when the unemployment rate in Germany was below 2 per cent. The initial policy goal was to provide instruments to solve the short-term employment problems of individuals in transition from one employer to another, and the legislation presupposed that there would be a situation of full employment in the future, the labour market would offer sufficient jobs, and only limited cyclical, structural or individual unemployment could be expected. Since then the situation has changed radically, and the AFG does not seem to perform its policy function any longer. To some extent this seems to be a consequence of the reduction of benefits and services by the BA in the 1980s, which was initiated by the Federal Government in order to reduce the structural deficit of the BA (Adamy 1994:32–40).

Conventional labour market policies in Germany have relied on two main instruments. First, macro-economic instruments have been used: Keynesian demand management strategies in the 1970s, and monetaristic fiscal policies in the 1980s and 1990s – but with questionable results. Second, the AFG continues to provide the basis for vocational training, job creating measures (ABM), early retirement schemes, and short-time work designed to overcome problems on the labour market – but with diminishing efficiency. In addition, purely passive measures of financial support for the unemployed are one of the increasingly questioned pillars of conventional German unemployment policies (for details on the passive and active instruments of labour market policy see Schmid 1987).

On the level of collective bargaining, conventional labour market policies are mainly restricted to attempts by trade unions to reduce standard working time and by employer associations to deregulate the employment system. From the point of view of trade unions, collective bargaining is mainly a matter of improving or at least defending working conditions for the employed. In other words, primarily, the system of collective bargaining takes care of the interests of the employed, while any potentially negative external effects on prospects for the unemployed are not considered, or at least not directly.

These initial observations support our suspicion that the two central labour market institutions have become increasingly inefficient in fighting unemployment, and in addition practise a division of labour which reduces their efficiency even more: the BA is responsible for the unemployed, the system of collective bargaining is designed for the employed. The influences of one system on the other are obvious, but they are of secondary importance to the primary interests of both institutional settings.

Table 2.1 Radical unemployment policies in Germany

Strategy	Measure
Reduction and restructuring of working time	Industry-wide reduction of working time Temporary working time reduction on the company level Flexibility of working time Part-time employment
Secondary labour markets	Labour cost subsidies Labour promotion and training companies in the West and ABS-Companies in the East Contract labour
Institutional reforms	Reform of AFG law Decentralising of collective bargaining

RADICAL UNEMPLOYMENT POLICIES

The spectrum of radical unemployment policies, defined as those which are outside the EU policy consensus, new at the national level, and designed to significa ⁿly reduce unemployed, can be grouped into three categories: reduction and restructuring of working time; secondary labour markets; and institutional reforms. The first of these involves mainly actors within the institutional framework of collective bargaining, whereas the second is mostly related to the institution of public labour market administration. The third topic encompasses both institutional domains.

Reduction and restructuring of working time

The reduction and restructuring of working time, which can be summarised under the term 'work-sharing', plays a prominent role in the discussion on labour market policy. In general an increasing erosion of standard working time schemes can be observed. As a consequence, industry-wide skeleton contracts increasingly define only the framework within which decentralised agreements on working time can be negotiated between individual employers and work councils, who are jointly responsible, within the German system, for local (company) level agreements, although they are not allowed to engage in any form of collective bargaining or dispute.

Industry-wide reduction of working time

General reductions in working time constitute a 'classical' demand by trade unions. Initially the issue was discussed as a matter of workers' protection.

In the 1980s this aspect moved to the background and considerations relating to job creation via this instrument came to the fore. In 1985, after hard bargaining, the union and the employers' association of the metal industry reached an agreement on a successive reduction of working time from 40 to 38.5 hours per week. A further reduction to 35 hours until October 1995 has also been agreed on. The effects of such measures are disputed, and statistical analyses on the amount of actual job creation yield considerably different results. On the one hand this is a consequence of methodological problems, on the other hand the selection of models for estimation may be influenced by different political preferences (see Seifert 1991; Bach/Spitznagel 1994).

The main problem relating to working time reduction is the question of who is going to pay for it. If working hours are cut but wages are not – working time reduction with full wage compensation – then hourly labour costs for employers must rise. Because rising productivity is generally not sufficient to compensate for this, employers reject reductions of working time with wage compensation. In this context it is obvious why the employers' organisation in the metal industry (Arbeitgeberverband Gesamtmetall) has published studies which demonstrate that only 21 per cent of the hours lost as a result of working time reductions in the 1980s have been made up by hiring additional labour. Trade union results, by contrast, claim a 70 per cent substitution rate (Seifert 1989:157). Given employer concern over increased labour costs, trade unions cannot demand radical working time reductions without having to fear decreasing support by their members, since lower wage rises, rising intensity of work, increased pressure for flexibility etc. are the probable consequences of such reductions.

Temporary working time reduction on the company level

Recently there have been moves to introduce temporary, decentralised reduction of working time to overcome a crisis on the company level. The substantial reduction of working time, limited to two years, at the Volkswagen Company (VW) since January 1994 can be taken as paradigmatic for such a model. These have proved easier to agree on than industry-wide working time reductions, but only as a preventive measure and only under certain circumstances.

Facing massive economic problems in 1993, VW planned to reduce personnel expenditures by around DM 2 billion (about £1 billion), which would have resulted in a reduction in the number of employees of around 30,000 (around 30 per cent of the staff). The options of early retirement had been already exhausted prior to this, so that the only alternatives were mass dismissals or large-scale short-time work. Short-time work has to be approved by the BA, which then grants wage compensations out of the unemployment insurance fund. Employees are paid for hours lost over a period of six months at a level approximately equivalent to 60 per cent of the last full-time wage.

Apart from considerations concerning the social and political consequences of mass dismissals, financial aspects had to be taken into account. In the case of lay-offs the VW contract provided for high social expenditures (Sozialpläne) to be paid by the company, which would have limited the short and medium term financial benefits considerably (Rosdücher/ Seifert 1994:4). Furthermore, due to clauses in the contract, the young and productive employees would have had to be dismissed first. Finally, after an economic recovery of the company in the future, high transaction costs in terms of training of new employees would need to be added to the overall bill. Economic reasons also spoke against short-time work. VW would have had to contribute to the payments for short-time work by the BA to allow the income of the employees to reach 90 per cent of their past average net income. In addition, the company would still have had to pay social security contributions.

Given these facts, the VW management reversed its position and suggested a reduction of working time limited to two years in order to save the jobs. An agreement was reached after only 14 days of bargaining in November 1993. The solution was a reduction of working time of 20 per cent from 36 hours per week to 28.8 hours with a proportional wage reduction. Although this 20 per cent wage cut had to be expected, it was partly compensated for by a complicated rearrangement of special bonuses and wage increases, so that annual wage losses amounted only to 12 per cent to 13 per cent (for further details see Rosdücher/Seifert 1994).

Compared to other disputes over reductions of working time, such as the general reductions from 40 to 38.5 hours with wage compensation, this case was handled with a surprisingly low level of conflict, despite the fact that the negotiated matters were far more risky with respect to potential losses for both sides. On the one hand this low level of conflict was due to the need to overcome the crisis as soon as possible: under 'normal' circumstances employees would probably not have been prepared to accept losses of annual income of around 12 per cent (see also Meinhardt *et al.* 1993). On the other hand the existing specific contract at company level (Haustarifvertrag), which provided for higher wages than the relevant industry agreement as well as a high level of social protection, contributed to the success of this model. In addition, the costs for the company in the case of dismissals or short-time work would have been higher than those incurred for the reduction in working time.

Although the VW case cannot easily be transferred to other companies, it served as a reference model for the collective agreement in the metal industry that has been in operation since April 1994. In cases of imminent mass dismissals or short-time work the agreement allows for temporary reductions of working time from 36 to 30 hours per week without wage compensation, although compensations can be agreed upon and have to be offset against annual incomes. In return employers are supposed to renounce dismissals as long as reductions of working time are in operation for all employees. In cases where reductions of working time apply to only a part of the staff, wage compensations are introduced (1 per cent in case of 35 hours; up to 7 per cent for 30 hours) and dismissals are allowed (iwd 1994/36:6). The objections put forward by employers, that companies would suffer from production bottlenecks if highly skilled workers and middle management were needed for more hours than those agreed on, were taken care of by the provision that 13 per cent to 18 per cent of the personnel could work for up to 40 hours per week.

Despite the unquestionably positive effects which these measures can yield, it should be noted that the reductions have only been accepted in the political context of job protection and not in the context of job creation, which was the objective in the 1980s. This demonstrates the lack of representation of the unemployed in the process of developing and forming labour market policy objectives within the institutional framework of collective bargaining.

Flexibility of working time

The demand to increase flexibility of working time has strengthened considerably during the 1990s, focusing on the distribution of working hours (structure of working time) and the duration of working time (for example part-time employment). As with the debate on reduction of working time, the discussion on increasing flexibility of working time shows that the objectives of decentralisation, deregulation and individualisation are moving to the centre of labour market policies. Of primary interest to employers are models of flexible adjustment to the specific conditions of individual companies; industry-wide agreements with fixed standard working hours are criticised as not being adjusted to companies' needs.

Employers have repeatedly pointed out the need for increasing flexibility in the distribution of working time (for example Handelsblatt, no.20, 27./28.1.1995, p.5). If a standard working time no longer exists, wage supplements for paid overtime disappear and working time can be adapted to the requirements of machinery and production processes as well as to the fluctuating volume of work (fluctuations over a day, week, month, or year). In short this implies a substantial reduction of labour costs. Thus the Federal Organisation of Employer Associations (Bundesvereinigung der Arbeitgeberverbände) calls for collective agreements which specify only the number of working hours per year and demands a fundamental reform of legal restrictions in this field, for example the abolition of working time regulations that protect female workers from night work. Because trade unions are afraid of disadvantages for the employees, such as cuts in extra bonuses for shift work and work on Saturdays, they are not willing to agree to an extensive flexibilisation of working time in general, although the

Federation of German Trade Unions (Deutscher Gewerkschaftsbund – DGB) recently indicated willingness to negotiate on flexibilisation if combined with working time reduction with differentiated wage adjustments.

Part-time employment

Compared with international standards Germany has a low ratio of part time employment (iwd, Jg.20, Nr.10, 10.3.1994, S.8), although it is assumed that the demand is much higher (Sozialpolitische Informationen 1994/ 15:1). Thus proposals to expand part-time employment, in the context of increasing flexibility of working time, represent a radical change in policy direction. Various models are suggested: sabbaticals (blocks of free time), spacious 'working time corridors', rolling 'four-day weeks' (in which five employees share four jobs), and flexible working time over a lifetime (for example reduction of working time with age). First attempts to settle this collectively can be observed in the chemical industry, where unions and employers' representatives agreed on 'working time corridors', which provide the individual with flexible arrangements for working time in the corridor of 30 to 40 hours per week.

Employers particularly profit by such agreements because flexible part-time employment actually means a reduction of working time without wage compensation. In addition it means increased flexibility of the structure of working time with all its positive implications. Trade unions, however, see part-time employment from a more critical viewpoint. On the one hand the hope is that these measures will generate a higher supply of jobs on the labour market (Schreiner 1994:164), and they are aware that the number of employees interested in part-time jobs is increasing, but on the other hand they fear an erosion of the standard employment situation: often part-time jobs are less well paid, and chances of promotion, qualification opportunities, and social insurance contributions are reduced for part-time employees, which means a reduction in the level of pensions and unemployment benefits (under 10 hours no contribution is made at all). In the face of these problems the DGB demands the same rights for part-time employees as for full-time employees (Arbeit und Recht, 1992/9:267–271). However the government has not yet taken an initiative to change the legal framework for part-time employment, which would be a prerequisite for DGB support.

Secondary labour markets

In accordance with Keynesian economic policy, job creating measures (Arbeitsbeschaffungsmaßnahmen – ABM), such as taking care of the handicapped and keeping public parks clean, were introduced by the AFG in 1969 to fight cyclical unemployment by increasing the public demand for labour. In the 1980s the purpose of these measures changed and the fight against long-term and structural unemployment became the central policy objective. Under the pressure of severe structural problems on the labour market in East Germany, the AFG was partly modified (§§91–99, 249h), leading to the creation of employment and training companies (Beschäftigungsgesellschaften) and new types of labour cost subsidies. Furthermore, new ways of combining training and secondary labour markets are aimed at fighting qualification mismatches and preventing increasing 'de-qualification' of the long-term unemployed.

Secondary labour markets are often criticised by economists and employers for blocking the provision of 'regular' jobs. They fear that all kinds of wage subsidies distort competition, thereby weakening the private sector in the long run (see also Sperling 1994). These reservations are the reason for two requirements set by the BA which have to be met by any kind of measure in the secondary labour market supported by labour offices: 'being in the public interest', and 'additional' (that is, the job would not be done otherwise).

Trade unions criticise both the time limit set by the BA on conventional ABM and the requirement that potential participants must be entitled to unemployment benefits, which means that they must have been paying unemployment insurance contributions for at least one year. Thus unemployed people who have never had the chance to work under labour contracts which include provisions for unemployment insurance contributions are excluded. Furthermore, unions demand a legal right to claim ABM plus a specific collective agreement defining the employment conditions. The latter is an attempt by trade unions to establish collective bargaining rights on secondary labour markets.

Labour cost subsidies

Labour cost subsidies (AFG East §249h/West §242s) of up to the value of unemployment benefits for twelve months are paid to the employer of a previously unemployed person. The difference compared to the standard wage must be paid by the employer or by other means. Labour should be in the public interest, which in the East for example, could mean environmental redevelopment or protection, social services, youth welfare, culture and reconstruction of monuments. Entitlement to subsidies is restricted to employers of unemployed persons who receive benefits and have not been employed for at least three months, short-time workers, or those who have participated in ABM before. Special attention is paid to those who cannot be placed easily. Labour cost subsidies are granted only if the wage level is 10 per cent lower than the one for 'regular' comparable work, or when working time is reduced to 80 per cent of the standard working time, in order to weaken the tie between wages in the secondary and primary labour markets.

It is often claimed that these kinds of subsidies provoke 'pocketing' by employers or allow for 'windfall' gains. But it has also to be taken into account that such subsidies are supposed to provide incentives for potential employers to employ those previously unemployed, as opposed to those moving from other jobs. In order to prevent employers dismissing the workers as soon as subsidies run out, employers are obliged to keep them on for at least twelve additional months after the subsidies have been stopped.

Labour cost subsidies are particularly attractive to the BA because of the institutional conditions under which it has to operate, that is, the budgetary problems caused by the obligation to grant active and passive measures at the same time. In face of a tight budget, these measures are devices to change passive into active labour market policies without additional expenditures. Labour cost subsidies were initially planned exclusively for the five new federal states, as part of the response to the massive labour market problems there, but positive results with the measures and a tightened budget led in 1994 to their introduction in the West as well.

Labour promotion and training companies in the West and ABS-companies in the East

At the beginning of the 1980s trade unions and local governments have developed ideas for public or private employment and training companies. All variants of these companies constitute an innovation insofar as: (1) they are independent institutions, (2) they are financed by combining resources from different funds (BA, industrial regional policies, social funds etc.), and (3) they combine different measures of labour market policy (training, work, support for self employment etc.) (Bosch/Knuth 1992:431). While employment and training companies which are connected to private firms are designed to take care of those employees who would potentially become unemployed as a consequence of a severe economic crisis of the company, employment and training companies that are related to communes (municipalities) are supposed to reintegrate unemployed (especially long-term unemployed) into the labour market again.

Ideally, firm-related employment companies are set up in such a way that private funds and public resources are combined. During the existence of the employment company the management is supposed to restructure the firm and to re-employ the personnel again thereafter. In the meantime employees will be trained to adjust their qualification to the 'new' needs of the company. In this way expensive training measures for new personnel after the restructuring of the company can be avoided.

Employment and training companies which are associated with public authorities were formed as a reaction to increasing social benefit expenditures for those unemployed who are not entitled to claims on the BA (usually the long-term unemployed). A positive side-effect of this so-called 'help for work' (§19 Bundessozialhilfegesetz BSHG) for the municipality is that the participants are entitled again for benefits from the BA when the measure is finished. Moreover, employment and training companies operated by municipalities can absorb the long-term unemployed and other 'problem groups', who often cannot be easily integrated into every-day work processes and for whom ABM measures are not adequate, and, by providing opportunities and facilities, prepare them better for a job on the primary labour market.

In spite of considerable success for such measures, the BA has not shown very much interest in them in the past because the incorporation of other actors is perceived as an interference with its bureaucratic autonomy and control (Widmaier 1991). Employer reactions vary depending on whether the companies have a corporatist or an etatist structure: the latter is crit-icised for blocking structural change, the former for depriving managers of decisional autonomy. But the potential to overcome a crisis within a company via such a model is also acknowledged (Bosch/Knuth 1992:436).

In general the structure of the AFG represents an obstacle for employ-ment companies:

- The AFG only supports individuals, while employment and training companies are supposed to employ and support collectivities.
- According to the AFG, the BA should not support combined measures. For example, in the case of short-time work combined with qualification measures, the employer has to pay for the qualification part (§63, 4 AFG).
- The BA is reluctant to subsidise qualification measures and training which are tailored to the specific needs of a company. The insurance systems' logic is to insure individual risks, which means payments for the unemployed rather than payments towards the economic recovery of individual firms. Therefore the BA only contributes (1) if the qual-ifications can be used on external labour markets as well and (2) at the discretion of the local labour office, in cases of imminent dismissals.
- In principle the BA grants subsidies only if dismissals have already been decided. This means that preventive measures are difficult to implement.

To meet the specific needs of the East German labour market conditions a special variant of employment and training company was developed: the Companies for Labour Promotion, Employment and Structural Develop-ment (ABS companies). ABS companies can be placed in between employment and training companies associated with firms and those connected to local authorities.

Since the reconstruction of companies in the new Länder is often impossible due to the lack of the necessary economic preconditions, ABS companies are often preoccupied with the exploitation of the bankrupts' assets (dismantling and recultivation of the former site, preparation for new enterprises etc.). In addition, they search for new fields of economic activities on the local or regional level (Knuth 1994; Wagner 1994). These include the establishment of industrial and technological centres, advice for the promotion of economic development, planning of infrastructure, tourism etc. Such tasks are elements of regional development. This strong link between private economic interests and publicly supported structural development – which is not in accordance with existing AFG logic – is a consequence of the specific situation in the East (see Knuth 1994; Bosch/Knuth 1993).

A significant trend here is that ABS companies in the East are supported by the BA and other institutions applying a relatively liberal interpretation of the legal framework. The specific problems in the East led to a situation in which nearly every activity seemed to be of 'public interest' and 'additional' (ibid.), the preconditions for receiving support from the BA.

It is too early to assess the long-term efficiency and effectiveness of the ABS-companies. However, short-term benefits, such as providing jobs in regions where over 30 per cent of the workforce are unemployed, can be observed. Positive effects probably also exist in the long term since the companies provide training to the participants. Moreover, it can be assumed that the close relationship between municipal administrations, the regional economy and the employment companies render the latter interested and effective in the placement of the unemployed in other (private) companies (Knuth 1994:181).

Contract labour

Another model in the field of secondary labour market policies is based on the possibilities of contracting labour. The more recent publicly supported models provide ways of contracting out the long-term unemployed to companies under the conditions of normal labour contracts. Like the Dutch original this is administrated by a network of agencies. The unique programme of START Contract Labour Co. Ltd. (START Zeitarbeit NRW GmbH) has been in operation since February 1995, tests having been undertaken from 1992–1994 on the local level (Weinkopf/Krone 1995). START is a corporate initiative of the government of North-Rhine-Westfalia, the BA, the DGB, employers' associations, chambers of commerce, communities and the Dutch foundation START. The company consists of 22 offices in NRW which cooperate closely with the labour offices in order to establish regional networks.

The Contract Labour Act (Arbeitnehmerüberlassungsgesetz) provides for unlimited (standard) labour contracts between the START company and the unemployed. Therefore START has to employ and place employees again in cases where they have not been hired by the company to which they have been contracted out. At the beginning, and in periods when the employees are not contracted out, they are trained and qualified. For that reason START is intended to serve as a central instrument for the reduction of long-term unemployment. Because it is often difficult to integrate long-term unemployed people into regular labour processes, this project provides the opportunity to have more than one attempt. In addition, it provides an opportunity for employers to overcome prejudices against potential employees by giving them the chance to 'sound out' long-term unemployed without being restricted by the normal employees' protection against dismissals.

START is a non-profit organisation and for this reason should therefore not be compared with commercial contract labour companies. The estimated costs of 11 million DM are provided jointly by the federal and the regional governments during the first three years. Thereafter the agencies are supposed to be self-financing. Potential profits are to be used for improving the qualifications of the employees. Although up to now unions have generally opposed contract labour, START is accepted by the DGB because it is a public organisation which has signed a collective agreement with the public service union (Öffentliche Dienste, Transport und Verkehr – ÖTV). The Minister of Labour plans a fundamental revision of the AFG in autumn 1995 to enable the BA itself to contract out unemployed people to companies.

Institutional reforms

The suggestions and proposals for reform discussed so far are all hampered by institutional constraints which lead to suboptimal results even if there is relatively widespread consensus among all actors on the desirability of a certain policy. These institutional deficits became especially obvious as a result of the extremely critical situation in the East German labour market.

As a consequence, within the institutional domain of public labour market policy almost all actors now demand a reform of the AFG. Even the Federal Government seems to be convinced, and the Minister of Labour has announced a fundamental revision of the law. The probable directions of the reform appear to be as follows (Bosch 1994:32ff):

- A combining of labour market policies and industrial restructuring, and better coordination of regional development, ABM and qualification measures.
- An increase in the proportion of active measures, as opposed to passive measures, and an extension in the entitlement of the unemployed to assistance by the BA.
- A strengthening of preventive measures; in the first place this means qualification of short-time workers and of employees whose jobs are endangered.
- A more flexible coordination of various labour market policies. The existing AFG distinguishes strictly between measures which depend on

different prerequisites and which therefore cannot be combined. A standardisation of criteria for support, and more flexible administration, should enable the creation of 'measure-bundles'.

- Decentralisation of labour market policies by the allocation of funds to regional and local labour offices for their discretionary use (for example investment in equipment for ABM).
- Reform of financing modalities, including (a) obliging civil servants and the self employed to contribute to unemployment insurance; (b) financing active labour market policies from general revenue; (c) financing payments which are outside the direct responsibility of the insurance system from general revenue (for example funding to solve specific problems on the East German labour market or to facilitate the integration of immigrants).
- Abolition of the BA monopoly on the placement of the unemployed in order to generate more competition, thereby improving the relationship between labour offices, the unemployed and employers. This measure has already been implemented (see Basedow 1992; Engelen-Kefer 1992; Walwei 1994).

In summary, the legislature is being asked to make the instruments of the BA more flexible and to break away from principles of central governance. At the same time, trends in the direction of self-regulation, flexibilisation and decentralisation can already be seen. In this connection the BA is increasingly dependent on corporatist arrangements on the local level, such as those relating to employment and ABS companies, START, etc.

With respect to the institution of centralised collective bargaining, the debate on institutional reform centres around the question of whether centralised collective settlements are still compatible with the diverse needs and requirements of individual companies. Employers and managers argue that structural economic change has increased the pressure for flexible solutions, especially with regard to employment conditions in a 'high wage country' like Germany. In addition, lower economic growth rates have reduced the distributional possibilities for collective bargaining, which increases the redistributional character of the negotiations. Furthermore, the consequences of structural economic change generate substantial processes of differentiation for the conditions of employment in companies both quantitatively and qualitatively.

These developments have led to a heated debate between unions and employers over the need for decentralised bargaining. Collective agreements are supposed to set guidelines only, which are then filled in by firm-specific settlements. Recent agreements on flexible working hours are an example here. But such firm specific strategies contain the danger of social closure against collective regulations and external labour markets. They imply that interest-representation at firm level by work councils

(Betriebsräte) would rise in importance. If unions wanted to keep their leading position in representing the interests of the employed in such a decentralised system, they would have to re-define their function and restructure their organisation.

POLITICAL DYNAMICS

The proposals for radical changes in unemployment policies in Germany as presented above can be grouped into specific policy arenas. Following classical policy analysis (Lowi 1972; Salisbury 1968), we posit that the relative degree of conflict and consensus, and therefore the chance of acceptance of a new labour market policy, is dependent on whether the policy is primarily distributive or redistributive in nature, and divides the possible institutional arrangements into predominantly regulative or predominantly self-regulative.

The distinction between distributive and redistributive policies relates to the question of whether we are dealing with a zero-sum game in which the losses of one actor are the gains of the other. It is obvious that the degree of conflict increases as the redistributive character of the arena increases, so that we can expect that policies which are distributive in character and contain gains for all actors, or at least no losses, are more likely to be accepted than redistributive policies. As far as the distinction between predominantly regulative or predominantly self-regulative is concerned, the salient distinction is whether the arena is primarily characterised by state/public (governing) structures or by associative/private (bargaining) patterns.

Agreement, acceptance or resistance to a policy is thus mainly a question of the distributive or redistributive character of the policy arena, rather than whether it is regulative or self-regulative. However, it will become clear that the latter distinction may also be relevant in this respect.

Of course to classify in this way is to simplify the 'real world' in an 'ideal-typical' way. Actual policies are mostly conducted in more than one arena. Nevertheless, it serves the essential theoretical purpose of generating dynamic predictions concerning the potential for reform and transformation, that is, the chances of radical unemployment policies being accepted and put into practice.

In the remainder of this section we will discuss these four arenas in greater detail and demonstrate their specific problems. This theoretical exercise should also provide an answer to the central question of why, in the light of increasing structural differentiation coupled with rising uncertainty about future states and behaviour and the growing diversity of problems and transactions, existing institutions are no longer capable of fulfilling their functions in a satisfactory manner.

The question of institutional efficiency is the classical domain of transaction-cost theory (Williamson 1985). This assumes that the efficiency

Character of the Arena

		Distributive	Redistributive
	Regulative	Rebuilding the East	Modes of financing
Institutional arrangement	*Self-regulative*	Arrangements on the local level	Collective bargaining

Figure 2.2 Four potential arenas to conduct unemployment policies in Germany

(cost) of a transaction varies with the institutional arrangement. In our case the question is whether it is more efficient to take on a new employee or to buy the needed product or service on the market. Which institutional form is optimal in saving costs depends, among other things, on the properties of the good to be exchanged (such as the skills offered by the new employee and the wages and working conditions offered by the employer). Most important are the criteria of specificity of the transaction (that is, its single or multiple-purpose use), uncertainty about future states and the behaviour of the partner(s), and the frequency of transactions of the same kind. Institutional forms are associated with costs based upon their design. Spontaneous and anonymous forms of coordination such as markets are cheaper ways than bureaucratic control mechanisms of conducting a transaction in a way that avoids opportunistic behaviour on the part of the partner(s). The intensity of incentives in the sense of an immediate reward after the transaction, the capacity to adapt to changing conditions, and the costs of establishing and maintaining an institution all vary with the institutional arrangement chosen. The question in relation to the German labour market is whether the AFG-based labour market administration and the system of collective bargaining still represent efficient institutional arrangements for transactions on the labour market.

Redistributive/regulative: the 'shunting yard logic' of financing unemployment policies

Active labour market policy can be financed by general revenue or by contributions to an insurance system. While the first option tends to cut payments and services in times of financial crises, the second tries to get rid of high risks. Because in Germany we have a mix of both systems

– as described above – we can observe both reactions (see Bruche/Reissert 1985:125; Schmid/Reissert/Bruche 1992 for details). Furthermore, because the different systems of financial support (unemployment benefits, benefits for registered unemployed and social benefits) are administered by different agencies – the Federal Government, the BA and the municipalities respectively – the result can be described as a 'shunting yard of costs' among them. 'Shunting' is done horizontally (Federal budget – BA) as well as vertically (Federal – municipal).

The reason for this can be found in regulative rigidities as well as in financial problems. The basic resources to finance labour market policies run by the BA are individual contributions made equally by the employers and the employees. Continuing high levels of unemployment produce a structural budget deficit and thereby reduce available funds for active labour market policies. Active measures then become more selective because their provision is not legally mandatory, in contrast to individual unemployment benefits (see Widmaier 1991 for details).

Aside from this 'budgetary cutting logic', the Federal Administration pushes financial burdens on to other state levels. A recent proposal by the Federal Government to limit the social benefits of registered unemployed (Arbeitslosenhilfe) to two years is an example of such a policy, as it would imply a considerable redistribution of costs to the local level by obliging the unemployed to resort to the municipally-financed social welfare benefits earlier than they do at present. Other regulative measures by the Federal Government (extending periods until claims can be made, reducing periods of payment) have reduced the population able to claim benefits and other services from the BA (the relative share not absolute numbers). The consequence of this policy is again an increasing number of unemployed dependent on social welfare benefits. Another financial burden which increasingly hits the municipalities stems from the reductions in contributions at the Federal level for employment in job creation measures (ABM). Municipalities are dependent on the labour of those employed on such schemes in order to provide for a number of public services, and, ironically, a reduction would automatically show up in the communal budget for social welfare benefits. In addition, persons employed on such schemes for a while are then entitled to unemployment benefits, which are financed by the BA.

In other words, we are dealing with a policy arena in which initiators and promoters of measures can externalise costs to other institutions. The real losers, however, are the unemployed who are pushed into other policy arenas (social policy) and therefore are longer officially considered as being participants in the labour market.

Due to the logic of the insurance system, the institutional form in which the BA conducts its transactions (passive and active measures) is that of an individualistic, quasi-labour contract, the minimum standards of which are defined by the AFG and other regulations. However this creates a number of inefficiencies. First, there is the problem of opportunistic behaviour, especially with respect to qualifying for unemployment benefits, which the BA tries to control with a bureaucratic apparatus. Second, we face the problem of uncertainty with regard to training and qualification measures: it is necessary to qualify the unemployed for jobs without knowing precisely the required skills and the demand for them. Third, from a legal and regulative point of view the insurance system implies benefits in the case of unemployment to insured individuals but excludes financial support for structural measures or investments which are not directly related to individuals. Despite the fact that individual rights to financial support have an important protective function for the individual, this seems to be the most serious deficiency of all.

Observing all these inefficiencies, the question has to be posed as to whether the modes of financing and the principle of individualistic support on the basis of centrally defined rules can meet the requirements of flexibility, differentiation and adaptation required in modern labour markets. In fact, the discussion on reforms of the AFG, as well as actual practice (regional industrial policy, ABS-companies, START), are moving towards greater decentralisation, flexibilisation of instruments and a closer integration of activities of local labour offices into more encompassing strategies to fight unemployment.

Redistributive/self-regulative: the 'social closure logic' of the institution of collective bargaining

Examination of the workings of the German system of collective bargaining suggests that institutions with a self-regulative character in an arena with shrinking distributional options are increasingly divorcing themselves from the claims and interests of third parties. They are probably following a radical policy for the employed, but not for the employment chances of the unemployed. From this perspective the system of self-regulation does not prove in itself to be an efficient institution for the supply side of the labour market. As long as it is impossible to break the logic of zero-sum games the outsiders will always be the losers in the distributional struggle.

The coordination problem between micro and macro level, which appears from a union and employer association perspective as an increasing opportunism of individual employers and work councils at the firm level, has been subject to discussion particularly in connection with the bargaining power and potential for collective action of industry-wide unions. The frequently used term 'company syndicalism' (Hohn 1988; Keller 1989) may serve as an example. The collective good and solidarity problem constitutes not only an organisational challenge and a problem of associational discipline for encompassing unions but also – probably even more dramatically– for employer associations as well. The increasing differentiation of conditions, and the resulting requirements for the specific regulation of work at company level, cause a kind of 'productivity syndicalism' (Wiesenthal 1987:318) which is to a large degree liberated from the collective good problem on the collective bargaining level, thereby promising a higher rationality of interest mediation on the company level. A possible consequence is the weakening of 'collective rationality' in the sense that chances to settle on solidaristic goals – like employment opportunities for all – are becoming smaller. In addition, the chances of reaching predictable, politically calculable standardised solutions are diminishing.

Although this situation leads to increasing relevance for the work council, it can also imply a reduction of its potential for action since the work council lacks bargaining power, especially in small and medium-sized firms (see also Keller 1989; Widmaier 1993). Because it is placed at the interface between productivity and solidaristic interests it finds itself rather powerless and 'structurally irresponsible' (Wiesenthal 1987:317) in representing collective interests. This is also true of the individual company within employer associations.

From the perspective of the labour market this situation implies a danger of closing internal labour markets, for example by negotiating agreements on overtime instead of hiring additional employees. This mechanism reduces the chances of the unemployed to find new employment. The content of some of the company agreements achieved up to now, such as that at VW, supports this hypothesis. In times of shrinking demand for labour the danger of closing the employment system against the entitlement of the unemployed to work grows. The possibility exists that 'productivity coalitions' will be formed between employers and employees on the company level which reduce even further the possibilities of the unemployed getting a job.

In the longer term we have to expect that the declining relevance of collective agreements and of supporting organisations (unions) will weaken employee protection and increase deregulation. This will be particularly the case in small and middle-sized businesses. This could generate 'American labour relations' which could give new chances to the unemployed, albeit based on considerably less solidaristic conditions.

The theoretical perspective of transaction cost efficiency also demonstrates an increasing number of problems caused by the institution of industry-wide collective agreements. For example, such agreements disregard the increasing specificity of investment and its consequences for employment and therefore produce inefficiencies with respect to the intensity of incentives to realise transactions (for example hiring an unemployed person) and their adaptability to company specific conditions. In the meantime, and contrary to its original function the existing institution reduces the number of transactions instead of facilitating and increasing them – that is, it reduces the chances of new employment. Under this perspective dismissals can also be seen as a strategy to avoid transaction costs which would show up if the alternative was the probably unsuccessful ex-post renegotiation on cuts in wages and salaries under the existing regime of the collective agreement. Company specific developments which have led to wage cuts via the reduction of working hours are remarkable in this context. It is not by chance that the most prominent example is based on a decentralised company level agreement (VW).

Distributive/regulative: the 'field experiment' in the East

German reunification clearly showed the deficits of conventional labour market policies, and in addition created the conditions for a 'field experiment' with new, or altered policies. Policies became more distributive, and seem to provoke less conflict than their 'classical' redistributive predecessors.

One of the economic results of German reunification was a widespread de-industrialisation of the former GDR accompanied by dramatic losses in employment (especially among women). Unemployment figures of unprecedented levels called urgently for radical unemployment policies. In order to control the situation and to be in a position to conduct any policy, the authorities in West Germany decided to transfer its political-institutional order to the East in all fields of public policy. But the special situation in the former GDR required exceptions and modifications which in retrospect can be regarded as offspring of often underrated innovations. Examples can be found in science, law and the labour administration, including the system of financing through a compulsory insurance system with contributions not only from employers and employees but also from the Federal Government. It is obvious that the situation required substantial public contributions. This *de facto* change to a publicly-financed labour market policy helped to change the character of the policy arena from a rather redistributive to a more distributive one. Subsidies for the East have been put together into a large package called Gemeinschaftsaufgabe Aufschwung Ost to which all governmental levels have made their proportional contribution. This again is an important difference from the situation in the West, where budgets relevant to labour market policies are separate and very often dominated by conflicting political interests.

Even before the reunification, the so-called AFG-GDR law introduced in June 1990 included special regulations in order to take care of the special labour market structure in the East. After the reunification a number of these 'specialities' – some limited in time – were included in the AFG itself. But despite the modifications and the important differences mentioned, the transfer of an administrative-legal system to a totally different situation does not solve the institutional problems which – as we have demonstrated – have been apparent in the context of the old

FRG. Nevertheless, it is fascinating to see how the predominantly state-financed active labour market policy in East Germany changes the character of the policy arena. The financial resources for labour market policy are integrated into other public programmes and are thereby no longer affected by the chronic budgetary and regulative problems of the BA.

This type of financing has also made it possible to depart from the individualistic logic of active labour market policy. For example it is now possible to finance investments in equipment for employment and training companies. Furthermore, firms which guarantee employment for those otherwise unemployed can be subsidised as well as specific persons (under special conditions in order to avoid 'pocketing').

Notwithstanding the fact that such companies are supposed to avoid direct competition with private activities, it is of central importance that they are designed to be open to market influences and as similar as possible to private companies. If these aspects are neglected there would be a significant danger that such collective projects would turn into entrenched activities of the secondary labour market with all the long-term consequences for those employed in such organisations. It is also necessary to invent new forms of ownership, responsibility and financing in order to create businesslike organisations which develop specific, marketable know-how, thereby enabling a gradually decreasing dependence on public subsidies. Even models which operate on a public loan base for certain investments, which would have to be repaid later in case of economic success, are conceivable. The kind of new direction that active labour market policy could take, given the challenges in the East, is demonstrated by the Structural Promotion Programme Brandenburg – Work instead of Unemployment (Strukturförderungsprogramm Brandenburg – Arbeit statt Arbeitslosigkeit). Based on the simple thought that too much money is paid for financing unemployment and not enough on creating new jobs, a large variety of policies can be introduced. They are based on mixed ownership and innovative modes of financing with the goal of promoting structural change in the region. They clearly deviate from the existing institutional logic and are therefore considered as radical.

Distributive/self-regulative: cooperation at the local level

Local labour markets are often characterised by a mismatch between the qualifications of the labour force and those demanded by employers. Such a situation can lead to overlapping interests on the part of different actors. Companies are looking for additional labour force, the local (regional) labour office wants to place unemployed people into new jobs, and the local administration wants to improve its image and reduce the number of social benefit recipients in the future. Successful unemployment policies in this field depend first on the identification of common interests and on communication (see Bandemer/Stöbe 1992 for details). Second, they demand the participation of a greater number of interested parties (unions, employer associations, chambers of commerce) and third, the scientific evaluation of the steps and measures taken. The combination of decentralisation and the intense participation of the directly affected actors in political processes seems to be a solution to these problems. We can assume that such a self-regulative mechanism will not only lead to better acceptance of policies but will also be more effective since a more flexible coordination of different interests is possible.

It is important to realise that only specific and visible indications of progress guarantee continuation of interest and participation in such corporatist structures. Models to qualify the long-term unemployed at the communal and regional level (employment companies) have recently attracted a substantial degree of interest. A central feature of these models is their closeness to the actual working process in firms, since otherwise they neither generate important motivational pressure on the part of the unemployed nor reduce reservations on the part of the firms about the social and occupational skills of such job applicants. In order to reduce the risk for the private actors involved, employment companies operated by public administrations employ the long-term unemployed on the basis of a regular labour contract. After a period of training these people are contracted out to employers on the basis of a limited contract in the hope that both sides can settle on a regular contract after getting to know each other. The initial results of this START are promising (Weinkopf and Krone 1995).

The creation of similar models on a decentralised base in as many local settings as possible in the future will furnish the political arena of radical unemployment policies with a set of new institutions. They are based on features like cooperation and integration and display a stronger distributive character in their political style. Simultaneously such institutional innovations also imply the building of stronger linkages between unemployment policies and regional economic processes thereby making the former more market-oriented. Finally, this can also redefine the role of the BA away from the 'administration' of unemployment towards active support for the unemployed on their difficult road to new employment.

OUTLOOK

It can be seen that our theoretical perspective helps to explain why the two central institutions of the employment system in Germany, industry-wide collective agreements and the BA, have increasingly failed to solve the employment problems in modern labour markets characterised not only by differentiation and individualisation but also by segmentation. On the one hand these institutions are too deeply rooted in the regulative policy model and on the other they emphasise strongly the redistributional character of policy arenas. By doing so they tend to widen the gap between the employed and the unemployed. We can expect that in the future the costs of policy failure will be too high for all actors, so that industry-wide working time reductions, for example, and a mere continuation of policies along the principles of the AFG seem to be unlikely.

The enormous scale of the problem in the East and the pressure to act have generated a labour-market policy with more innovative concepts and models. At the same time they have demonstrated how different instruments can change the perspective of a policy. This holds true on the one hand for the switch from passive to active support, in the case of wage subsidies instead of unemployment benefits and, on the other hand, for the financing of projects instead of individuals in the case of employment and training companies. It also allows for the integration of programmes into a regional reconstruction policy. In addition, the scale and manifold of programmes have also changed the policy field into a distributive arena in which the state 'distributes' instead of 'redistributing' internally. This constitutes a significant difference compared to the character of the policy arena in the West.

The corporatist, non profit-oriented models of contracting out labour on the communal level in the West point in a similar direction. If these models are successful in integrating associational and private actors more strongly into efforts of this type then there is hope that unemployment policy will not remain a welfare policy for the unemployed, but change to an employment policy for the unemployed as well as for those currently employed. The chances of such models and programmes being put into operation improve dependent upon the extent to which participating actors perceive them as positive sum games.

The building materials for institutions which could change the character of labour market policy in Germany are a cooperative, interest mediating political style and a distributively structured policy arena. The problem with reforms of existing institutions is that they define the 'feasible set' (Elster 1986) in which solutions to newly arising problems are to be sought. The vested interests and organisational routines of the collective actors participating make radical deviations from the logic of existing institutions very difficult.

However not all functions of the old institutional regimes should be abolished or replaced. The protective function for the individual which collective settlements and individual entitlements provide is an example in this respect and should be kept.

The survival chances for innovative ideas to fight unemployment are therefore dependent on their developing and growing 'silently' under the regime of the old institutions. For that they need to have common elements with, and be deeply embedded in, these institutions. Only if they are accepted as legitimate offspring born under specific circumstances – the extraordinary magnitude of a problem for example – will they have a chance to change 'the system from within' (Leonard Cohen 1988).

REFERENCES

Adamy, Wilhelm (1994), '25 Jahre Arbeitsförderungsgesetz. Bilanz und Perspektiven aus der Sicht der Gewerkschaften', *Arbeit und Sozialpolitik*, vol. 48, no. 7–8, pp.32–94.

ANBA – Amtliche Nachrichten der Bundesanstalt für Arbeit, annual volumes.

ANBA (1994), *Amtliche Nachrichten der Bundesanstalt für Arbeit*, vol. 42, Sonderheft: Arbeitsmarkt 1993.

Arbeit und Recht (1992), 'DGB Thesen für ein Arbeitsverhältnisgesetz §9', *Arbeit und Recht* no. 9, pp.267–71.

Bach, Hans-Uwe, and Spitznagel, Eugen (1994) 'Modellrechnungen zur Bewertung beschäftigungspolitischer Arbeitszeitverkürzungen', *IAB Werkstattbericht* no. 2, 25 January 1994.

Bandemer, Stephan von, and Stöbe, Sybille (1992), *Der 'Erste' Arbeitsmarkt im Visier lokaler Handlungsmöglichkeiten. Bedingungen für eine betriebsbezogene Arbeitsmarktpolitik*, Arbeitspapier des Instituts Arbeit und Technik, IAT-Z 08, Gelsenkirchen.

Basedow, Jürgen (1992), 'Arbeit durch private Vermittlung: Vom Ende des staatlichen Vermittlungsmonopols', *Wirtschaftsdienst*, vol. 72, no. 4, pp.180–2.

Bosch, Gerhard (1994), 'Aktuelle Debatten über eine Reform des Arbeitsförderungsgesetzes', in Heinelt, Hubert, Bosch, Gerhard and Reissert, Bernd (eds) *Arbeitsmarktpolitik nach der Vereinigung*, Berlin, pp.30–42.

Bosch, Gerhard, and Knuth, Matthias (1992), 'Beschäftigungsgesellschaften in den alten und neuen Bundesländern', *WSI Mitteilungen*, vol. 45, no. 7, pp.431–9.

——(1993), 'The Labour Market in East Germany', *Cambridge Journal of Economics*, vol. 17, pp.295–308.

Bruche, Gert, and Reissert, Bernd (1985), *Die Finanzierung der Arbeitsmarktpolitik*, Frankfurt, New York.

Bundesanstalt für Arbeit (1994) (ed.) *Strukturanalyse 1993*, Nürnberg.

Elster, John (ed.) (1986), Introduction to, *Rational Choice*, Oxford, pp.1–33.

Engelen-Kefer, Ursula (1992), 'Arbeitsvermittlung verbessern – nicht privatisieren', *Wirtschaftsdienst*, vol. 72, no. 4, pp.175–7.

Handelsblatt, no. 20, 27./28.1.1995, p.5.

Heinelt, Hubert, Bosch, Gerhard and Reissert, Bernd (eds) (1994), *Arbeitsmarktpolitik nach der Vereinigung*, Berlin.

Hohn, H.W. (1988), *Von der Einheitsgewerkschaft zum Betriebssyndikalismus. Soziale Schließung im dualen System der Interessenvertretung*, Berlin.

iwd (1994), Resonanz auf ein neues Modell, *iwd – Informationsdienst des Instituts der Deutschen Wirtschaft*, vol. 20, no. 36, p.6, Köln.

Keller, Bernd (1989), '"Krise" der institutionellen Interessenvermittlung und Zukunft der Arbeitsbeziehungen: Flexibilisierung, Deregulierung und Mikrokorporatismus', Hartwich, Hans-Hermann (ed.) *Macht und Ohnmacht politischer Institutionen*, Opladen, pp.135–57.

Knuth, Matthias (1994), 'ABS-Gesellschaften als dezentrale Akteure der Arbeitsmarkt-und Strukturpolitik: Problemlösung "vor Ort"?' in Heinelt, Hubert, Bosch, Gerhard and Reissert, Bernd (eds) *Arbeitsmarktpolitik nach der Vereinigung*, Berlin, pp.172–84.

Lowi, Theodor J. (1972), 'Four Systems of Policy, Politics, and Choice', *Public Administration Review*, vol. 33, pp.298–310.

March, James G., and Olsen, Johan P. (1989), *Rediscovering Institutions. The Organisational Basis of Politics*, New York.

Meinhardt, Volker, Stille, Frank and Zwiener, Rudolf (1993), 'Weitere Arbeitszeitverkürzungen erforderlich – Zum Stellenwert des VW-Modells', *Wirtschaftsdienst*, vol. 73, no. 12, pp.639–44.

OECD, *Employment Outlook*, annual volumes, Paris.

Rosdücher, Jörg, and Seifert, Hartmut (1994), *Die Einführung der '4-Tage Woche' in der Volkswagen AG*, Berlin.

Salisbury, Robert H. (1968), 'The Analysis of Public Policy: A Search of Theories and Roles', in Ranney, Austin (ed.) *Political Science and Public Policy*, Chicago, pp.151–75.

Schmid, Alfons, Krömmelbein, Silvia, Klems, Wolfgang and Gaß, Gerald (1994), 'Neue Wege der Arbeitsmarktpolitik: Modellarbeitsämter und Modellprojekte', *WSI Mitteilungen*, vol. 47, no. 2, pp.84–94.

Schmid, Günther (1987), *Arbeitsmarktpolitik im Wandel. Entwicklungstendenzen des Arbeitsmarktes und Wirksamkeit der Arbeitsmarktpolitik in der Bundesrepublik Deutschland, Wissenschaftszentrum Berlin für Sozialforschung*, WZB discussion paper IIM / LMP 87–17.

Schmid, Günther, Reissert, Bernd and Bruche, Gert (1992), *Unemployment Insurance and Active Labor Market Policy. An International Comparison of Financing Systems*, Detroit.

Schreiner, Ottmar (1994), *Arbeit für alle? – Wege aus der Arbeitslosigkeit*, Köln.

Seifert, Hartmut (1989), 'Beschäftigungswirkungen und Perspektiven der Arbeitszeitpolitik', *WSI-Mitteilungen*, vol. 42, no. 3, pp.156–63.

——(1991), 'Perspektiven tariflicher Arbeitszeitpolitik', *WSI-Mitteilungen*, vol. 44, no. 3, pp.164–9.

Sozialpolitische Informationen (ed.) (1994), *Bundesministerium für Arbeit und Sozialordnung*, vol. 28, no. 15, 4 October 1994.

Sperling, Ingeborg (1994), 'Probleme des zweiten Arbeitsmarktes', *Wirtschaftsdienst*, vol. 74, no. 8, pp.396–402.

Wagner, Alexandra (1994), 'Gesellschaften zur Arbeitsförderung, Beschäftigung und Strukturentwicklung (ABS) im Transformationsprozeß Ostdeutschlands', *WSI-Mitteilungen*, vol. 47, no. 2, pp.73–83.

Walwei, Ulrich (1994), 'Reform der Arbeitsvermittlung in den OECD-Ländern: Modernisierung öffentlicher Dienste und Zulassung privater Anbieter', *MittAB*, vol. 27, no. 2, pp.94–107.

Weinkopf, Claudia, and Krone, Sirikit (1995), *START Zeitarbeit – sozialverträgliche Arbeitnehmerüberlassung als arbeitsmarktpolitisches Instrument*, Ministerium für Arbeit, Gesundheit und Soziales des Landes Nordrhein-Westfalen (ed.) Gelsenkirchen, Düsseldorf.

Wiesenthal, Helmut (1987), *Strategie und Illusion. Rationalitätsgrenzen kollektiver Akteure am Beispiel der Arbeitszeitpolitik 1980–1985*, Frankfurt a.M.

Widmaier, Ulrich (1991), 'Segmentierung und Arbeitsteilung – Die Arbeitsmarktpolitik in der Bundesrepublik Deutschland in der Diskussion', *Aus Politik und Zeitgeschichte*, B34-5, pp.14–25.

—— (1993), 'Arbeits- und tarifpolitische Konsequenzen und Perspektiven flexibler Fertigung', *Flexible Arbeitsysteme und neue Informationstechnologien: Veränderung der Produktionsarbeit*, Ringvorlesung Ruhr-Universität Bochum/ IGMetall 1992–93; IGMetall Vorstand/Ruhr- Universität Bochum (ed.), 1993.

Williamson, Oliver E. (1985), *The Economic Institutions of Capitalism*, New York.

3 France

Susan Milner and René Mouriaux

INTRODUCTION

There has been no shortage of proposals for radical unemployment
policies in France. On the right, proposals to eliminate unemployment by
removing unemployment benefit have a long history, dating back to
Jacques Rueff's calls in the 1930s. Further right still, the equation 'number
of unemployed equals number of immigrants' has found a ready response
in some sections of the population, as Jean-Marie Le Pen's score of
15 per cent in the first round of the 1995 presidential elections showed.

There no longer seem to be any taboos in the discussion of unemployment policies. After fourteen years of the Mitterrand presidency, characterised by a succession of left and right wing governments each loudly
proclaiming its inability to do anything to halt the rise of unemployment,
the stage seems open for economists and politicians to come forward with
their proposals. A general sense of dissatisfaction with traditional policies
and a desire for radical change, strongly visible in the 1995 presidential
elections, have led to a questioning of orthodoxies. In April 1995, for
example, a 'manifesto for employment' signed by thirteen economists
(who themselves proposed a variety of differing partial measures or pack-
ages of solutions, highlighting the variety of responses on offer) called for
a radical overhaul of employment policies and an end to the prevailing
orthodoxy of 'growth-led employment':

> Unemployment will not fall by itself. ... A lasting return to growth of
> the French economy will not be enough to bring the unemployment
> rate down sufficiently. ... The measures implemented or planned to
> date have not been on an adequate scale. In order to combat the plague
> of unemployment, it is necessary to act strongly and in a coordinated
> fashion, on a financial, social and even cultural level simultaneously.
>
> (Boissard and Vittori 1995:48)

The 1995 presidential elections were dominated by the question of
unemployment, which various opinion surveys highlighted as the major
issue preoccupying voters: over 70 per cent of survey respondents cited
unemployment as the most important issue of the elections, and in some

surveys the figure rose as high as 90 per cent. Jacques Chirac was elected President because of his ability to capture this desire for policy change in his campaign. But despite this favourable climate, the chances of radical new proposals being implemented seem very remote indeed.

On the left as well as on the right, France has generated a series of radical unemployment policies which have been influential in a general sense, moving work-sharing into the arena of public debate not only inside France but across Europe. However very few of them have been put into practice, for reasons which will be explored in this chapter.

CONTEXT

To understand the environment within which the French debate on radical unemployment policies has taken place, it is necessary to look at the institutional framework, the unemployment benefit system, recent developments in unemployment and unemployment policies, and the vocational training system.

Institutional framework

The Ministry of Labour is the main branch of government responsible for employment policy, although other ministries, such as the Civil Service Ministry and the Agriculture Ministry, also regulate employment in the relevant sectors. There are three state institutions which report to the Ministry of Labour: the External Services for Work and Employment, the National Employment Agency, and the National Agency for Adult Vocational Training.

The External Services for Work and Employment (Services Extérieurs du Travail et de l'Emploi, or SETE) represent government policy at the level of the département, under the authority of the prefect. They are concerned mainly with the monitoring of aid to companies in difficulty, redevelopment schemes, and various start-up initiatives for business creation.

The National Employment Agency (Agence Nationale pour l'Emploi, or ANPE) was set up in 1967 as the central state placement agency. It employed a staff of 12,000 in 1990 (Laroque 1990:202). It works with job-seekers in order to try to find suitable employment for them through information and guidance, and with employers to fill vacant posts. A separate agency for management and supervisory staff (Agence pour l'Emploi des Cadres or APEC) was set up within the ANPE in 1969 to deal with this specific category of job-seekers. When the ANPE was originally established, job placement was a state monopoly, but a decree of December 1986 opened the way for the ANPE to sub-contract activities to approved outside agencies. The ANPE found it difficult to cope with the situation of rising unemployment since the early 1970s and came increasingly under fire in the late 1980s and early 1990s. It was reorganised by Labour Minister Martine Aubry during the period 1991–2 and ordered to pay more attention to individual employment needs, but in fact in recent years it has increasingly been run along the lines of a private placement agency and has preferred to leave cases of poorly qualified workers with real employment difficulties to social service agencies. The nomination of Michel Bon as director of the ANPE in August 1993 exacerbated this trend.

The National Agency for Adult Vocational Training (Agence Nationale pour la Formation Professionnelle des Adultes, or AFPA) was set up after the war in order to assist the ANPE by offering training and retraining courses to job-seekers. With its staff of 10,000 it provided training for 138,000 people in 1990 (Laroque 1990:202). Like the ANPE, it has experienced problems trying to keep pace with the demands placed on the employment services by rapidly rising unemployment.

Unemployment benefits

The system of unemployment benefits is organised separately, outside the Ministry of Labour or for that matter the Social Security department. The insurance-based unemployment compensation scheme was established in an agreement between employers and trade unions on 31 December 1958, under which locally based Associations for Employment in Industry and Commerce (Associations pour l'Emploi dans l'Industrie et le Commerce, or ASSEDIC) were created to adminster the insurance funds. At national level, the Union for Employment in Industry and Commerce (Union Nationale pour l'Emploi dans l'Industrie et le Commerce, or UNEDIC) coordinated the local ASSEDIC. Benefits were paid out according to payments made, and the state financed only a subsidiary part. However, the insurance fund was unable to finance the growing demand for unemployment benefit in the 1970s, and in January 1979 the social partners' insurance scheme and state benefits were merged into the UNEDIC, which retained its joint management structure whilst now incorporating state financing. The new system did not last long: in 1984 it was reformed again and the two modes of financing – insurance managed by the social partners and state 'solidarity' benefits – were separated.

Since 1984 the UNEDIC agreement has been amended seven times. The agreement of 1 January 1993 established a single, graduated benefit comprising a sum calculated as a proportion of former daily pay and a fixed sum. The duration of benefit varies according to previous contributions; after a certain time the amount decreases until it runs out altogether. The period of eligibility for benefits varies from four to sixty months. Once entitlement to unemployment benefit has been exhausted, claimants may qualify for various targeted social assistance payments, dependent upon the level of previous contributions.

In order to cater for the growing number of 'new poor', which includes the increasing masses of youth who have never held a contribution-paying job in their lives, the Minimum Income (Revenu Minimum d'Insertion, or RMI) was introduced in December 1989. Those over the age of 25 whose income falls below a certain level receive a basic allowance and in return must make themselves available for 'labour market integration' jobs made available by the local authorities. Since 1990 the number of 'RMIstes' has almost doubled, from 422,102 in 1990 to 803,303 in 1994 (*Le Monde*, 13 December 1994).

According to a report on the French economy prepared for the Commission of the European Communities (CEC 1991:10), 'Unemployment benefits in France appear to be fairly generous as regards availability, duration and level. There is, therefore, a relatively strong incentive to prolong the search period for employment and a high risk that workers meanwhile lose important working abilities.' However, the French system was devised for an environment in which employment was relatively rare and of short duration. Despite the panoply of social assistance benefits available, many unemployed people evidently slip through the net and are forced to live on inadequate means. UNEDIC figures showed that 82 per cent of the unemployed had a monthly income of less than 5,000 francs (about £660) in 1994, and almost half (46.29 per cent) received less than 3,000 francs (about £400). Nearly 500,000 unemployed young people under the age of 25 had no access to benefits whatsoever (*Le Monde*, 12 January 1995).

Recent developments in unemployment and unemployment policy

When France was hit by economic crisis and rising unemployment in the 1970s, government reaction was first of all to alleviate unemployment with retraining and restructuring schemes whilst waiting for a return to growth. When it became clear that growth was not around the corner, mainstream unemployment policy hinged on a reduction of wage costs and moves towards greater labour market flexibility, particularly numerical flexibility.

The Socialists came to power in 1981 with a mandate for radical change. They proceeded to tackle unemployment with an ambitious reflationary package based on the nationalisation of industrial champions and much of the financial sector, a wages and social benefits boost to fuel consumer demand, and a reduction of working time from 40 to 39 hours per week, with the aim of a gradual decrease to 35 hours. Despite the beneficial effect on the unemployment figures, the Socialists' programme fell foul of the international economic climate of austerity, which made foreign goods cheaper than French goods, and led to a flight of capital abroad. Successive governments introduced unemployment plans which were little more than cosmetic adjustments to existing training schemes, and continued after 1985 to encourage labour market flexibility (numerical and temporal) and

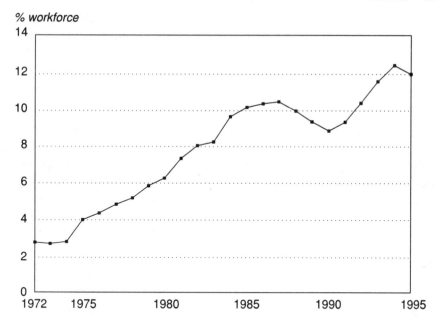

Figure 3.1 Unemployment in France, 1972–1995

Source: OECD 1992 (1972–87), OECD 1995 (1988–95)

Note: Standardised unemployment rates to 1994, projection based on commonly used definition 1995

'precarious' forms of work. Most of the training and 'solidarity' agreements (replacement of older workers through early retirement with new trainees) involved employer wage subsidies, as did many of the measures to encourage the use of part-time employment. The following table shows the increase from 1993 to 1994 in 'precarious' forms of employment contract based on government unemployment measures alone (i.e. leaving aside the rise in other forms of precarious employment such as fixed-term contracts and temporary work).

Despite his promises in the election campaign, Jacques Chirac's new presidency has shown little tendency to move away from this mainstream policy. The main measure in the plan unveiled by Prime Minister Juppé on 22 June 1995, heralded as a revolutionary new approach to long-term unemployment, was the Contrat Initiative-Emploi (CIE) (Employment Initiative Contract). Replacing the 'return to work' contract, the CIE offered employers taking on an unemployed person a bonus of 2,000 francs per month (about £260) as well as complete exoneration from social contributions on that part of the salary over the minimum wage (SMIC). In addition, the Juppé plan aimed to encourage youth employment by an extension of existing subsidies for apprenticeship schemes, and reduced

Table 3.1 Trends in 'precarious' forms of employment in France, 1993–1994

Type of precarious employment	Number employed	Increase	
'Insertion' contracts	700,000	+143,131	+28%
'Work-solidarity' contracts	430,000	+ 65,058	+18%
Tax relief for companies employing part-time workers	212,176	+ 29,468	+13%
'Qualification' contracts	143,000	+ 12,000	+ 9%
'Return to work' contracts	187,801	+ 64,266	+18%
'Adaptation' contracts	45,000	+ 3,000	+6%
'Insertion' training schemes	31,176	+ 5,934	+19%
'Orientation' contracts	6,495	+ 2,118	+32%

Source: INSEE

social security contributions on low wages. The extent of the CIE subsidy as well as its intention to tackle long-term unemployment (whereas earlier schemes had concentrated on youth training) signalled some steps in a new policy direction, but in general the plan remained within the orthodox policy of employer wage subsidy and an increase in taxation to finance 'insertion' schemes. Unemployment figures dropped slightly in July 1995, helped by the decision contained in the Juppé plan to exclude those working over a certain number of hours from the unemployed register (300,000 in July 1995), but rose again in August and September 1995.

Vocational training

Improved training as a means of ensuring a better fit between labour supply and demand has become part of a new orthodoxy uniting right and left-wing politicians, although very few specific measures have accompanied the 'new skills discourse'. Instead, measures have all too often used the rhetoric of upskilling to accompany youth training programmes which are little more than cheap labour replacement schemes but have the advantage of taking people off the official unemployment register. Few doubt that a problem exists at various levels. The 1991 EC Commission report pointed the finger at 'the transition from school to professional life [which] is very poor and apprenticeship is poorly developed' (a major source of concern for France's youth, as seen in the numerous protest demonstrations which have taken place in recent years), as well as France's relatively low level of spending on active labour market programmes genuinely aimed at matching local labour market supply and demand.

Moves towards reform of initial training have been patchy, partly because of the bureacratic inertia within the educational system which acts as a brake on change and partly because politicians have preferred to let the social partners agree on reform rather than impose it from the centre. The 1971 law on vocational training, based on a prior agreement between employers and trade unions, was revised following a similar consultation process in 1991. Subsequently, politicians have expressed the desire for a boost in apprenticeship schemes but have done little to activate such change themselves (although the 1995 Juppé plan constitutes a step in this direction). Companies have also been slow to spend money on continuous training for those who need it most (despite the existence of a training levy), preferring to concentrate training expenditure on those already qualified and to buy in lower-level qualified staff as required.

Radical economists have focused on continuous training as part of a wider programme to change the nature of work and work organisation. Thus, the influential French regulationist school has pointed to various options for 'post-Fordist' society: a liberal/dual scenario (characterised by highly segmented labour markets and the persistence of large-scale unemployment or under-employment), a mixed 'tempered liberal' scenario, and a 'wage democracy' scenario in which a balance is sought between technological, organisational and social innovation (Coriat 1990:268–85). In this respect, vocational training is not a radical employment policy in itself but part of a wider policy aimed at reshaping work and society. The keystone of this programme is work-sharing. Several companies which have introduced agreements on skills training (such as Péchiney and Renault) have linked it to reorganisation of work and a reduction in working time; however, such experiments remain limited to a handful of large public and private companies with strong links with government.

RADICAL UNEMPLOYMENT POLICIES

As we have already seen, radical unemployment policies have been many and various in France. In this section we will concentrate on radical unemployment policies of the left: in particular, work-sharing.

Repatriation of immigrants

As mentioned earlier, Jean-Marie Le Pen's 1995 presidential campaign concentrated almost exclusively on this theme. The slogan of 'French preference' in jobs was also the focus of his party's 1995 municipal election campaign, leading to the election of three National Front mayors (in Marignane, Orange, and, for the first time, a city of over 100,000 inhabitants, Toulon). The theme is not a new one – indeed, no less a figure than Jacques Chirac, as Prime Minister in January 1975, publicly declared that with one million unemployed and one million immigrants, France had the answer to its unemployment problem staring it in the face – but it has acquired added resonance in a country increasingly rent by social inequalities and spatial segregation. Le Pen is not alone in attributing France's unemployment to immigration: Nobel prize-winning economist Maurice Allais (admittedly known for his idiosyncracies, but nonetheless influential

Table 3.2 Radical unemployment policies in France

Strategy	Measures
Repatriation of immigrants	(Not implemented)
Cutting benefits/workfare	(Not implemented)
Personal services	Fiscal incentives
	Service employment vouchers
Measures aimed at preventing company lay-offs	Compulsory social plans
	Levy on intensified productivity (not implemented)
Work-sharing	Solidarity agreements on early retirement
	Part-time work
	Shorter working week (not implemented)
	Aznar twenty options, based largely on 'second cheque' (not implemented)

enough to command column space in the major newspapers for his views) has unequivocally laid the blame for unemployment at the door of immigration, as well as the European Union's free trade and monetary policies (*Le Figaro*, 7 July 1995). It is unlikely that a repatriation policy would be put forward as a radical unemployment policy, since apart from Allais no major economist takes the argument seriously and the practical difficulties involved in even the limited repatriation scheme which already exists make it unworkable on a large scale, but it is significant as a demagogic response to social discontent arising from mass unemployment.

Cutting benefits/ 'workfare'

One characteristic political response to each successive funding crisis involving unemployment benefits is a call to 'workfare'. Michel Bon, the new ANPE director, has made several public statements in support of 'workfare' policies whereby unemployment benefit would be dependent on public service labour. The RMI in particular has come under fire from the right because of the difficulties experienced in providing work experience placements for recipients. It is clear that the right sees the RMI as a form of 'workfare'. Michel Godet claimed in an article in *Le Figaro* (1 June 1995) that 'passive benefits create a culture of non-work and welfare dependency which is dangerous for society'. Various other right-wing politicians have also attempted to draw public attention to misuse of RMI benefits, rather like the 'dole fraud' arguments which are a perennial theme of the right in Britain. The idea has also been taken up by government: Eric Raoult, Minister for Integration, stated on 25 June 1995 that RMI expenditure would be more usefully spent 'recycled into programmes of social utility' (*Le Monde*, 26 June 1995). However, the costs of providing real jobs for welfare recipients (and the organisation of such jobs, which falls to the departmental social services) are such that no government would seriously contemplate 'workfare' schemes in France; rather, such remarks tend to serve as a justification for administrative cost-cutting.

'Emplois de proximité': Personal services

The idea of developing personal services, launched by André Gorz, has been advanced in recent years by the economist Pierre Héritier, a leading figure in the Confédération Française Démocratique du Travail trade union. In his book *Nouvelle croissance et emploi*, published in 1988, Héritier argued that by validating qualifications in this sector (home and personal services such as childminding, care of elderly or sick dependents, and house repairs, which are often discouraged by present tax arrangements or which fall increasingly outside the 'official' economy) and placing such activities within a coherent and conducive regulatory regime, a significant number of jobs could be created. According to this scenario, job creation arises from two processes: the professionalisation of service activities involving a shift from unpaid work (such as household activities) to paid work; and fiscal incentives to encourage demand for services, leading to a freeing-up of supply. In his preface to Héritier's book, Gorz noted the author's intention to give a new value and prestige to jobs which are often undervalued, but raised doubts about the feasibility of transforming activities based on human relationships into jobs without fundamentally altering their meaning. In an interview on 27 March 1995, Héritier explained that he wanted to draw a sharp distinction between 'emplois de proximité' and the precarious forms of work developed by successive governments, particularly the right-wing government under Jacques Chirac from 1986 to 1988, under which the laws introduced by Labour Minister Philippe Séguin encouraged flexibility of working hours and brought in more youth training schemes.

However, the distinction between professionalised personal services and low-grade, precarious jobs has sometimes been difficult to discern. In 1991 Martine Aubry attempted to encourage personal services through fiscal incentives in her employment plan, but was widely criticised by trade unions and the left for further eroding employment stability. Similarly, in its contribution to the 1995 presidential election debate, the French employers' association (the Conseil National du Patronat Français or CNPF), called for the development of service jobs as one of its three unemployment policy proposals, alongside labour flexibility and the reduction of non-wage labour costs, raising fears among trade unionists about employers' use of such service employment.

The idea of generating personal service jobs still has some attraction for economists and politicians. Philippe Séguin, the maverick right-wing politician (now President of the National Assembly), whose star has been in the ascendancy since his outright opposition to President Mitterrand over the Maastricht agreement, has often referred to 'unexploited reserves' of potential job creation, particularly in personal services: 'There is a real demand which could be met with a supply which most of the time the market no longer provides spontaneously ...' (*Le Monde*, 22 March 1995). Lionel Jospin's manifesto for the 1995 presidential elections also contained measures aimed at developing personal and community services, especially in the area of ecology and conservation, within the framework of a concerted job creation programme.

In December 1994, the Balladur government introduced a 'service employment cheque', enabling households to apply for vouchers to be exchanged for services, as one of the measures in its five-year employment plan. By the end of the same month, almost 50,000 applications for the vouchers had been registered (Ministère du Travail 1995). Three months later, some 165,000 vouchers had been delivered to employers of service personnel. In two thirds of these cases, the vouchers represented new jobs which had not previously been notified to the tax authorities. However, some experts have asked whether the measure simply represents a regularisation of informal jobs rather than the creation of new jobs (*Le Nouvel Economiste*, 21 April 1995:27). The results so far from various government fiscal measures and the 'service employment cheque' have not suggested any measurable effect on unemployment levels. Using econometric forecasts, the Paris-based Observatory on the Economic Climate (Observatoire Français de la Conjoncture Economique, or OFCE) estimated that the creation of 100,000 service jobs exempt from employers' social security contributions and remunerated at 80 per cent of the minimum wage would result in a reduction of only 40,000 in the number of unemployed, since jobs would be lost elsewhere because of the resulting price rises. In addition, it pointed out that such measures could be carried out only on a small scale due to the limited number of real gaps in service provision (OFCE 1993).

Measures aimed at preventing company lay-offs

In 1986, Philippe Séguin repealed the law requiring companies to submit planned mass redundancies to the labour inspectorate, which had been introduced as a first reaction to rising unemployment by Jacques Chirac in 1976. The 1986 measure gave satisfaction to a key demand of the main employers' association, whose president Yvon Gattaz promised that the flexibility it gave employers would result in significant job creation. On the contrary, unemployment rose perceptibly in the months following Séguin's decision. In response, the government called on employers and trade unions to negotiate a compromise solution which would obviate state action, but negotiations were slow in coming (talks between the social partners on unemployment did not start until 1995).

Meanwhile, a requirement for companies to submit a 'social plan' out-lining employment plans was introduced. The 'social plan' obliged employ-ers not only to inform the authorities of plans for large-scale redundancies, but also to show that they had explored all possible opportunities for rede-ployment or retraining of workers.

Martine Aubry's law of January 1993 made this obligation more precise: in companies with over fifty employees, any plans to lay off ten or more workers would be declared invalid unless details of opportunities for retraining for jobs elsewhere were submitted beforehand to workplace representatives. The Balladur government, hit by a succession of redun-dancy announcements, continued to use the 'social plan' as a means of putting pressure on employers and controlling the extent and timing of redundancies. Thus, in the case of the electronics giant Thomson, the company withdrew its social plan prepared in September 1993, which had been criticised by Balladur, and replaced it with a new version in which there were no outright redundancies but a mixture of early retirements, short-time working and reduced working hours. In other cases, however, a sceptical press warned that revised social plans might simply be a means of postponing unpopular decisions or introducing them in phases to soften the blow.

The 'social plan' initiatives are aimed at developing a 'social responsi-bility' in the business world. Politicians like Martine Aubry have found support for this approach among some sections of France's big business community, especially the public sector employers who so often share a common background with the political élite. Aubry's former business associate Jean Gandois, formerly head of Péchiney, won the presidency of the main employers' association, the CNPF, by promising a break with his predecessors' more confrontational style and a move towards a con-sensual approach. It was largely thanks to Gandois that national-level talks between employers and trade unions took place in 1995.

More controversially, economist Patrick Artus has suggested that politi-cians have waited far too long for employers to take the initiative on job creation and that a more punitive approach is needed. Artus, director of the economic and financial study unit of the state's public investment office, has proposed a tax levy on employers who intensify productivity rather than take on new workers, in order to subsidise low-productivity job creation elsewhere (see Boissard and Vittori, 1995:51). However, such a move would require real political courage; in any case, most observers concede that any measure seen as punitive could well be counter-productive if the aim is to encourage a sense of shared responsibility.

Solidarity agreements

As Aznar (1993:178) notes, it has become increasingly rare for workers over the age of 55 to stay in full-time employment. Early retirement schemes involving the replacement of older workers by younger workers were promoted by the government in the early 1980s and form part of the panoply of state anti-unemployment measures, alongside training schemes and wage subsidies. The financial burden fell on the unemployment benefit scheme (UNEDIC) rather than on individual companies, which exchange experienced labour for inexperienced, lower paid labour. As a result, the success and spread of early-retirement schemes depended largely on the willingness of the three parties involved (employers and employees through their contributions, and the state) to shoulder the burden. This limited the use of 'solidarity contracts'.

However, some larger companies, notably Rhône-Poulenc and Fleury-Michon, began to develop other forms of 'solidarity contract'. Under these agreements, workers of 55 years or over may opt for partial retirement. During their part-time work, they act as 'tutors' for the young workers who replace them. The French state responded to these company initiatives by agreeing to pay 30 per cent of the worker's former wage. The company pays 50 per cent of the worker's wage, leaving only a 20 per cent wage loss. In 1990, 4,500 workers opted for early, part-time retirement under such agreements, thus opening up an equivalent number of full-time jobs. Aznar (1993:179–80), noting the relatively small number of workers concerned, attributed the limited impact of the measure to workers' desire to maintain their standard of living. Since such measures tend to involve manual workers at the lower end of the pay scale, a 20 per cent drop in wages can make a big difference to their standard of living. In order to make the schemes more attractive, Aznar proposes a gradual decrease in working time involving no wage loss. The wage compensation would be financed through the state retirement scheme. This could be recouped by extending the move into retirement beyond the age of 60. In other words, the company and the state share the burden over a longer period, whilst the worker works for a longer period in return for no wage loss. Aznar points to American companies such as IBM which have pioneered this type of flexible retirement, but it has not yet caught the imagination of French companies.

A further move towards 'solidarity pacts' was made in September 1995 with the signature of an agreement between all five major trade union confederations and the CNPF. This agreement, hailed as a 'first' in French labour relations, allows workers over the age of 57½ to opt for full early retirement, provided s/he has made pension contributions for forty years, and receive 60 per cent of his/her former wage. The 'early pension' is to be financed by the UNEDIC unemployment fund, the retiring worker's job will be filled by a young unemployed worker. Trade unions estimate that the measure could create up to 100,000 jobs.

From a reduction in working-time to 'unemployment-sharing'

The theme of work-sharing was developed in France in the 1970s by thinkers close to the new left and ecologist movements, especially André Gorz and Guy Aznar. Aznar's 1980 book *Tous à mi-temps!* (*Let's all go part-time!*), a rousing call to rethink the very basis of work in post-industrial society, provided the basis for many new ideas on work-sharing. The debate was reopened when the Socialist government came to power in 1981 on a manifesto promising a reduction in working time to 35 hours. However, disagreements soon arose over the question of wage compensation, which proved to be the major sticking-point in the debate. An immediate reduction from 40 hours to 39 (with no wage loss) came into effect, with the expectation that further reductions would follow once the productivity gains from this initial reduction had become clear and all parties had thought through the effects of the experiment. No further reduction followed. Instead, the debate shifted towards 'reorganisation' of working time, with laws in 1985 and 1986 designed to give employers greater temporal flexibility.

However, calls for a reduction in working time did not go away. In 1988 André Gorz relaunched the debate with his book *Métamorphoses du travail*. Consultants Bernard Brunhes and Dominique Taddéi, who remained close to President Mitterrand's inner circle of advisers, produced reports on the reduction and reorganisation of working time in the late 1980s (Taddéi 1988, Brunhes 1993). Taddéi's report was taken up by the (then Socialist minority) government, which introduced a law offering tax relief to companies prepared to reorganise work to allow maximum machine capacity. Although the Taddéi law was taken up by only a handful of guinea-pig firms, his and Brunhes's ideas (particularly on the beneficial effects of a coordinated European reduction in working time) have been influential in shaping the policy environment at national and European level.

The debate resurfaced in 1993 with the five-year plan on employment presented by Labour Minister Michel Giraud. Early expectations that the plan would move towards a phased reduction in working time were confounded; instead the government chose to continue the well-worn path of reorganisation of working time (facilitating part-time work). However, the plan did at least reopen the debate. An amendment calling for a 32 hour week (over four days) was killed off in the upper chamber. However, it emerged again in the spring of 1994 when five MPs presented an (unsuccessful) motion to that effect.

Outside government circles, other actors had also taken up the call for a reduction in working time. The episcopacy of the Catholic Church in France produced a report on work-sharing in 1982, which it updated in 1993 (Commission sociale de l'épiscopat, 1993). Some of the French trade unions also took up the issue. The Confédération Générale du

Travail (CGT, close to the French Communist Party) campaigned for a 35 hour week with no wage loss. The CFDT, on the other hand, was more prepared to negotiate on the question of wage compensation and more inclined to argue for a reduction of working time on the grounds of solidarity with the unemployed. At its 43rd congress in March 1995, the CFDT voted to campaign for a framework law establishing a 32 hour week.

In 1993, Guy Aznar returned to the offensive with a new book on work-sharing in which he assessed the progress to date and attempted to evaluate the chances of success of the programme he put forward. The book, *Travailler moins pour travailler tous* (*Let's work less so we can all work*), represented an attempt to get away both from the utopian over-tones of the 1970s work-sharing debate and the political quagmire of the issue of working hours. Like Brunhes, who called for an imaginative approach using a variety of possible measures adapted to individual circumstances (*Libération*, 3 November 1993), Aznar argued that work-sharing covered a multitude of options, some more appropriate to certain circumstances than others. He formulated twenty possible options in the book, some of which stood more chance of gaining acceptance than others (see Tables 3.3 and 3.4).

Central to work-sharing is the idea of the 'second cheque' (an idea developed by Gorz): a compensatory income which is not directly financed by employers (except in cases where productivity gains can clearly cover the loss induced by the reduction in working time) but borne to a small extent by the worker (who benefits through increased leisure) and to a greater extent by wider society (whether directly in the form of an allowance or indirectly through tax cuts etc.).

According to Aznar, the proposals by the Greens in France for a 35 hour week (propounded notably by economist Alain Lipietz) were seen as incredible by public opinion because they failed to take into account the economic hardship they would cause to specific groups of workers or employers. The Paris-based Observatory on the Economic Climate (Observatoire Français de la Conjoncture Economique, or OFCE) studied the Greens' proposal in a report in March 1993 and concluded that it would lead to economic disaster without a massive reorganisation of work (shift-working), because of pressures on investment leading employers to squeeze wages further. In this report, the OFCE studied three unem-ployment policies: a 'left-wing' reflationary strategy (with an estimated gain of 200,000–300,000 jobs), 'right-wing' reorganisation of work (labour market flexibility) (with similar estimated results), and a Green-inspired work-sharing policy.

The idea behind the Green proposals is a general, immediate move towards a 35 hour week with no wage loss, then a 30 hour week by the year 2000. Wage compensation would be differential, with higher wage-earners receiving less compensation. Those volunteering to work part-time

Table 3.3 Guy Aznar's 1993 proposals on work-sharing

Strategy	Proposed measures	Examples
Reduce working time with no wage loss, financed by productivity gains and partial state funding	(1) second shift	IBM, Printemps, Hewlett Packard
	(2) three-day weekend	
	(3) fourth shift (2 × night shift)	
Reduce working time with wage cuts ('unemployment sharing')	(4) reduced working time +% wage cut	many!
Voluntary part-time work ('chosen time') with partial state funding	(5) job-sharing	
	(6) parental p/t leave	
	(7) elder care p/t leave	
	(8) progressive early retirement	Rhône Poulenc Fleury Michon Hewlett Packard
	(9) p/t training leave	
	(10) p/t work experience for unemployed	
	(11) public sector p/t quotas (13–25%)	Crédit Lyonnais UAP, AGF
	(12) sabbatical year	
	(13) training leave	
	(14) temporary work (as a means of forestalling redundancy)	
Make youth work part-time	(15) alternance (work/training for all 16–18 year olds)	
	(16) civilian national service for all youth (M/F) (12 mths)	
Eliminate long-term unemployment by creating 'insertion' companies	(17) new 'insertion' companies at local level (e.g. associations, works committees)	
Create jobs	(18) job quotas (e.g. in retail: employees per m2); policies to discourage total automation	
	(19) employer incentives for innovative practices	
	(20) penalise overtime	

Source: Aznar 1993

(less than 30 hours per week) would receive public aid ('second cheque'). According to the OFCE, this work-sharing policy could generate around two million jobs. By itself this would not be sufficient to absorb all of France's unemployment, but complemented by other measures it represents the best chance of solving the problem (OFCE 1993; see also Lipietz 1995).

Table 3.4 Estimated job creation potential of work-sharing proposals in France

Work-sharing proposal	Part-time jobs created	Full-time equivalent
Four-day week	400,000	200,000
Progressive (p/t) early retirement	200,000	100,000
Part-time parental leave	200,000	100,000
Part-time elder care leave	200,000	100,000
Part-time training or sabbatical	200,000	100,000
Public sector part-time quotas	600,000	300,000
Youth part-time work	500,000	500,000
Elimination of long-term unemployment	n/a	500,000
Job creation	200,000	100,000
Total		2,000,000

Source: Aznar 1993:223

The question is not whether the work-sharing solution is economically viable, since many reliable reports have now confirmed its effectiveness, but whether it is acceptable to the key people concerned – workers and employers – and also politically acceptable, i.e. whether politicians are sufficiently convinced that there is political capital to be made from policies which require at least partial sacrifices.

POLITICAL DYNAMICS

Public opinion on work-sharing has fluctuated considerably according to economic and political circumstances. The onset of durable, mass unemployment has created an awareness of the complexity of the problem and to some extent a willingness to make sacrifices to help solve it. For the first time, the unemployed themselves have become visible actors, with a series of marches for employment organised under the auspices of a new movement, Agir ensemble contre le chômage, or AC! ('Act together against unemployment', the abbreviation AC being a homophone of 'assez!' – 'enough!').

However, as Lipietz (1995) admits, recent revelations about company profits and top management salaries, together with widespread disillusionment caused by numerous financial and political scandals, have reinforced a feeling that sacrifices are shared unequally, making individuals reluctant to choose leisure time over wages and boosting the 'old-style' trade union demand for a reduction in working time without wage loss. Thus whereas 71 per cent of people interviewed in one survey in 1993 declared themselves willing to accept a wage cut in exchange for a general reduction in working time, only 53 per cent expressed the same willingness in a survey carried out by the same organisation in early 1995, and 47 per cent categorically rejected the idea (*Le Nouvel Economiste*, 24 February 1995).

Even these figures seem high. Another survey, carried out in August 1992, shows only 32 per cent of people willing to accept a reduction in working hours with a corresponding wage cut ('in order to give the unemployed access to a job'), with 51 per cent refusing (Aznar 1993:165–6).

Workers seem divided on the issue depending on their position in the labour market. Women tend generally to prefer the option of part-time work when questioned in surveys, although in reality they shun such work for financial reasons. The unemployed, students and workers on temporary work contracts are the groups most in favour of a general reduction in working hours. Around two-thirds of those in employment put the maintenance of income before an increase in leisure time; this holds true for all categories of wage-earners, but particularly for manual workers (Ministère du Travail 1995). On the other hand, Lipietz notes that the idea of work-sharing has gained acceptance among the middle classes.

According to Aznar, three basic conditions are required for the implementation of the 35 hour week: shift-working must be developed to amortise capital equipment; companies must pay only a fraction of the costs, which must be borne essentially through fiscal distribution; and the reduction in working time and attendant reorganisation of work must be negotiated by employers and trade unions at all levels. Shift-working has been developed in many French companies, but the 1989 Taddéi law failed to mobilise extra efforts in this area.

Trade union opposition to shift work is understandable: it is obviously not popular with workers because of the health and particularly social aspects. Considerable incentives would have to be introduced to compensate for these. Fiscal redistribution is undoubtedly urgently needed anyway, and a rethink of taxes and social contributions has already begun, particularly in relation to low wages. Nevertheless, changes in trade union attitudes are likely to be a slow process and a reactive rather than innovatory one. The weak link here is the under-development of collective bargaining in France. The CFDT counted 208 collective agreements on the reduction of working time, with a total of 4,500 jobs created and 11,000 jobs saved as a result (*Le Monde*, 24 February 1995). In a further study of 197 company-level agreements concerning employment issues signed by the confederation in 1993 and 1994, the CFDT noted the limited impact of such agreements and severely criticised their content and implementation. For the trade unions, there are considerable risks involved in signing employer-led agreements on employment:

> Most companies have no real employment policy. . . . The trade unions do not contest the economic strategies of the companies. . . . Trade unions risk being perceived as an actor attempting to make constraints on employees palatable, without being able to influence choices. . . . Their chances of altering company strategies are low and their ability

to play a significant part in implementing and following up decisions is inadequate.

(CFDT report on 'La CFDT face à l'emploi', quoted in *Le Monde*, 31 October 1995)

There are nonetheless signs that the trade union movement has woken up to the issue of unemployment and is taking it seriously, particularly in the CFDT, which emerged from the Catholic trade union movement in 1964 and has remained close to a progressive Christian, 'new left' current of thought in France. At a low level, some initiatives are emerging. Under the CFDT's presidency of the UNEDIC, 500 billion francs per year were set aside for unemployed workers to claim benefits whilst seeking work through 'work experience' schemes. CFDT activist Daniel Labbé has documented several cases where trade unionists, often through workplace representative councils, work with local unemployment associations to create jobs. According to Labbé (1994), 'the fight against exclusion has become a central debate within the trade unions'. The problem is that the framework for a concerted approach to unemployment is lacking in France; trade unions are weak, with an estimated membership rate of only 7 per cent of the workforce, the lowest in EU Europe. Employers are able to use labour flexibility to cut costs rather than to create jobs, in the absence of effective counterweights or state surveillance. Thus, a recent report on work-sharing in practice shows that private-sector companies have used flexible working time as a means of creating a peripheral part-time workforce rather than as a means of reducing working time overall. In the public sector, on the other hand, working-time flexibility has been used together with early retirement formulae to create diversified working patterns. According to the author of this report, work-sharing 'has very little place in this dual system of work organisation' (Ramaux 1994).

At a higher level, there are some signs of change. The summit-level talks between the CNPF and the leading trade union confederations in 1995 quickly ran into employers' refusal to discuss reduction of working time; however, the employers later returned to the table. The 7 September 1995 agreement on early retirement was heralded as a breakthrough in labour relations and the dawn of a new spirit of compromise 'à l'alle-mande'. But on the issue of working time, the trade unions were forced to accept the employers' position based on flexibility rather than job creation: an agreement signed on 31 October 1995 allowed employers to modulate working hours within annual limits. The trade unions had all previously expressed their dismay at the employers' position, and Force Ouvrière called the agreement a 'relative failure'. The CGT refused to sign it. There is little sign that the employers are ready to move from their position in favour of flexibility towards discussing more ambitious work-sharing proposals. After all, theirs is a position of strength since it has been official government policy for the last decade and beyond.

Politically, the 1980s and 1990s have seen an expectation of change, fostered by the close links between some political circles and radical economists, but no real change, creating a sense of frustration among the public which was evident during the 1995 presidential election campaign. In June 1993 Philippe Séguin captured this frustration with his comparison between the employment situation and the politics of appeasement of the 1938 Munich agreement. He called for a referendum on unemployment policies. A window of opportunity appeared in 1993 with the discussions surrounding the 'Giraud plan' on employment, leading to an unsuccessful parliamentary motion on a 32 hour week. Instead, the government preferred to steer the discussions back to the classic policy of labour flexibility. The debate was opened but left unresolved in the absence of political will.

In this debate, there is increasingly a recognition that solutions must be sought within a wider European context. Proponents of radical unemployment policies, including the Greens, have pointed to the need for a concerted European approach to unemployment, in line with some of the early reports prepared for the Commission's 1993 White Paper. In 1994, former planning commissioner Jean-Marcel Jeanneney's book *Vouloir l'emploi* called for a European strategy to tackle unemployment, and the OFCE published similar outline strategies for European growth and employment (Dreze and Malinvaud 1994). Similarly, both Dominique Taddéi and Bernard Brunhes have produced reports for the European Commission on the employment gains of a concerted reduction and reorganisation of working time. One of newly elected President Jacques Chirac's first moves was to turn to the Cannes EU summit in June 1995 for a new European anti-unemployment strategy. However, in the absence of new EU plans for tackling unemployment there is a real danger that 'Europe' simply serves as an alibi for inaction at home, whilst the Maastricht convergence criteria serve as an effective policy straitjacket for governments wishing to justify inactivity, which is electorally less threatening than radical change.

OUTLOOK

To some extent the failure to apply radical unemployment policies in France reflects the powerlessness of the left. The Communist Party has lost its former power to represent the marginalised masses of society and is cut off particularly from the young people who are bearing the brunt of the dualised French employment system. It has also lost contact with intellectuals and innovative ideas on employment. Since 1993, the Socialist Party has appeared more interested in regaining political power than carrying out the necessary rebuilding of grassroots support and rethinking policies. Lionel Jospin's 1995 campaign for the French presidency showed some willingness to consider new initiatives on employment (including a reduction in working time), but was marked by extreme caution.

Even in the unlikely event of the Socialists coming to power in the near future, they would be weakened by a lack of clear policy direction and a reluctance to foster radical change. The most interesting changes are currently taking place in the trade union movement, especially the CFDT. Small-scale local initiatives may help to pave the way for the kind of multi-faceted approach called for by Gorz and Aznar.

With the election of Jacques Chirac to the French presidency, large question marks remain over the ability of the right to 'manage change', as Chirac has undoubtedly been mandated to do, and indeed even to manage its own internal divisions. The expectations created during the campaign, which were deliberately fostered by Chirac's explicit promises to sweep away the old approach to employment, have intensified the sense of urgency evident since 1993. Alain Juppé's employment plan, as we have seen, indicated some willingness to change direction but did not constitute radical change. If he fails to create the 700,000 jobs promised in eighteen months time (*Liaisons Sociales* 1995), and if street protests continue to intensify (seen in 1995 in a series of trade union strikes, following the youth demonstrations of 1994 which badly damaged the Balladur government), there is every chance that the established actors of the right will be discredited and new actors will emerge. This, at least, is the scenario on which Philippe Séguin is banking. Meanwhile, Séguin's proposal for a referendum on employment was taken up by Chirac during the election campaign, and the French parliament voted in July to allow the President to call referenda on economic and social affairs. This could provide the long-awaited opportunity for a fresh approach to unemployment policies. Or it could simply be another way of avoiding political responsibility for the central issue on which his presidency and his government will be judged by the French electorate.

REFERENCES

Aznar, G. (1980), *Tous à mi-temps!* Paris, Seuil.

—— (1993), *Travailler moins pour travailler tous*, Paris, Syros.

Boissard, D. and Vittori, J-M. (1995), 'Les dossiers de la présidentielle: le chômage. "Nous, économistes, déclarons, que ..."', *Le Nouvel Economiste*, no. 993, 21 April, 48–53.

Brunhes, B. (ed.) (1993) *Choisir l'emploi*, Paris, La Documentation Française.

(CEC) (Commission of the European Communities) (1991), *Economic Papers (no. 5). Country studies: France, Luxembourg*, Official Publications Brussels.

Commission sociale de l'épiscopat (1993), *Face au chômage. Changer le travail*, Paris, Centurion.

Coriat, B. (1990), *L'atelier et le robot*, Paris, Christian Bourgois.

Dreze, J. and Malinvaud, E. (1994), 'Croissance et emploi: l'ambition d'une initiative européenne', *Revue de l'OFCE*, no. 49, April, pp.247–88.

Gorz, A. (1988), *Métamorphoses du travail et quête du sens*, Paris, Galilée.

Héritier, P. (1988), *Nouvelle croissance et emploi*, Paris, Syros.

Jeanneney, J-M. (1994), *Vouloir l'emploi*, Paris, Editions Edile Jacob.

Labbé, D. (1994) *Syndicalistes et comités d'entreprise face à l'exclusion*, Paris, Conseil national de l'insertion par l'activité économique.

Le Figaro

Le Monde

Le Nouvel Economiste

Liaisons Sociales (1995), 'Plan d'urgence pour l'emploi', *Documents* no. 59/95, 29 June.

Libération

Lipietz, A. (1995), 'Une politique de l'emploi centrée sur la conquête du temps libre', in Brovelli, L. et al. *Quelle économie pour l'emploi?*, Paris, Editions de l'atelier.

Laroque, M. (1990), *Politiques sociales dans la France contemporaine*, Paris, Editions STH.

Ministère du Travail, de l'Emploi et de la Formation Professionnelle (Direction de l'Animation de la Recherche, des Etudes et des Statistiques) (1995), *Premières synthèses*, no. 83, February.

—— (1995) *Recueil d'études sociales*, no. 43, April.

OECD (1994), *Statistiques trimestrielles de la population active*, no. 2.

OFCE (1993), *1993–1998: veut-on réduire le chômage?* Lettre de l'OFCE no. 112(3), March.

Ramaux, C. (1994), 'Le partage du travail: où en est-on? Le prisme de la flexibilité', *Revue de l'IRES*, no. 14, Winter, 85–118.

Taddéi, D. (1988), *Le temps de l'emploi*, Paris, Hachette.

4 Italy

Elisabetta Gualmini

What we are looking for is not a convincing sequence of exceptional events, but an explication of their development in terms of human institutions.

(K. Polanyi 1944:7)

INTRODUCTION

'One million more jobs' was the daily slogan of Berlusconi's electoral campaign in March 1994. Both the right coalition, which officially formulated the proposal, and the left coalition, committed to denouncing its lack of realism, recognised the political salience of unemployment.

Since 1992, Italy has been experiencing a substantial fall in employment. Whereas in EC countries in general employment decreased by 2 per cent on average in 1993, in Italy it fell by 4.8 per cent. In January 1995 unemployment reached the historical high of 12.2 per cent: 22 per cent in the South against 7.2 per cent in the North. Long-term unemployment also significantly increased, amounting to 7.6 per cent of the total unemployment rate (*ISTAT* 1995).

The employment trends of the 1990s seem in fact to go in the opposite direction compared to the 1980s, when job creation, although insufficient to keep pace with the growth of the labour force, was significantly above the EC average. Between 1980 and 1991 total employment rose by more than 1.5 million, and the annual rate of growth averaged 0.6 per cent, compared with 0.4 per cent in the European Community as a whole (*European Economy* 1993). This low cyclical sensitivity to economic activity and to international output fluctuations is largely due to some structural disadvantages that put the Italian labour market in a unique economic and political condition compared with the rest of Western Europe.

The territorial, economic and social dualism between the South and the North, the sectoral dualism between competitive and non-competitive sectors, the low level of youth and female employment together with a de-institutionalised system of professional training, make the Italian case

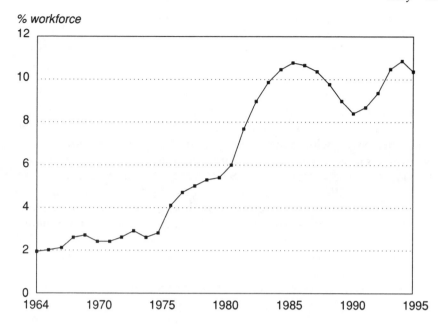

% workforce

Figure 4.1 Unemployment in Italy, 1972–1995

Note: Standardised unemployment rates to 1993, commonly used definition for 1994, projection based on commonly used definition 1995

Source: OECD 1992 (1972–87), OECD 1995 (1988–95)

a peculiar one. This peculiarity is moreover enhanced by a remarkable degree of social security that historically assures high income protection, thanks to the compensatory function of public spending. Consequences of this process include the well-known phenomena of a huge public deficit, persistent high inflation (5.5 per cent in May 1995), public sector ineffi-ciency, and the dominance of a culture of public assistance, often turning into clientelism (La Palombara 1964; Graziano 1974; Ferrera 1984).

The 1990s, however, are a period of both hard economic recession and multiple transition. Deep changes are taking place in the social and polit-ical arenas, including the political transformations that occurred in 1992, due to the action of 'Mani Pulite' (Clean Hands), which threw most of the ruling class out of office on grounds of corruption. The introduction of the majority electoral system, the new social pacts of 1992 and 1993, and the reform of collective bargaining are just some examples of the attempt to create more stability and greater rationalisation. Though pre-liminary steps in a wider political learning process, they open new areas of action with direct repercussions on labour policy innovation.

This chapter is organised as follows. The next section briefly presents the context and the historical development of labour policies. The following section focuses on radical unemployment policies, considered as new programmes outside the set of national mainstream instruments, that were introduced in the 1990s to tackle increasing unemployment. Special attention is paid to solidarity contracts and a case study is selected, Fiat's 1993–94 bargaining processes, in which work sharing was a central issue. The final section examines the influence of the political dynamics on employment regulation.

The theory this chapter utilises can be defined as institutional, the central argument being that policies are to be explained on the basis of the structural and historical features in which they are embedded (Granovetter 1985; Steimno *et al.* 1992; Streeck 1992; 1994; Soskice 1994). Innovations are filtered by the existing institutions, always modified and adapted. Politicians do not autonomously choose new policies on the basis of their rational forecasted outcomes, but adopt a logic of normative appropriateness (March and Olsen 1989) in conforming their strategies of action to the set of rules, norms and conventions 'incorporated' in the institutional structures.

As in the German case, radical and unorthodox programmes require a politics of institutional reforms. They are path-dependent on the institutional context of constraints and opportunities that surround the whole labour market. That is why theoretical explanations have to be sought not only in strategic choices, but also in the 'inertial choices' (Pérez-Diaz and Rodriguez 1994) that innovations paradoxically enact.

CONTEXT

Italian unemployment policies have always been characterised by high fragmentation and lack of coordination. These policies have varied according to a large number of parameters: the time they are introduced, the applicable legal procedures, the industrial sectors to which they refer, the territorial level on which they are mainly implemented, and the responsible authority. A brief historical perspective is needed for a better understanding of this particularistic and contingent logic.

The Italian government was one of the first, soon after the British one, to introduce unemployment insurance in 1919, but the level of insurance has remained very low in comparison with other European countries. After the Second World War a series of sectoral measures were introduced in order to make up for this lack. During the 1940s the state assisted in the creation of temporary wage subsidies via the Cassa Integrazione Guadagni (Cig) scheme, which are extended year after year until they are transformed into permanent benefits. In 1949 public labour agencies were established at the national and the provincial level. In the 1950s wage subsidies were again diverted from their original function and transformed into extraordinary subsidies for crisis-ridden industrial sectors. In the period of the so-called 'social mobilisation' from 1968 to 1973 (Regalia

1984), a quantitative explosion of labour measures occurred which included the introduction of early retirement for some *ad hoc* categories of workers, the establishment of a special fund (GEPI) for the rescue of crisis firms, and the extension of insurance to the building sector. The 1970s, a period of economic recession, were characterised by the introduction of the Regional Order, whereby training competences were transferred from the state to the regions and a number of new instruments, dovetailing with the existing national programmes, were created in order to cope with the rising number of unemployed at the local level.

In political and social literature pertinent to this area there is a consensus that Italian unemployment policies are based on a very sectoral and incremental logic. They frequently juxtapose and overlap, and moreover are often intertwined with policies in other policy sectors, as when early retirement and receipt of invalidity pensions became functional substitutes for unemployment insurance in the 1970s and 1980s.

At the end of the 1980s, after the social pact of 1983 but before the employment crisis of 1988, the list of mainstream labour policies can be summarised as follows (Table 4.1).

The system of income support policies is built around the functioning of the wage subsidies fund or Cig scheme, in itself a radical policy compared to other European countries. This is a very generous and flexible instrument comprising both temporary and permanent payments.

Ordinary wage benefits were introduced, as noted above, in 1945, and provide for compensation of earnings at a level of 80 per cent of income in the case of temporary interruption of a firm's activity (companies with more than fifteen employees), for a maximum of three consecutive months. The fund is located and administered by the National Institute for Social Insurance (Istituto nazionale della previdenza sociale), and employers' contributions vary between 1.9 and 2.2 per cent of incomes, depending on

Table 4.1 Mainstream labour policies at the end of the 1980s in Italy

Policy type	Policy action
Income support policies	Unemployment insurance (1919; 1986) Ordinary wage subsidies: ordinary Cig scheme (1945) Extraordinary wage subsidies: extraordinary Cig scheme (1968) Early retirements (1981) Solidarity contract legislation (1984) Ban on collective hiring (1977)
Active policies	Work and training contracts (1984) Professional training regulation (1978) Part-time working (1984) Apprenticeship (1955; 1987)

the size of firm. In addition, when employers use the ordinary Cig scheme they are obliged to pay 8 per cent of the compensation paid to their employees (4 per cent in companies with less than fifty employees).

Extraordinary wage subsidies were introduced in 1968 in the years of increasing social mobilisation in order to respond to the situation of crisis and industrial restructuring, and are a veritable bulwark against unemployment, almost unique in Europe in their generosity and duration. This is why they are frequently used as ordinary measures, transforming their original structural connotation into a conjunctural one. In the case of economic difficulties these subsidies can be extended to a maximum of one year, while in the case of industrial restructuring, benefits last up to two years and can be extended to a maximum of four years. Wage subsidies contribute 80 per cent of gross income, and are financed mostly by annual state transfers as provided for in the financial law. In addition, workers who use the extraordinary subsidies contribute 0.6 per cent of their taxable income, and other employees 0.3 per cent. The employer's contributions of 4.5 per cent of the wage replacement benefit (3 per cent for firms with less than fifty employees) double after two years of benefits (Bentivoglio 1994).

Other social shock-absorbers play a subsidiary role and are very rarely used, except for cases where firms are no longer eligible for the Cig scheme.

In the group of active labour policies the most significant instrument is the system of work and training contracts. These are two year contracts for people under twenty-nine which offer social contribution discounts to employers provided that work is combined with on-the-job training.

Vocational training is regulated in the general law of 1978, which designates the regions as the responsible institutions. It is theoretically sought as an instrument capable of remedying mismatches between supplied skills and labour demand, but a lack of communication with the public education system regulated by the Ministry of Education, combined with low intra and inter-regional coordination and a lack of financial resources, have a negative impact on the efficacy of the programmes, and make the Italian vocational training system one of the main obstacles to employment growth. It should also be noted that Italy has a low level of general educational attainment compared to the other OECD countries, especially in the South, where in 1988 fewer than 25 per cent of the population had more than a basic secondary education (Rhodes 1995:23).

Part-time working is regulated in the law 864/1984. In Italy it is almost exclusively women who work part-time – 75.3 per cent of total female employees in 1990 compared with only 24.7 per cent of men – and far more women than men opt to turn full-time work into part-time work, especially in the sector of services (*Rapporto* '93–'94).

Active policies play a minor role compared to income support subsidies. The whole system is unbalanced by a logic of public assistance that provides for a high level of income protection without boosting job creation. Social shock-absorbers, particularly the Cig supplementation fund, are in fact instruments of resource allocation and distribution that do not incite any active creation of jobs. Policies are at the same time regulative and distributive: they define a regulatory framework for the actors and at the same time give out benefits and resources (Regalia and Regini 1994). Thus the state is a prominent institutional actor in the labour market. The Ministry of Labour, often with his under-secretary, is used to directly intervening in the social agreements that allocate resources and benefits. During the tripartite labour accords in 1983 and 1984, for instance, labour policies were exchanged with tax allowances and special investments in the South.

As the recession worsened in 1988, doubts began to creep in as to whether the traditional system of unemployment policies was still adequate. The need for innovation in labour policies moved to centre stage in the policy debate. The dimensions of the public deficit, the level of unemployment (by mid 1995 approaching 11 per cent) and the gradual termination of public funds made government aware of the necessity for deep changes.

RADICAL UNEMPLOYMENT POLICIES

During the 1990s changes took place in three different but related directions: deregulation of employment conditions, drawing lessons, even though delayed (Haas 1992; Rose 1991; Regonini 1993), from the anglosaxon experiments of the 1980s; institutional reforms and qualification policies; and working time reduction. These programmes are all radical in that they are qualitatively innovative at the national level, outside the mainstream of West European economic policy, and meant to be capable of significantly reducing unemployment.

Deregulation of employment conditions

The core objective of deregulatory policies is to affect the protective nature of labour policies in a country where the labour market has hitherto been heavily regulated. The national employers' association (Confindustria) has always complained about the rigidity of the Italian labour market. The voice of employers found scientific support in the well-known economists and academic professors whose opinions inform the most prestigious Italian economic newspaper, *Il Sole 24 ore*, which is sponsored by the Confindustria. Even though flexibility is traditionally employers' philosophy, the unions, concerned about widespread evasion of regulatory norms, did not contest this view.

Law 223/91 (Norms on wage subsidies fund, mobility, unemployment benefits, EC directives and other measures for the labour market) introduced three substantial innovations: it redesigned the system of social

Table 4.2 Radical unemployment policies in Italy

Policy type	Policy action
Increasing demand for labour	Deregulation of employment conditions and procedures Modification of the system of social shock-absorbers Juridical recognition of collective dismissals
Institutional reforms and qualification policies	Reform of collective bargaining Abolition of wage indexation Plant level flexible agreements New regulation of apprenticeship Modification of work and training contracts
Decreasing supply of labour	Part-time working Solidarity contracts

shock-absorbers, modifying the whole set of passive policies; modified the procedures of placement by introducing the so-called 'nominative call' in place of the compulsory call; and recognised collective dismissals as a possible solution to firms' crisis situations. The introduction of a new instrument, mobility insurance (a longer form of early retirement), together with the modification of eligibility criteria for, and the duration of, the extraordinary Cig scheme should be noted.

But it is in relation to hiring procedures that this law has everywhere been welcomed as a liberalising step, because of the dismantling of the public guarantees inaugurated in 1949 (law 264). The reform of the 1940s had established a public monopoly on the management of the demand and supply of labour by making workers' hirings dependent on a compulsory list. Law 221 introduces the principle of the free choice and, in so doing, improves employers' available options. The removal of the ban on collective dismissals is also to the employers' advantage.

More recently, following the tripartite labour accord between the government and the social actors in July 1993, law 236/93 (Urgent interventions for employment support) introduced a series of rules aimed at extending the instruments of income protection, in view of the recession, by introducing an exceptional employment fund, for the period 1993–1995, extraordinary subsidies for the Mezzogiorno, and the augmentation of employment insurance levels.

As for job creation, the law 451/94 regulates the so-called 'public utility works'. Public administrations and some private organisations, identified by the Ministry of Labour, are allowed to promote projects for works of public interest in innovative sectors such as culture, environmental protection and public services.

During the period in office of the Berlusconi government a number of other measures were taken, although to a lesser extent than promised. A prize was introduced for young employers starting new enterprises: they are allowed to choose an alternative fiscal regime (2 million lire (about £800) for the first year, 3 million for the second, 4 million for the third), that substitutes for all existing taxes except for IVA (added-value tax). The prize is moreover accompanied by hiring incentives, such as a fiscal bonus of 25 per cent of the gross income of the new employees.

Among proposals not yet being implemented, but present on the agenda of at least the last three governments (Ciampi, Berlusconi, Dini), is the notorious issue of *ad interim* jobs, which would permit employers to rent workers from specialised agencies, as in France. By mid 1995 the proposal was close to realisation, having become a central issue of both the last bill of Labour Minister Treu and of the Labour Commission in the Chamber of Deputies.

Institutional reforms and qualification programmes

In 1992 and 1993 the government and the social actors undertook the series of non-stop negotiations which led to the tripartite labour accord of 23 July 1993. This can justifiably be considered as the most innovative step in Italian industrial relations since the Workers' Statute of 1970 and the experiments in concerted action of the 1980s. In the face of rising unemployment and slow economic growth, a number of drastic solutions were agreed, notably the abolition of wage-indexation and the reform of collective bargaining, including specification of the bargaining agents and of the responsible institutions (*Rapporto* '93–'94). The agreement aims to keep wage increases within the projected rate of inflation.

The new structure of collective bargaining is organised on the basis of two levels of bargaining: the national level (contratto collettivo nazionale di lavoro) and the plant or territorial level. The reform intends, on the one hand, to eliminate the chaos of overlapping levels of bargaining that have hitherto impaired Italian industrial relations; on the other, to respond more sensitively to local unemployment crises. The national level is now supposed to fix general standards on the determination of salaries, leaving the regulation of specific contents to decentralised bargaining. The agreement also introduces tripartite negotiations based on two annual meetings: the first, in May, on the objectives of the forecasted budget policies and the annual employment trends; the second, in September, on the regulation of income policies before the approval of the budget. In addition, a special Observatory has been established with the purpose of controlling prices.

The 1993 agreement also provides for the reform of qualification policies and vocational training. A reorganisation of the apprenticeship system is sought, in order to render it more adaptable to the different needs of different firms, and work and training contracts are strongly encouraged. In the law 451/94, following the agreement, the age of the beneficiaries was extended from 16 to 32 years of age and a clearer distinction was made between contracts for the acquisition of high and intermediate skills and those aimed at facilitating the entry of young people onto the labour market.

Working time reduction

It is worth noting that the law regulating working time dates back to 1923 and established a maximum limit of 48 hours per week. Since then, several proposals have been formulated but none formalised.

Nevertheless, working time reduction is an important feature of the Italian labour market. It is encouraged in at least three different ways. First, under the Cig scheme working time can be temporarily reduced from 80 per cent to 10 per cent, with wage compensation as outlined previously. Second, there is part-time working, to which Italian firms have increasingly resorted in the 1990s. The third form of shorter-hours working is represented by solidarity contracts, a radical instrument compared to the others: workers accept reduced working time in order to save jobs. Solidarity contracts can be applied to all categories of workers (as the term solidarity suggests) and work can be shared.

Solidarity contracts were first introduced in 1984 (law 864) on the wave of enthusiasm following the national corporatist agreement between the government and the social actors in 1983, with the explicit purpose of boosting labour demand and tackling youth unemployment in a period of rapid technological transformation. Trade unions, particularly the Catholic centre-moderate CISL, have always struggled for the introduction of solidaristic instruments to cope with unemployment ('Work less to let all work', in the words of the French philosopher Guy Aznar, whose essay, translated into Italian in 1994 with the title *Lavorare meno per lavorare tutti*, was a great success). This was of course anathema to employers, who have always feared the repercussions of work-sharing on the inner organisation of companies. In 1983, however, unions exchanged wage moderation for the recognition and the regulation of work-sharing.

Solidarity contracts are a form of working time reduction based on agreements between the firm and the unions. Two kinds can be distinguished: internal and external contracts. The former, also called 'defensive contracts', are used inside the company to avoid dismissals by increasing internal mobility; the latter 'active' contracts provide for work-sharing in order to create new employment.

For internal (defensive) contracts the Ministry of Labour provides employees, apart from managers, with wage compensation benefits amounting to 50 per cent of the wages foregone as a result of working-time reduction, for a period of twenty-four months (Bentivoglio 1994).

If the reduction of working time is higher than 20 per cent, employers' social security contributions are reduced by 25 per cent, (30 per cent in the South), rising to 40 per cent when the reduction of time is higher than 30 per cent. The beneficiaries are industrial and trade companies with more than 100 employees.

In the case of external contracts, for each new hire employers receive state subsidies equal to 15 per cent of the employee's income for the first year, 10 per cent for the second and 5 per cent in the third year. When employers hire young workers, between the ages of 15 and 29 through working hours reductions, they receive the same advantageous insurance and pension treatment that applies to the apprenticeship scheme.

The study of solidarity contracts is particularly worthwhile because of three major but partly contradictory reasons. First, for more than ten years working time reductions were very rarely demanded, whereas the Cig subsidies fund was increasingly utilised. Second, up until now the only type of contracts that have been used are the defensive ones; no active contracts exist. Finally, in the 1990s the situation radically changed and working time reductions suddenly emerged as a burning political issue. It is in this sense that solidarity contracts are a radical unemployment policy.

Today these measures are more and more widespread. By February 1994 55,000 workers were involved in solidarity contracts, including 30,000 metallurgists and mechanics (Alenia, Piaggio, Olivetti, Iveco, Italtel, Fiat) and 10,000 textile workers, and their use has permitted 20–25,000 jobs to be saved (D'Aloia e Magno 1994). In 1993 the government spent 12 billion lire (about £10 million) of the annual budget for solidarity contracts, and in 1994 requests for working time reductions reached a total amount of 10 billion lire, far beyond the annual sum forecast (inforMISEP, 1994). This has resulted in efforts by Labor Minister Tiziano Treu to come up with other types of funding sources.

POLITICAL DYNAMICS

The reason why solidarity contracts were not demanded at all during the 1980s relates to the functioning of the existing mainstream policies, in particular the Cig scheme. As mentioned above, the preference for this instrument is easily explained by the generosity and the flexibility of the subsidies it provides, plus the fact that the cost rests mainly on the state's shoulders. Solidarity contracts only become a plausible alternative when the high cost of unemployment benefits stimulate authorities to look for other instruments. In the Fiat plants the employer agreed to introduce work-sharing mainly because the company's eligibility for wage subsidies was running out.

The exclusive use of defensive contracts restricted to protecting existing jobs, to the great disadvantage of job creation, is consistent with the institutional features of the Italian welfare state: the culture of public assistance, the prevalence of passive policies for income support and the fear of redestributive programmes hamper a pro-active attitude towards external challenges. A vicious circle enhances the protection of those already protected at the expense of the perennial exclusion of those outside the system.

For about ten years solidarity contracts, which require preliminary intra-firm collective bargaining, were not part of the official policy paradigm despite being provided for by law: significant changes occurred only after the introduction of law 223 nearly ten years later as a consequence of the tripartite social pact of July 1993, which provided substantial incentives for employers. In the fifth article of law 223 three substantial innovations were introduced, valid until the end of 1995: first, the benefits were elevated from 50 per cent to 75 per cent of the foregone salary lost as a consequence of working hours reductions; second, employers benefited from a contribution equal to one-quarter of the lost salary. Last but not least, greater flexibility was promoted by a provision that the reduction of time could be based on daily, weekly, monthly or annual hours. As a result of these modifications it is easy to understand why the use of solidarity contracts began to spread across many companies (Iveco, Italtel, Ilva).

But in 1994 new arrangements introduced further significant changes. It was at this point that the strategies of the government and the interests of Italy's biggest automobile company intersected. The Fiat crisis of November 1993, with the dismissal of nearly 16,000 workers on grounds of overcapacity, shows how the labour market can effectively be described as a complex system of regulation within which public and private actors interact. It also shows how the history of solidarity contracts and of the legislative evolution is inextricably connected to the preparedness of big firms to accept them.

In August 1990 Fiat informed the unions that after years of great success (1989 was the record year for sales) it was forced to have recourse to ordinary wage subsidies. In the firm's view the crisis was of a conjunctural nature and the strategic line adopted was 'incremental strategy' (incremental adjustments), based on the gradual but continuous use of ordinary wage subsidies while waiting for favourable market changes. Unions agreed with this strategy, since the absence of more definitive measures allowed social tensions to be contained. This 'incremental strategy' continued for the whole of 1991, while foreign automobile industries announced deeper restructuring plans. In 1992 Fiat realised it faced not only an external crisis in terms of economic recession, but its own internal crisis in terms of declining market shares and a budgetary deficit. At the same time the new technological investments planned for its Melfi plant resulted in overcapacity. A reorganisation process was required and three plants were quickly closed: Maserati (49 per cent of which is owned by

Fiat), Desio and Chivasso. Meanwhile unions were struggling against any kind of layoff. Once again the company applied to the state redundancy fund, but only temporarily, since law 223/91 establishes a maximum of 52 consecutive weeks for subsidies. The situation exploded in June 1993 when all the available subsidies came to an end and budget constraints forced managing director Romiti to go to Mediobanca for recapitalisation. The transition from conjunctural to structural crisis was marked formally on 22 June 1993 when Fiat officially announced the need to resort to extra-ordinary wage subsidies.

A second and more serious phase of the crisis started in November 1993, curiously at the same time as the VW agreement in Germany on the four-day week. Fiat presented a restructuring plan which proposed massive layoffs, immediate closure of the Sevel Campania and Arese (ex-Alfa Romeo) plants, and, for the very first time, dismissal of white collar workers. In response, unions asked for inter-plant redeployments and officially demanded work-sharing in order to avoid dismissals.

Bargaining therefore opened with very distinctive preferences apparent: on the employer's side, Cig subsidies at 0-hours (that is, dismissals) and eventually registration on the mobility lists (the so-called 'mobility pro-cedure' is a form of early retirement offering the workers the possibility of being hired again in case of future jobs); on the workers' side, work-sharing and industrial restructuring.

The strategies were so incompatible that the Ministry of Labour was immediately called in. It is important to note that the incumbent Minister, Gino Giugni, was a highly respected professor of labour law, inter-nationally famous as one of the fathers of the Workers' Statute. In December he officially announced direct governmental intervention and the postponement of Cig subsidies at 0-hours, which had been scheduled for the following January.

Notwithstanding the intervention of the Minister and, later, of Prime Minister Ciampi himself in a meeting on the possibility of introducing the production of electric cars to reindustrialise old plants, the negotiations were suddenly interrupted in the middle of January. The interruption, probably precipitated by the company, was in fact the result of the inter-action of the different strategies: Fiat did not intend to renounce its objectives and the unions did not consider the existing proposals acceptable. The Minister of Labour, though he had attempted to find a consensual solution, had to stop in in the face of the irreconcileable preferences of the social actors. After nearly a month of suspension the bargaining process started again, and on the 24th of February it was officially concluded through a workers' ballot.

The central issue in dispute was the alternative between work-sharing, proposed by the unions, and the Cig scheme at 0-hours, wanted by employers. The consensual solution of the bargaining, as opposed to the unilateralism of the mass-dismissals of 1980, was due to the enactment of mutual adjustment strategies between the public actors and the employers, in which legislative accommodations played a primary role. This took two main forms.

First, an agreement was reached between the government and the firm which provided for direct public interventions in favour of the automobile industrial sector, such as financial aids for research projects concerning the production of electric cars, introduction of a special commission on industrial development at the Ministry of Transport, and extraordinary subsidies for the restructuring of the Sevel-Campania plant.

Second, a decree (40/1994) was issued soon after the interruption of the bargaining, encouraging the use of solidarity contracts by making them compatible with Cig subsidies. In other words, the law accommodated the requests of employers and at the same time changed the original nature of solidarity contracts.

The final result is a policy mix of four instruments, in which radical programmes overlap with mainstream policies: 6,500 early retirements (including, for the first time, 2,800 white-collar workers); 2,200 mobility insurances; 4,100 extraordinary Cig subsidies; and 3,500 solidarity contracts (for blue-collar workers only).

The role of the government, including legislation, appears to have been crucial. Not only do solidarity contracts become a legitimised part of the policy paradigm (Hall 1989; 1993) only after concerted social pacts, but their conditions continue to depend on direct intervention on the part of the government.

Moving a step further, it is possible to seek the political causes of the development of solidarity contracts in particular, and of radical policies in general, in the low compatibility of the new programmes with existing institutional imperatives. Four elements stand out as particularly relevant. These can be considered on the one hand as lock-in effects (Arthur 1989; North 1990) which hinder the full development of radical programmes, and on the other, as 'spaces of opportunity' that permit unusual (even random) courses of action. Furthermore, they have a structural nature, being that they do not depend on the strategies of institutional actors, but, rather, are historically rooted and thus capable of affecting the degree of innovation and learning in the labour market (Gualmini 1995).

The particularistic nature of labour legislation

In the Fiat case the bargaining was successfully solved when the firm decided to accept solidarity contracts after they were declared compatible with mainstream wage subsidies. In other words, a law was made in order to induce them to accept it. This strongly underlines the *ad hoc* nature of labour legislation (what we call 'leggine': small laws), which responds to the interests of the different actors involved. The incremental evolution of laws and decrees outside of a general framework tends to frustrate any attempt at coordination or radical reform. Labour legislation is torrential and overlapping in order to respond to local exigencies.

As can also be seen in the case of deregulatory policies, changes were introduced within several laws, each focusing on different instruments and on different aspects. The trend is even more evident for qualification policies where public decisions mix with collective bargaining agreements, giving rise to a multiplicity of rules and competences. The lack of a clear legislative framework – in contrast to countries such as Germany – obstructs any attempt at coordination.

The intertwining of private and public interests and the extended intervention of the State in the regulation of the labour market

The introduction of radical policies (solidarity contracts, reform of collective bargaining, qualification policies, deregulation of employment conditions) is clearly filtered through direct public intervention. Such intervention not only extends the public hand into the economic sector, but reflects and confirms the incapacity of the private actors to reach autonomous agreements. In a broad sense we can define this pattern of state regulation as highly interventionist and demand-side oriented. This is even more striking in that Italian governments are in no way strong governments compared, for instance, to the French ones; their weakness makes them permeable to particular interests. It also contrasts strongly with Germany, where during the Volkswagen negotiations in November 1993 the social actors were able to regulate themselves.

The widespread public intervention in the labour market has another important consequence, since the mainly juridical and formal culture of our public administrators tends to hinder effective radical reforms (Freddi 1989). The lack of horizontal coordination mechanisms between the ministries makes it difficult to reach collective decisions and to implement wide reforms, and the dominance of micro-interventions of a conjunctural nature, makes it hard to inaugurate structural interventions, such as, for example, high deregulation in a regulated labour market.

The weakly institutionalised industrial relations system

The low level of institutionalisation of industrial relations in Italy is widely recognised (Lange and Regini 1987), being particularly true at the national level. Things are different at the local level, where active voluntarism, frequently accompanied by the evasion of juridical rules, develops rather quickly (Regini 1995; Regalia e Regini 1994). The lack of homogeneous and coordinated action is, however, a major consequence. From an organisational standpoint, the trade unions' configuration is quite a complex one. Each federation is organised according to two different dimensions that often combine: the industrial dimension and the territorial dimension. There is a multiplicity of problems of cohesion and of unitary action, above all when unions have to assume a political role in relation to the government and employers. It is important to remember that one of the reasons why solidarity contracts in their original version were not accepted for so long was the required condition of previous collective bargaining. Even when, in some periods unions had the power to influence the political arena, they never benefited from allies in power who might have been more ideologically disposed to grant their requests (Reyneri 1990).

Despite the low degree of institutionalisation, however, it needs to be remembered that in 1993 the government and the social actors did reach an important agreement that seemed to open a new era in the industrial relations in which coordination between the groups is formalised.

Cultural obstacles to innovation

This dimension relates mainly to the long-established tradition of stable full-time jobs – the so-called myth of the guarantee – in the Italian way of life. The lack of job mobility, or rather the fear of new kinds of job organisation, leads to a perception that radical change has high costs for the individual's way of life. Dividing jobs, working fewer than 'normal' hours, and encouraging inter-job mobility all militate against the traditional proclivity for stability – especially for the majority of the Italian labour force who work in the public administration, where protection and immobility are central prerogatives.

OUTLOOK

The analysis of radical unemployment policies in Italy allows a number of conclusions to be drawn concerning the nature of policy innovation in the labour market.

As we have shown, policy failure in the form of persistent high unemployment has not been sufficient alone to stimulate substantial reform efforts. Institutions have their own interests, and these can become constraints on policy innovation. Most of the radical programmes examined above appear to suffer from a sort of institutional inertia that impairs their full development.

It is clear that this is the case for work-sharing, the radical policy on which we have concentrated. At Fiat, solidarity contracts were accepted by the employer only when they were accompanied by a profitable system of incentives. As a result they became a form of wage subsidy very similar to the Cig scheme, and lost their original function of applying solidaristically to all employees in order to provide new jobs relatively inexpensively. Even if the solidarity contract model now enjoys widespread acceptance, it is not likely to be extended to the national level due to the constraints identified in the previous section. Current trends suggest that its development will be totally dependent on the local decisions of different companies, as each company prefers to bargain for its specific kind of contract in order to best fit its own production exigencies.

As for deregulation, a curious paradox should be noted. From a formal point of view, it appears extremely difficult to introduce flexibility into the tight web of institutional rules devoted to employees' protection that distinguishes Italy as one of the industrial countries with the highest degree of employment rigidity. From an informal point of view, the widespread evasion of juridical rules, particularly at the local level, gives rise to considerable actual deregulation, or rather to a social micro-regulation that is difficult to control and evaluate. To say which of the two realities is more real is not an easy task. The interaction between the two systems of regulation is complex and varies according to the territory, the size of the firms and the sector of production. But it is probably this mix of different regulative regimes that characterises the Italian labour market.

With regard to institutional reforms and qualification policies, on the other hand, there do exist some interesting possibilities for innovation. It is worth noting that vocational training has recently assumed high electoral salience, becoming one of the favourite electoral themes of Romano Prodi, the new leader of the centre-left alliance. But reforms are still at a very preliminary stage.

It is therefore a rather complex task to construct a plausible scenario for the future acceptance and expansion of radical policies. It very much depends on the kind of programme and on the specific combination of opportunities within the political arena. The segmentation of the labour market and regional differences, although encouraging national patterns of innovation, enhance localism.

One way of viewing the Italian labour market is to depict it as a loosely coupled system (Weick 1976), in which the different parts and the different actors, despite influencing each other, nevertheless retain fairly independent behaviours: they are reciprocally connected, so that a change in one part of the system affects the other parts but not in a unilateral way. Random changes, serendipities and sudden events are also important variables. In this kind of system, political parties, economic interest groups, and national and local administrators try to pursue their strategies in a complex game whose solution never approaches a zero-sum.

In addition, the characteristics of the political system do not favour coordination. On the one hand, the instability of governments means that they cannot assure, because of their limited periods in office, the introduction of national policy guidelines; on the other, the fragmentation of legislation emphasises the 'personalisation' of the issues. It is quite obvious, for instance, that solidarity contracts have had an easier life under labour ministers close to the unions, such as Giugni and Treu. A scenario in which work-sharing can be extensively adopted should therefore probably include left or centre-left oriented governments, which might favour a corporatist collaboration between the social actors and the state.

In conclusion, Italian localism in policy formation and change seems to be the main explanatory variable. This is remarkable not only with reference to the national level, but also in relation to the European level: the guidelines outlined by the 1993 Commission White Paper on growth, competitiveness and employment, for example, did not produce any significant changes in Italian labour market policy.

In a long-run perspective, two elements appear therefore to be clear. First, radical policies require the active support of all the institutional actors on the labour market: they cannot be based solely on the political strategies of unions or on the views of some faction of Italy's fragmented epistemic community (Haas 1992). The government decision makers and the social actors need to find a field of reciprocal interaction where the different objectives – competitiveness for employers, living standards for employees, and public savings for the government – are integrated into a coherent and well-designed scheme.

Second, the problem of financing must move to the centre stage of the policy debate. It can not be taken for granted, as hitherto, that any kind of subsidy can make demands on public spending. The alarming problem of public debt makes it necessary to accompany the introduction of radical policies with a reform of the welfare state system.

REFERENCES

Arthur, Brian W. (1989), 'Competing technologies, increasing returns, and lock-in by historical events', *Economic Journal*, 99, 116–31.
Aznar, Guy (1994), *Lavorare meno per lavorare tutti*, Torino, Bollati Boringhieri.
Bentivoglio, Marina (1994), *Il mercato del lavoro*, Milano, Pirola Edizioni.
Camuffo, Arnaldo and Volpato, G. (1994), *Making Manufacturing Lean in the Italian Automobile Industry: The Trajectory of Fiat*, Discussion Paper, Venezia.
D'Aloia, Giuseppe and Magno, M. (1994), *Il tempo e il lavoro*, Roma, Ediesse.
David, Paul (1992), *Why are Institutions the Carriers of History*, Discussion Paper, Stanford.
European Economy (1993), 'Reports and study. The economic and financial situation in Italy', 1.
Ferrera, Maurizio (1984), *Il welfare state in Italia. Sviluppo e crisi in prospettiva comparata*, Bologna, Il Mulino.
Freddi, Giorgio (1989), *Scienza dell'amministrazione e politiche pubbliche*, Roma, La Nuova Italia Scientifica.
Granovetter, Mark (1985), 'Economic action and social structure: the problem of embeddedness', *American Journal of Sociology*, 91, (3):481–510.
Graziano, Luigi (1974), (a cura di), *Clientelismo e mutamento politico*, Milano, F. Angeli.
Gualmini, Elisabetta (1995), 'Apprendimento e cambiamento nelle politiche pubbliche: il ruolo delle idee e della conoscenza', *Rivista italiana di scienza politica*, 2:343–70.

Hall, Peter H. (1989), *The Political Power of Economic Ideas. Keynesism Across Nations*, Princeton, Princeton University Press.

—— (1993), 'Policy paradigms, social learning, and the State. The case of economic policymaking in Britain', *Comparative Politics*, 25, (3):275–96.

Haas, Peter M. (1992), 'Introduction: epistemic communities and international policy coordination', *International Organisation*, 46, (1):1–35.

InforMISEP (1994), 'Politiques', 47, Commission des Communautés Européennes DG 5.

ISTAT (1995), 'Revisione delle serie trimestrali relative all'indagine sulle forze di lavoro dall'ottobre 1992 all'ottobre 1994. Confronti e tecniche', Roma.

Lange, Peter and Regini M. (a cura di) (1987), *Stato e regolazione sociale*, Bologna, Il Mulino.

La Palombara, Joseph (1964), *Interest Groups in Italian Politics*, Princeton, Princeton University Press.

March, James G. and Olsen J.P. (1989), *Rediscovering Institutions. The Organisational Basis of Politics*, New York, The Free Press.

North, Douglas C. (1990), *Institutions, Institutional Change and Economic Performance*, Cambridge, Cambridge University Press.

OECD, *Employment Outlook*, 56, June 1994.

Pérez-Diaz, Victor and J.C. Rodriguez (1994), *Inertial Choices: Spanish Human Resources Policies and Practices (1959–1993)*, ASP Research Paper.

Polanyi, Karl (1944), *The Great Transformation*, New York, Holt, Rinehart and Winston Inc.

Rapporto '93–'94, 'Lavoro e Politiche della Occupazione in Italia', Ministero del Lavoro e della Previdenza Sociale, Roma.

Regalia, Ida (1984), 'Le politiche del lavoro' in Ascoli U. (a cura di), *Welfare State all'italiana*, Bologna, Il Mulino 53–86.

Regalia, Ida and Regini M. (1994), 'Industrial relations and human resource practice in Italy: between voluntarism and institutionalisation', forthcoming in Kochan R., Locke R. and Piore M., *Employment Relations in a Changing World Economy*.

Regini, Marino (1995), 'La varietà italiana di capitalismo. Istituzioni sociali e struttura produttiva negli anni Ottanta', *Stato e Mercato*, 43, (1):3–26.

Regonini, Gloria (1993), 'Il principe e il povero. Politiche istituzionali ed economiche negli anni ottanta', *Stato e Mercato*, 3, 361–403.

Reyneri, Emilio (1990), 'La politica del lavoro' in Dente B. (a cura di) *Le politiche pubbliche in Italia*, Bologna, Il Mulino, 237–55.

Rhodes, Martin (1995), *Unemployment in Europe's Southern and Western Peripheries: Towards a New Policy Mix?*, Paper presented to the 23rd ECPR Joint Session, Bordeaux.

Rose, Richard (1976), 'Risorse dei governi e sovraccarico di domande', *Rivista italiana di scienza politica*, 2, 189–230.

—— (1991), 'What is lesson-drawing?', *Journal of Public Policy*, 2, (1):3–30.

Soskice, David (1994), *Advanced Economies in Open World Markets and Comparative Institutional Advantages: Patterns of Business Coordination, National Institutional Frameworks and Company Product Market Innovation Strategies*, Draft Paper, WZB, Berlin.

Steinmo, Sven *et al.* (1992), *Structuring Politics, Historical Institutionalism in Comparative Analysis*, New York, Cambridge University Press.

Streeck, Wolfgang (1992), *Social Institutions and Economic Performance*, London, Sage Publications.

—— (1994), 'Vincoli benefici sui limiti economici dell'attore razionale', *Stato e mercato*, 41, 185–213.

Weick, Karl E. (1976), 'Educational organisations as loosely coupled systems', *Administrative Science Quarterly*, 21, 1–19.

Widmaier, Ulrich and Blancke S. (1995), *The Politics of Radical Unemployment Policies in Germany*, Paper presented to the 23rd ECPR Joint Session, Bordeaux.

5 Britain

Jonathan Tonge

INTRODUCTION

Britain has been afflicted by mass unemployment for much of the 1980s and 1990s. The return to the levels of unemployment associated formerly with the 1930s has failed to produce a consensus surrounding optimum solutions. The decline of the Keynesian economic paradigm has not been countered by the development of an alternative holistic model of employment generation.

An abandonment of the commitment to full employment was signalled by the Conservative Party in 1979. Elected on a manifesto devoid of specific targets in respect of unemployment, the Conservative Government's pursuit of a deflationary macro-economic strategy enshrined the control of inflation, rather than the pursuit of reductions in unemployment, as the primary economic goal.

Electoral survey data has indicated the continuing salience of unemployment as an issue of public importance, with the issue rated as the second most urgent item confronting the electorate during the last general election (Crewe 1993). However, the electoral durability of Conservative Governments presiding over high levels of joblessness appears to indicate the inability of unemployment to act as the decisive factor underpinning party choice. This inability, allied to the coexistence of economic growth and high unemployment, has impaired the development of radical unemployment policies in Britain. Caution rather than radicalism has characterised employment options, although alternatives have nonetheless been preferred which reject the notion of a permanent 'acceptable' level of unemployment.

CONTEXT

Unemployment in Britain between 1945 and the mid 1960s averaged only 400,000 or 1.8 per cent of the workforce (Glynn 1991). The curbing of unemployment dominated economic goals, a situation unchanged as unemployment rose to 900,000 by 1972. During that year the Conservative Government, under Edward Heath, confirmed the salience of

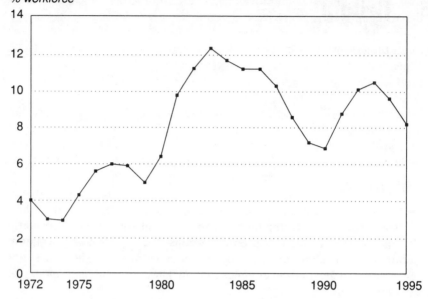

Figure 5.1 Unemployment in Britain, 1972–1995

Note: Standardised unemployment rates to 1994, projection based on commonly used definition 1995

Source: OECD 1992 (1972–87), OECD 1995 (1988–95)

unemployment as an economic indicator by reflating the economy in an attempt to ensure that the total number of jobless did not reach the politically sensitive figure of one million. Figure 5.1 indicates the higher levels of unemployment prevalent since the late 1970s.

The trebling of unemployment to three million during the first three years of the Thatcher Government elected in 1979 was not primarily a repudiation of specific supply-side, micro-economic measures aimed at reducing unemployment. Initially at least, the approach of the Conservative Government represented an attack upon previous macro-economic reflationary responses to increases in the numbers out of work. A refusal to reflate the economy characterised governmental responses during the 1970–82 and 1990–93 recessions. Supply-side measures were partly based upon the perception that labour market rigidities, heightened by the activities of trade unions, were detrimental to economic and employment growth. Accordingly, a series of legislative restrictions were placed upon trade unions.

Until the announcement of its merger with the Department of Education in July 1995, the Department of Employment was responsible for the development of labour market policy. The department also undertook the count of unemployed claimants. Financial allocations to the department were determined annually by the Treasury. Post-merger, responsibility for training, the labour market, employment and equal opportunities has been transferred to the newly-titled Department for Education and Employment, whilst the Central Statistical Office now produces employment statistics, including the monthly unemployment figures. Until 1990, employment and training schemes were run by the Manpower Services Commission followed by the Training Commission, under the direction of the Department of Employment. Subsequently, responsibility for training the unemployed has been devolved to a network of 82 local, employer-led Training and Enterprise Councils (TECs) (Local Enterprise Companies in Scotland). When created, the TECs were made formally accountable only to the Secretary of State for Employment (Tonge 1993).

Stress upon the importance of training provides the new orthodoxy in British employment policy, to an extent unseen since the mid 1960s when Industrial Training Boards were established by the Labour Government to improve skills training. Both the Industrial Training Boards and the Manpower Services Commission (created in 1973) were tripartite bodies, established during a period in which employment policy was characterised by a modest veering towards neo-corporatism (Farnham and Lupton 1994). Employment, training and labour market policies have since been government-dominated and based upon the 'empowerment of employers' (King 1993).

Within this restricted policy arena, employment policy has frequently been characterised by its lack of radicalism. Table 5.1 lists current mainstream unemployment policies.

Work training schemes are combined in a Training for Work package which displaced the previous Employment Training programme. A Work

Table 5.1 Mainstream unemployment policies in Britain, 1995

Policy	Policy deliverer	Policy target
Work training schemes	TECs	All unemployed
Work experience schemes	TECs	Long-term unemployed
Benefit conditioning	Department of Education and Employment	All unemployed
In-work child/family benefits	Department of Social Security	All unemployed with families
Childcare assistance	Employers (voluntary)	Unemployed with children
Jobfinder grants	Department of Education and Employment	Unemployed more than two years
Work trials	Department of Education and Employment	Long-term unemployed

Based Training programme provides training for 16–18 year olds, although fewer than half its trainees were in full time employment six months after leaving the scheme (*Hansard*, PQ, 7 July 1995). Schemes of direct work experience without training were common during the first recent period of high unemployment in the 1980s, via the Community Programme. The Community Action scheme, involving 40,000 work placements, amounts to an attempt to combine work experience with job training. This current work experience scheme does not provide remuneration at market rates, with participants receiving their benefit plus £10 per week.

The replacement of unemployment benefit by jobseekers allowance strengthens the condition that state support is dependent upon the unemployed 'actively seeking work'. The unemployed enter a 'jobseeker agreement' prior to the award of benefit. The benefit system has also been reshaped slightly in an attempt to assist those in work. Since July 1995, additional family credit has been payable to recipients taking a job of 30 hours or more weekly.

Little central state direction has been forthcoming to encourage those with children to work by promoting childcare arrangements. Instead, the voluntary, business-led Employers for Childcare, with thirty-one large member companies, has been encouraged to promote better childcare arrangements, in conjunction with TECs (*Employment News*, October 1994). However recent employment policy statements have indicated a switch towards work incentives for the childless, who comprise two-thirds of the long-term unemployed (Budget Statement, *Hansard*, 29 November 1994). Finally, the jobfinder grant scheme is designed to assist employment prospects by facilitating greater labour mobility. Lump sum payments are provided for those out of work for the previous two years upon their return to work. Up to 25,000 grants averaging £200 each have been allocated for the scheme, at a cost of £5 million annually.

Finally, work trials have been based upon the idea of 'selling' the unemployed to employers, whilst attracting the unemployed into work. Employers can take on people who have been unemployed for six months or more for a trial period of up to three weeks, without incurring costs, in an attempt to assess their suitability. The unemployed continue to receive their benefit during this period and may quit the job without benefit sanction. The scheme enjoys cross-party consensus and support from employer and claimant pressure groups and is being trebled in scope to cover 60,000 unemployed people by 1998.

RADICAL UNEMPLOYMENT POLICIES

Although employment policy in Britain has rarely been radical, several innovative policies have nonetheless been attempted, as Table 5.2 indicates.

Table 5.2 Radical unemployment policies in Britain, 1995

Policy	Policy action
Deregulation of employment law	Various, including removal of wage rigidities, diminution of employment protection
Employer incentives	Direct payments to employers recruiting the long-term unemployed
Local interventionism	Central-local urban regeneration partnerships
Part-time workers assistance	Payments to the long-term unemployed if they take a part-time job

Deregulation of employment law

While not new in the national context, deregulation in Britain is very much a radical policy compared to most of its European counterparts, and new innovations continue to be made.

Since 1979 deregulatory measures have formed the major component of employment policy, with ideological support backed by a specific series of legislative measures initiated by successive Secretaries of State for Employment. Often aimed at curbing trade union-based influence, these Acts also reversed the major thrust of employment legislation created by the Labour Government during the 1970s (Beharell 1992). Thus the Employment Protection Act of 1975 was partly neutered by the Employment Act of 1980 whilst the 1993 Trade Union and Employment Rights Acts abolished wages councils and their power to determine minimum levels of pay. The insistence of the Minister of State for Employment that 'terms and conditions of employment ... are a matter for employers and employees to decide' has characterised the government's approach, with the opt-out from the social chapter providing a further indication (Michael Forsyth, *Hansard*, PQ 5 July 1995). Recently, the aim has been to create 'a bonfire of red tape' (*Employment News*, March 1994). The Deregulation and Contracting Out Act 1994 was designed to effect this, whilst the Department of Trade and Industry has created a Deregulation Task Force designed to foster deregulation initiatives.

Employer incentives

Although financial incentives for employers to hire the unemployed are an established part of British employment policy, recently there have been some new departures in this area.

In 1986 the Conservative Government implemented the New Works Scheme, in which employers were given a subsidy for each unemployed 18–20 year old taken into employment. The subsidy amounted to a maximum of £20 per youth and was payable only to employers taking on workers at a rate below £65 weekly. Accordingly, the scheme was seen by critics as primarily an attempt to depress wages within the youth labour market.

Since June 1993, the Workstart Scheme has been in operation in pilot sectors of the adult employment market, based initially in east Kent, parts of London, Devon and Cornwall and Tyneside. Under this scheme, employers recruiting workers unemployed for two years or more (four in London) receive a subsidy of £60 per week per recruit for the first 26 weeks, followed by £30 per week for the next 26 weeks, up to an annual total of £2,430.

Responsibility for management of the scheme has rested with the Employment Service or, in one instance, the local TEC. The scope of the scheme has been modest, with 1,474 unemployed persons assisted in the first eighteen months of operation, although an extension to 5,000 subsidies was announced in the November 1994 Budget.

Furthermore, in 1994 the Chancellor announced that from April 1996 employers willing to hire a person unemployed for two years or more would be granted a national insurance 'holiday', whereby they would receive a full state rebate on the employer insurance contributions due for that worker for the opening year of employment. This development follows increased pressure from employer organisations, such as the Engineering Employers Federation, for such contribution exemptions, which are estimated to save employers £300 per employee (*Financial Times*, 30 November 1994). The annual cost to the Treasury is estimated at £45 million. For the Conservative Government, national insurance reductions represent an ideologically acceptable form of job creation, compatible with its belief that reductions in the overall burden of taxation upon employers are the most appropriate means of generating employment growth. It should be noted however, that there is cross-party consensus concerning the usefulness of national insurance holidays.

Local interventionism

Only a modest degree of local interventionism has developed as a policy response to unemployment, but there are a number of proposals to go further.

Central government remains the dominant actor in the initiation of ostensibly localist measures. However, the City Challenge Grant scheme allows local authorities to compete for funds to assist economic growth in a given area. To date thirty-one central–local partnerships, based upon five-year regeneration programmes, have been created under City Challenge. Local authorities compete with private sector developers for funding. In Scotland, the fusion of the work of the Scottish Development Agency and the Training Commission in the late 1980s signalled a slight switch towards the use of local initiatives (Moore and Richardson 1989). Such a development has been fostered by the Local Enterprise Companies, although here, as elsewhere in Britain, debate surrounds the most appropriate set of institutional arrangements for local interventionism. Furthermore, there has been little advocacy of large-scale regional approaches to curing unemployment, which had been common during the 1960s with the funding of assisted areas and the use of measures such as regional employment premiums.

Proposals for a more dynamic role for local authorities in reducing unemployment have suggested this could be achieved by a variety of methods.

First, there could be public schemes carried out by local authorities themselves in order to create employment, with authorities possessing their own industrial strategy. Such schemes were initiated by a number of urban councils in the 1980s, under the auspices of newly-established enterprise boards (e.g. the West Midlands and the Greater London enterprise boards). The 1990s has nonetheless seen the decline of this socialised, interventionist model of employment creation.

Second, local authorities could be more significant participants in joint public-private sector partnership models, a feature not always found in schemes sponsored by TECs. This would involve local authorities accepting loss of any remaining control of local employment and training initiatives in return for private investment in such programmes.

The main barrier to localism as an employment initiative is that there exists a lack of consensus over what constitutes 'local'. The absence of calls for regional employment solutions is perhaps surprising given the favouring of the creation of regional government by the opposition parties as part of a new constitutional settlement. Seemingly, the right to work has not yet become part of this revised package of citizenship rights.

Part-time workers' assistance

Assistance for part-time workers has developed in recognition that progress through secondary labour markets may be required for entry into the primary market. Under the Jobmatch pilot scheme that started in November 1993, individuals out of work for two years or more are paid a weekly allowance of £50 for six months when they accept a part-time job. The unemployed are matched to part-time jobs by TECs. Government intentions appear to be to develop part-time jobs as 'a stepping-stone to full-time work' (*Employment News*, January 1995). TECs, as policy deliverers, believe that the acquisition of sufficient part-time jobs to act as a substitute for full-time employment is a viable approach (*Financial Times*, 30 November 1994). The scope of the scheme is small, offering 3,000 such jobmatches in each of the three years 1995–96 to 1997–98.

POLITICAL DYNAMICS

Arguably the most striking feature of the unemployment policies described above is what is not present. There are no state-sponsored schemes to reduce working hours, share jobs or introduce sabbatical leave. The Job Release Scheme introduced in 1977 was designed to encourage early retirement, with replacements from the unemployed register. However, restriction of the scheme's retirees to individuals extremely close to retirement produced only a very marginal effect (Driver 1987).

The lack of radicalism in British unemployment policy has ensured that tentative pilot schemes, lacking comprehensive coverage, have characterised policy output. In explaining why, the particular balance of forces at the national level requires consideration. These include, among other things, current ideological directions, political and academic orthodoxies, the balance of power between political actors, and the particular strengths of institutions shaping employment policies. Such balances may be influenced by levels of unemployment, the success or otherwise of particular employment policies elsewhere and the electoral salience of unemployment.

I turn first to consideration of unemployment as a political issue, then examine the policy roles of the institutional framework and the dominance of training policy. This analysis is then applied to the questions of why there are no radical moves towards work-sharing in Britain, and the role in policy innovation of the piloting of radical measures.

The issue of unemployment

Unemployment in the past two decades has not possessed the political importance even of the early 1980s. The electability of a government presiding over a high level of unemployment was clearly demonstrated in 1983, when the Conservative Government won despite an unemployment figure approaching three million. In that contest, the Conservative Party increased its number of seats held in the 200 constituencies with the highest rates of unemployment from 33 to 44 (Grant and Nath 1984).

Debate over the true extent of unemployment also impairs the development of radical policies. Over thirty changes to the method of counting the unemployed were made between 1979 to 1994, all except one reducing the size of unemployment register. For example, most non-working married women and unemployed males over 60 years of age do not appear in the count. There has developed a politics of the unemployment statistics in which it is argued that the official jobless count underestimates the true extent of unemployment by nearly one million (Glynn 1991). This uncertainty, allied to the successful application of 'scrounger' perceptions towards a section of the unemployed, has impaired the creation of any populist 'back to work' campaigns. Indeed the response of the unemployed has been far more muted than during the previous era of mass unemployment in the 1930s, as unemployed activity has moved from protest to acquiescence (Bagguley 1991).

The institutional framework

Even more important barriers to the development of radical unemployment policies are provided by the institutional arrangements for employment policymaking. The Department of Employment has traditionally been seen as a lower-order ministry, with its abolition long threatened prior to its absorption into the Department for Education and Employment in 1995. The conclusion of trade union reforms ended the Department's specific labour market role. Throughout the 1980s and 1990s, the Department was not seen as a job creator. At best, its role was a labour market facilitator, responsible for the removal of perceived barriers to full employment. In so doing the Department of Employment was active in shifting the balance of power in labour relations decisively towards employers.

In achieving this, the last vestiges of corporatist employment policy formulation were removed during the 1980s. The replacement of the tripartite Manpower Services Commission by the Training Commission diminished trade union influence. TUC opposition to the implementation of the Employment Training Scheme in 1988 led to the abolition of the nominally tripartite Commission. The TUC opposed the scheme on the grounds that it did little to retrain the unemployed and paid only £10 above benefit levels, amounting to a form of cheap labour. Such opposition led to the transfer of the functions of the Commission to the Secretary of State for Employment. Ostensibly, this narrowing of the employment policy network concentrated great powers with the Employment Department. However, the department proved persistently vulnerable to Treasury desires for reductions in the funding of training and employment programmes, particularly during the 1990–92 recession. These reductions were criticised by employer organisations such as the Confederation of British Industry, which condemned the 'hand-to-mouth' existence of TECs (Banham 1992).

The dominance of training policy

In addition to institutional barriers to the development of radical unemployment policies, differing policy objectives have also had a negative impact. During the early 1980s, proactive employment policy, extending beyond the removal of alleged barriers to employment, largely comprised temporary work experience schemes, known as the Community Programme. These amounted to temporary public works schemes which were abandoned due to their prohibitive cost. Their replacements were training schemes, such as Employment Training, which reduced the unemployment count but achieved mediocre long-term results. For example, in 1989 42 per cent of participants in the main adult scheme, Employment Training, returned to unemployment upon completion of training (*Hansard* 26 January 1990, 221W).

The extension of training schemes heralded the current orthodoxy in employment policy, which is centred upon the need to retrain the unemployed as part of a 'skills revolution' (Department of Employment 1988). Alongside the recurring theme of deregulation, training has become the instrument of employment policy, to the virtual exclusion of other supply-side measures. Changed institutional arrangements have reflected this new orthodoxy, with responsibility for training the unemployed now devolved to the creation of a local employer-led network of Training and Enterprise Councils. As Farnham and Lupton (1994) argue, the establishment of TECs represents an attempt to privatise and decentralise Britain's unemployment problem.

Political consensus over the need for training solutions to unemployment has been evident, based upon the belief in the significance of skills shortages. Specific training levies have been advocated by the Labour Party, amounting to 1 per cent of the profits of selected companies, as part of a training and employment package calculated as likely to achieve a reduction in the unemployment total. A similar solution has been offered by the Liberal Democrats, who advocate collection of a training levy of 2 per cent of company payrolls through the tax system. Proceeds would be hypothecated to training and allocated through regional governments to employer organisations.

Outside political parties, consensus over the need for training is not complete. On the right, The Institute of Economic Affairs rejects the economic utility of training (Institute of Economic Affairs 1992). Indeed the new right is far from united in its outlook upon the need for skills training (Evans 1994). A thinktank of the left, the Institute for Public Policy Research, believes that cyclical recovery and full employment can occur despite skills shortages (Haskell and Martin 1994). Amongst employers, only 2 per cent of CBI firms reported skills shortages in 1992 (*The Times*, 8 September 1994).

Governmental acceptance of the need for the retraining of the unemployed has however been characterised by political and institutional arrangements which inhibit the development of radical unemployment policies. Henley and Tsakalotos (1995) suggest that corporatist modes of interest-mediation permit the development of alternatives to the acceptance of unemployment as a crude anti-inflationary device. In Britain, the absence of such political arrangements acts against the coordination and comprehensiveness of employment policy. Indeed the creation of the TEC network possesses the features of voluntarism and state detachment which characterise the broader policy arena. Participation by employers within the activities of TECs remains voluntary. Reluctance to impose employment policies upon TECs is based upon opposition from such bodies, on the grounds that compulsion does not equate to commitment. Furthermore, there is ideological antipathy to the creation of an alleged training bureaucracy.

Accordingly, there has developed a two-tier approach to employment policy. This is based upon a self-regulative institutional sphere, in which employer participation, TEC composition and innovation are self-determined at the local level. Such arrangements are juxtaposed with regulative approaches in, first, the financing of activity, which remains highly contingent upon national economic conditions; and, second, in relation to the participation of the unemployed, an increasingly work-welfare system (King 1995). The latter feature has ensured a lack of support for aspects of the retraining programme, exemplified by the opposition of the TUC to aspects of the Training for Work programme (TUC 1993). Allied to such criticisms is opposition to the use of training as a replacement for the development of more dynamic employment policies.

Overall barriers to the development of radical policies are summarised in Table 5.3.

The absence of radicalism: work-sharing

The above factors help to explain the absence of specific policies in respect of work-sharing. Since the demise of the Temporary Short-time Working Compensation Scheme in March 1984, a measure designed to prevent redundancies through work-sharing, there has been an absence of state attempts to utilise work-sharing to increase the number of people employed.

Table 5.3 Constraints upon the development of radical unemployment policies in Britain

Level	Nature of constraint
Ideological	New right conservative commitment to free economy; anti-interventionist approach.
Economic	Hostility to Keynesian reflationary approach (now cross-party); dominance of supply-side. Treasury opposition due to cost.
Political	New orthodoxy centred upon training. Lack of electoral salience. Abandonment of full employment commitments. Debate over extent of unemployment.
Institutional	Absence of specific department for employment. Employer domination of TECs. Non-existence of corporatist frameworks. Voluntarism of participatory arrangements.

This is perhaps the most glaring omission from employment policy in Britain. Suggestions to reduce unemployment by shortening the working week have been actively resisted by the Conservative Government on the grounds of the potential to reduce output and increase costs to industry. Britain's opt-out from the EU social chapter formed part of a defence of autonomy over working hours. Although there are no formal barriers to the instigation of a work-sharing scheme in Britain, government antipathy towards business regulation ensures that there is no prospect of enforcement, or even financial inducement, for such a programme. A lack of government activism concerning work-sharing is reinforced by employer hostility, labour organisation indifference and academic scepticism.

As Cripps and Ward argue, the problem associated with work-sharing is not so much how to redistribute work, but instead how to achieve the redistribution of income necessary as part of any plan (Cripps and Ward 1994). Work-sharing is therefore somewhat easier to implement in high income countries. In low-wage economies such as that in Britain, it is more difficult to construct any populist agenda based upon the idea. Only Italy has a lower benefits to average wages rate among EU countries, which means that any work-sharing proposal that created reliance upon benefit payments on non-working days is unlikely to gain popular support (Layard and Philpott 1991).

Trade union ambitions have been directed not towards work-sharing in the narrow sense but towards reductions in the working week without financial disadvantage. The defence of individual income, conducted by citizens and representative labour organisations makes work-sharing a distant prospect. Fear of inadequate income generated by part-time employment provides an important attitudinal barrier, with only 20 per cent of employed males willing to consider part-time work as an adequate replacement for current full-time employment (Burchell *et al.* 1994). Indeed, in a low-income economy such as Britain, the preference for more pay rather than shorter hours has been a persistent trend, in contrast to the situation found in countries such as Denmark and the Netherlands (Driver 1987).

The political right suggest that compulsory work-sharing is economically damaging. Lack of support among the employed means that without compulsion, work-sharing would be ineffective. The centre and left fear that part-time work, without concomitant employee protection measures, increases the casualisation of labour, ensuring greater long-term vulnerability for the workforce.

Treasury opposition to work-sharing has been based upon three contentions. First, there is likely to be a loss of competitiveness. Second, any scheme would be costly to implement, whilst increasing the marginal costs of labour. Third, the Treasury has accepted the view of those economists who maintain that work-sharing is not a cure for unemployment, as it rests upon what Layard describes as the 'lump of output' fallacy (Layard

1986: 157). Output is not given, therefore there is no measurable amount of work that can be divided upon a more equitable basis among the workforce. The favoured solution therefore is to increase output and employment, by increasing demand for output through fiscal means. The Treasury has also been a willing player in the subordination of a specific unemployment policy to a broader deflationary strategy.

Nevertheless, the possibility of work-sharing initiatives in the future cannot be entirely excluded. One idea in respect of helping reduce standard working time has been that the benefit system be overhauled to reflect the switch towards part-time employment. A recommendation of the Borrie Commission on Social Justice in 1994 was that a new part-time workers benefit should be introduced (Commission for Social Justice 1994). This would allow greater proportions of other benefits to be retained in the event of part-time work being undertaken, ensuring that those undertaking such employment should be able to maintain a reasonable level of income per head. Present regulations are seen as a deterrent to part-time employment, participation in which has a punitive impact upon social security benefits. The Borrie Commission provided a redefinition of the commitment to full employment, supporting the principle but emphasising its attainment through part-time work, work-sharing and short-term contracts. These measures, allied to early retirement, are seen as the optimum way to increase output and employment.

The piloting of radical measures

Given the constraints upon the development of radical unemployment policies, how is the recent development of some such measures explained?

Employer incentives and deregulation have been measures universally applied within the labour market. Both have the support of the main actors – government department, Treasury, employer organisations and TECs – within the employment policy arena, and both accord with the ideological direction of the government and its belief that relief of non-wage costs will facilitate employment growth; furthermore, national insurance relief is a low-cost employment policy for the Treasury. However there remains doubt over the extent to which such relief will reduce unemployment. Employers' national insurance for workers earning less than £200 is less than £10 per week. As these low-wage jobs are the type likely to be offered to the unemployed, reductions in national insurance may make little difference to employers' recruitment decisions.

The other radical policies adopted thus far have been introduced only on a localised basis. In part, this reflects the new policy-delivery arena, which, through the introduction of TECs, allows a local focus and a small measure of area innovation. For example, the introduction of the job-match scheme designed to help workers into part-time employment as a 'stepping-stone' to full-time work followed an experiment conducted by

Lincolnshire TEC. Furthermore, employment policies have become some-what more radical in recent years, with the embryonic development of wage subsidies providing one example.

Indeed the former Employment Department appeared to endorse the findings of the Institute of Employment Studies which suggested that the 'Workstart' pilot subsidy programme had made a substantial difference to employment recruitment patterns. The IES found that nearly half of employers participating in the scheme would not have recruited workers without the available subsidy (IES 1995). However, the universal adoption of such schemes is opposed by the Treasury on grounds of cost. Academic arguments that subsidy schemes could be self-financing through insurance and taxation gains have not yet held sway (Snower 1993).

OUTLOOK

Few formal barriers to the development of radical unemployment policies exist in Britain. Indeed, 'flexible legalism' allows frequent changes in employment policy compared to countries such as Germany (Rose and Page 1990:77). Measures can be enacted rapidly by the relevant depart-ment and given retrospective legitimacy through subsequent legislation. This explains the ease with which a plethora of training and employment schemes have developed and indicates how tripartite policymaking structures were so quickly dismantled.

If an absence of constitutional impediments provides a promising leg-islative framework for the development of radical unemployment policies, their formulation will not occur without ideological and institutional changes. With regard to ideology, neo-liberal principles have been applied, in that there has been state disengagement from direct responsibility for the unemployed.

A first principle underpinning the development of radical unemploy-ment policies needs to be a reacceptance of the political and social imperative of a commitment to full employment. As Grieve-Smith (1992) declares, full employment needs to be seen as a concept no more out-dated than universal suffrage. On this basis, policies can be adopted on a cost-benefit basis. A second requirement is the development of a con-sensus over the measurement of unemployment. There remains no guar-antee that the use of different counting methods showing an alternative unemployment figure of four million will heighten the development of radical unemployment policies (Wells 1995), but statistical agreement would prevent diversion of discussion of employment solutions towards debate over the true extent of the problem.

Certainly there has been a shift away from the absolutist ideological and economic beliefs of the early 1980s. Crude monetarism has long been displaced, whilst a broader range of employment policies is utilised at the micro-level. However, the new orthodoxy, that comprehensive training policy allied to greater benefit conditionality is the optimum solution to Britain's employment problem, has impaired the search for radical unemployment policies. Current 'employment' policy has thus been summarised as:

> the creation of a neo-liberal training regime in which employer-led training directs policy to problems of labour market disincentives and rigidities and to the short-term political need of reducing unemployment and away from the realisation of full employment.
>
> (King 1993:235)

There remains little prospect of a return to the tripartite institutional arrangements which formerly characterised employment policymaking. Trade union representatives form only 5 per cent of the board membership of TECs. However, this need not preclude the development of radical policies; indeed, the conservatism of trade unions did little to assist such ideas as work-sharing, persistently favouring early retirement as the most appropriate, minimalist form of such a measure. Work-sharing policies may need to be developed via a 'snowball' effect at local or sectoral levels prior to their national application. Pilot schemes can encourage work and income sharing, but employee participants may require financial inducement.

Recent changes in institutional arrangements offer some scope for radicalism in employment policy. Devolution of policy delivery to TECs may be followed by greater autonomy in policymaking. However, given that TECs possess no compulsory powers over employers, local employers may simply reject schemes such as work-sharing. In addition, there remains no guarantee that the activities or composition of a TEC accurately reflect the local labour market. Greater employee participation is required if radical employment policies are to be fostered, although the TECs may be useful in promoting local interventionism as a means of employment growth. Finally, the development of radical employment policies requires the creation of a single powerful employment department to promote such schemes. The British experience has been precisely the reverse.

REFERENCES

Bagguley, P. (1991) *From Protest to Acquiescence? Political Movements of the Unemployed*, Basingstoke, Macmillan.

Banham, J. (1992) 'Taking forward the skills revolution', *Policy Studies*, 13, (1).

Beharell, A. (1992) *Unemployment and Job Creation*, London, Macmillan.

Burchell, B., Elliott, J. and Rubery, J. (1994) 'Perceptions of the labour market: an investigation of differences by gender and by working-time' in Rubery, J. and Wilkinson, F. (eds) *Employer Strategy and the Labour Market*, Oxford, Oxford University Press: 298–325.

Commission for Social Justice (1994) *Strategies for National Renewal*, CSJ.

Crewe, I. (1993) 'Voting and the electorate' in Dunleavy, P. *et al. Developments in British Politics 4*, London, Macmillan: 92–122.

Cripps, F. & Ward, T. (1994) 'Strategies for growth and employment in the European Community' in Michie, J. and Grieve-Smith, J. (eds) *Unemployment in Europe*, London, Academic Press.

Department of Employment (1988) *Employment for the 1990s*, London, HMSO Cmnd 540.

Driver, C. (1987) *Towards Full Employment: A Policy Appraisal*, London, Routledge and Kegan Paul.

Employment News

Evans, B. (1994) 'Neo-liberalism and training policy 1979–92: a rejoinder to Desmond King', *Political Studies* 42, (3):480–5.

Farnham, D. and Lupton, C. (1994) 'Employment relations and training policy' in Savage, S., Atkinson, R. and Robins, L. (eds) *Public Policy in Britain*, London, Macmillan: 96–115.

Glynn, S. (1991) *No Alternative? Unemployment in Britain*, London, Faber and Faber.

Grant, W. and Nath, S. (1984) *The Politics of Economic Policy-Making*, Oxford, Blackwell.

Grieve-Smith, J. (1992) *Full Employment in the 1990s*, Institute of Public Policy Research, London.

Haskell, J. and Martin, C. (1994) 'Will low skills kill recovery?', *New Economy*, Autumn 1994, Institute for Public Policy Research.

Henley, A. and Tsakalotos, E. (1995) 'Unemployment experiences and the institutional preconditions for full employment' in Arestis, P. and Marshall, M. (eds) *The Political Economy of Full Employment*, Aldershot, Edward Elgar: 176–201.

Institute of Economic Affairs (1992) *Training Too Much? A Sceptical Look at the Economics of Skill Provision*, London, IEA.

Institute of Employment Studies (1995) *Evaluation of Workstart Pilots*, Institute of Employment Studies Report 279.

King, D. (1993) 'The Conservatives and training policy 1979–1992: from a tripartite to a neo-liberal regime', *Political Studies*, XLI, (2):214–35.

—— (1995) *Actively Seeking Work? The Politics of Unemployment and Welfare Policy in the United States and Great Britain*, Chicago, University of Chicago Press.

Labour Party (1992) *It's Time to get Britain Working Again*, Labour Party manifesto 1992.

Layard, R. (1986) *How to beat Unemployment*, Oxford, Oxford University Press.

Layard, R., and Philpott, J. (1991) *Stopping Unemployment*, London, Employment Institute.

Moore, C. and Richardson, J. (1989) *Local Partnership and the Unemployment Crisis in Britain*, London, Unwin Hyman.

Rose, R. and Page, E. (1990) Action in adversity: responses to unemployment in Britain and Germany', *West European Politics*, 13, (4):66–84.

Snower, D. (1993) *The Future of the Welfare State*, London, CEPR.

Tonge, J. (1993) 'Training and Enterprise Councils: the privatisation of Britain's unemployment problem?' *Capital and Class*, 51:9–15.

Trade Union Congress (1993) *TUC Unified Budget Submission 1993*, London, TUC.

Wells, J. (1995) 'Unemployment, job creation and job destruction in the UK since 1979' in Arestis, P. and Marshall, M. (eds) *The Political Economy of Full Employment*, Aldershot, Edward Elgar.

Wilson, T. (1987) *Unemployment and the Labour Market*, London, Institute of Economic Affairs.

6 Spain

Martin Rhodes

INTRODUCTION

Spain currently confronts one of the most serious employment crises in the EU. Its response to this problem in the 1990s has been to embark on a programme of radical deregulation in the labour market. Although radical in the Spanish context, given the preservation of many of the paternalist and protective employment regulations of the Franco era, the thrust of reform has remained quite consistent over the last decade. Prioritising the deregulation of contracts for new recruits, while leaving the arrangements which buttress permanent contracts in place, only lip service has been paid to other areas of labour market policy such as training and education. As a result there has been an expansion in the use of precarious, fixed-term contracts, continued growth of the informal, unregulated economy – which fixed-term contracts were meant to counteract – and an accelerated increase in unemployment during the most recent recession, concentrated among younger workers and women. The following analysis seeks to explain this unbalanced approach to employment policy and considers the prospects for a different, more solidaristic, strategy.

CONTEXT

In an era of recession and high rates of unemployment in Europe, Spain stands out as a country with some of the continent's most serious labour market problems. Not only does it have the highest rate of unemployment in the European Union (EU) – an official rate of 24 per cent at the end of 1994 – but it also suffers from one of the highest rates of long-term unemployment: 53 per cent of unemployed people have been without work for one year or more. Although a large informal economy absorbs a proportion of those out of work who may also be claiming benefits, the real rate of unemployment is still estimated at over 20 per cent (Dolado and Jimeno 1995).

Furthermore, Spain's unemployment is persistent: even in the second half of the 1980s, when an average annual growth of 4.25 per cent was only surpassed by Japan in the OECD, it did not fall below 15 per cent.

% workforce

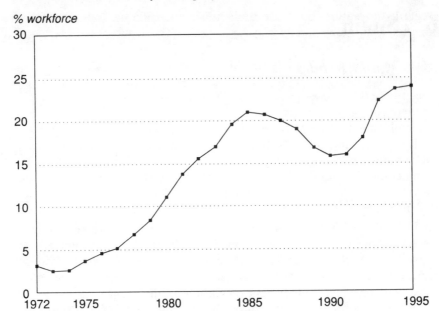

Figure 6.1 Unemployment in Spain, 1972–1995

Note: Standardised unemployment rates to 1994, projection based on commonly used
definition 1995

Source: OECD 1992 (1972–87), OECD 1995 (1988–95)

Taking account of a low participation rate (by EU standards), less than
half the working age population – 47 per cent in 1993 – were employed,
compared with an EU average of 59 per cent. And of these, more than
a third are now employed on fixed-term contracts, producing the most
unbalanced labour market in the EU (Rojo Torrecilla 1994). The consequence of an incomplete and idiosyncratic approach to labour market
reform undertaken since the mid 1980s, the proliferation of such contracts
has provided a partial, short-term solution to the problem of youth and
female unemployment, but, as will become clear, it has had longer-term,
negative consequences for the economy as a whole.

  The persistence of Spanish unemployment indicates the structural
nature of the problem. This has its origins in the rapid restructuring of
the Spanish economy after its post-Franco liberalisation, the massive
destruction of agricultural employment, the impact of the twin oil shocks
of the 1970s, and the substantial increase in female workforce participation
triggered by social and cultural modernisation. But, as already indicated,
explanations for the persistence of Spanish unemployment and employment disequilibria should also be sought in the way in which the labour
market is regulated and in the unidirectional nature of reform. In this

regard, the nature, structure and interrelationship of state and labour market institutions clearly plays a key role. The institutional framework of the labour market in Spain has its origins in the Franco regime when wage bargaining and conditions of work were closely controlled by the state. Many elements of that system have remained in place until quite recently – the consequence of Spain's method of reconciling economic modernisation with democratic consolidation. Indeed, to some extent unemployment is the price that Spain has paid for that compromise.

The actors, and the industrial relations framework which govern relations between them, emerged in the turmoil of the early years of democratic transition. The poorly institutionalised system that resulted helps explain the subsequent problems of developing a coherent and balanced approach to the labour market. The illegality of free associations of workers and employers under Franco explains to some extent the weakness of their organisations in the democratic era. The two most important unions – the UGT (Unión General de Trabajadores), which, until the late 1980s, was closely linked to the Socialist Party (PSOE) and the CCOO (Confederación Sindical de Comisiones Obreras), traditionally close to the Spanish Communist Party – currently represent only between 10 and 15 per cent of the workforce. Their defence of laws protecting permanent employees should be understood in part as a means of defending their own existence, since the fixed-term, unemployed and informal workforce remains beyond their reach (see Estivill and de la Hoz 1990). As for employers, although the formal membership of their peak organisation, the CEOE (Confederación Española de Organizaciones Empresariales) is high (its density rate is around 75 per cent) it is also divided: between an indigenous capitalist class and foreign capital (multinationals account for around half of industrial turnover and employment in major Spanish industries); and between large companies and small and medium-sized firms which, organised in an affiliated association, CEYPME (Confederación Española de la Pequeña y Mediana Empresa) account for 80 per cent of all employment in Spain (Lucio 1991).

Employment policy has been shaped by a 'strategic neo-corporatism' linking the state, employers and unions via a series of social pacts from the late 1970s to the mid 1980s. Union acceptance of wage moderation and marginal reforms of the labour market was gained by the preservation of the Franco regimes' paternalist system of employment protection (for workers on permanent contracts) and the reduction of wage differentials. The 1980 Workers' Statute (Estatuto de Trabajadores) followed a similar logic by layering a new set of regulations on the old in order to guarantee union consent. The willingness of unions and employers to cooperate with the state was based in part on their organisational weaknesses and their joint concern to avoid social conflict given the fragility of democracy (demonstrated in 1981 by an abortive coup d'état). But since 1986, the adoption of austerity policies by the government and a growing polarisation between the parties on labour market issues has seen a parallel demise of tripartism, which has been replaced by a less institutionalised and shifting set of relationships between the state, employers and trade unions. In the subsequent period, industrial relations – like the labour market itself – has become increasingly 'disorganised'.

While the unions have become ever more distant from their base, employers have revealed themselves to be fragmented and rarely capable of playing a constructive public role. Moreover, both unions and employers perform a quasi-political function, for while the rightward shift of the Socialist Party has encouraged the unions to behave as its alter ego on the left, equally the centrist, almost Christian Democratic character of the political right has persuaded the CEOE to present itself as the guardian of the market economy. A consequence of this politicisation of the peak associations of capital and labour has been a parallel politicisation of employment policy and the labour market (see Lucio and Blyton 1995). Meanwhile, the government – controlled by a majority Socialist government between 1982 and 1993, and subsequently by a minority Socialist administration backed by the Catalan nationalist group, Convergence and Unity (CiU) – has attempted to unload responsibility for labour market policymaking onto the social partners. When, as in the case of the most recent (1993) reform package, this has failed, the government has implemented radical policies unilaterally. All in all, this context has proven to be far from conducive to a balanced, consensual approach to Spain's unemployment problems.

RADICAL UNEMPLOYMENT POLICIES

'Radical' in the Spanish context may be considered somewhat less than radical elsewhere. But in Spain, labour market reform of any kind is highly politicised given the symbolic and practical significance that employment regulation has had in that country's transition from an autarkic, authoritarian regime to a modern, capitalist democracy. Given the sensitivity of unions and the political left to any shift in the balance of power between capital and labour, regulatory reform of any kind is likely to be difficult and limited: all attempts at reform since the mid 1980s have provoked general strikes. Dismantling or renovating any part of Spain's complex and rigid regulatory structure in the labour market is therefore a 'radical' step.

There are four main types of radical unemployment policies in Spain: deregulation and the reduction of labour costs; strengthening work incentives; working time reduction; and institutional reform.

Deregulation and the reduction of labour costs

The deregulation of labour law and practices has provided the main thrust of employment policy reform in Spain during the past decade. Under

Table 6.1 Radical unemployment policies in Spain

Type of policy	Policy
Deregulation and reduction of labour costs	New forms of employment contracts Relaxation of dismissals regulations
Work incentives	Stronger incentives for unemployed to seek work
Reduction of working time	Early retirement Part-time work Restrictions on overtime Shorter standard working hours
Institutional reform	Decentralisation of employment policy administration Concertation

Franco, permanent jobs were protected by high dismissal costs, in terms of redundancy payments and administrative authorisation procedures, but these were partially offset by a degree of flexibility in wages and the use of overtime. Work organisation was strictly governed by the *ordenanzas laborales* (labour regulations) which were a substitute for collective bargaining. With the transition to democracy, collective bargaining was formally introduced and the regulation of contracts modified under the Moncloa Pacts (1977) and the 1980 Workers' Statute, which legalised fixed-term employment even before its use was made more flexible (Toharia 1988). But the high degree of protection of permanent contracts and the *ordenanzas laborales* remained in place – indeed, both were reinforced in the 1970s and 1980s – and the flexibility of wages and overtime was drastically reduced. Meanwhile, the Workers' Statute introduced new restrictions on functional mobility (between fixed occupational categories, i.e. demarcation lines) and geographical mobility.

Hence the determination of employers to have the vestiges of Francoist labour regulation – as well as the new layer of restrictions – removed: the high costs of dismissals, they claimed, deterred them in recruiting new workers and the limitations on functional and geographical mobility prevented adjustment to market conditions while adding to labour costs. For the unions, however, both were essential to guard against the exercise of unilateral employer power in a labour market where workers' representation is highly uneven and the authoritarian/paternalistic employer is still very much in evidence.

New forms of employment contracts

The substantial package of labour reform introduced by the Socialist government at the end of 1993, in the form of a decree-law on 'urgent measures to promote employment' and a bill on amendments to the 1980 Workers' Statute, represented consolidation as well as radical change in the sense that a radical reform of contracts had already been introduced by the Socialist government ten years earlier. At that time, a vast range of new contracts was introduced as a means of counteracting both the rapid rise in unemployment then occurring and the expansion of the informal economy. The bulk of these were employment-promoting in intent (training and apprenticeship contracts, for example), but, since they incurred annulment costs of twelve days pay per year, only around a fifth of all fixed-term contracts registered in the early 1990s were of this type. The great majority (60 per cent in 1992) were of the ordinary variety, used for specific tasks and seasonal work. Most of the one-third of the work force now employed on a fixed-term basis have been recruited on such contracts, which are renewable for up to three years, incur zero annulment costs, and fall outside the regulations limiting functional mobility.

The 1993 reform allowed those contracts which expired that year to be extended for a further eighteen months, but otherwise new temporary contracts are now limited to six months only. Earlier that year, an employment subsidy of Ptas 250,000 (approximately £1,438) was introduced for each fixed-term contract converted into an open-ended contract. At the same time new apprenticeship contracts have been introduced with low wages and reduced social security contributions attached as incentives.

Relaxation of dismissals regulations

While the restrictions on functional and geographical mobility in the Worker's Statute have been relaxed and employers and unions obliged (by a state-fixed expiry date) to negotiate the replacement of the labour regulations with collective agreements, some of the most important reforms concern dismissals legislation.

Until now, Spanish employers have been faced with some of the most restrictive dismissals procedures and costs in Western Europe. Originally justified by the paucity of unemployment benefits, these have become a *cause célèbre* – even an obsession – for employers. For individual dismissals, there is a minimum of twenty days pay per year of service, up to twelve months, for workers on standard contracts. However, a higher sum is usually agreed to prevent an employee claiming unfair dismissal – in which case the employer has the option of reinstating the employee or paying forty-five days pay per year of service. If the claim arises from a worker's refusal to accept changes in working conditions or work location, then the cost to the employer can be anywhere between twenty and forty-five days pay per year of service.

In the case of collective redundancies, defined as dismissals involving more than two workers, regardless of firm size, administrative authorisation procedures can last between fifty and seventy-five days and the outcome depends on there being valid economic or technological reasons as well as on prior agreement between the employer and the union. The latter usually entails redundancy payments of around fifty days pay per year of service for each worker affected (Garcia Perea and Gómez 1993:70–71). In 1992, the average cost of a redundancy payment in companies with over 200 employees was Ptas 4.5 million – then £22,000 (EIRR 1995:16).

Under the new post-1993 reforms, in the case of failure to reach agreement with the unions, the labour administration is required to reach a judgement on the employer's application for dismissals' approval within fifteen days; 'organisational and production' reasons have been added to economic and technological exigencies as objective grounds for collective redundancies; and collective dismissals have been redefined as those which over a period of 90 days affect at least 10 workers in firms with less than 100 staff, 10 per cent of workers in firms with between 100 and 300 staff, and 30 workers in large companies (those with 300 workers or more).

Although the unions led a general strike on January 1994 against what they described as an 'unprecedented deregulation of industrial relations', the employers were distinctly unimpressed with the timid nature of these reforms (EIRR 1994). They are calling for the full abolition of authorisation; but a more radical approach has been ruled out by outright union opposition and divisions in the government between the Minister for the Economy, who has been keen to abolish authorisation to help boost investment, and the Minister of Labour, who has been concerned not to upset the present balance of power between capital and labour (EIRR 1993a: 25). Modifying the contractual entitlements of those already in permanent positions would clearly also be a major vote loser, which explains the timidity of even conservative politicians when confronted with this issue. Thus, the Catalan conservatives (CiU) – whose support has kept the Socialists in office since the 1983 general elections – have called for a compromise solution: a new indefinite contract which can be broken, without authorisation, by the employer on payment of twenty days salary per year of service. In keeping with tradition, those already on permanent contracts (the core work force) would not be affected.

Stronger incentives for the unemployed to seek work

One of the most controversial reforms of the 1990s – provoking general strikes in May and October 1992 – has been the modification of entitlements to unemployment benefit to provide individuals with greater incentives to seek work. Part of the state's Programa de Convergencia (Plan for Economic Convergence), designed to prepare Spain for the third and final phase of European Economic and Monetary Union, was the decree-law that introduced the changes. This was roundly denounced by politicians both to the left and the right of the governing Socialists, as was the statement by the Minister for Economics, Carlos Solchaga that the measures were designed to eradicate 'social parasitism' (EIRR 1992:13).

The disincentives to work, especially for low and average-wage blue collar workers, have been noted in the Spanish case by numerous analyses. Alongside an expansion of unemployment benefit cover from 25 to 70 per cent of the workforce between 1983 and 1993, unemployment benefits became more generous: untaxed (until January 1994), they are paid on a sliding scale of 80 per cent of previous income in the first six months, 70 per cent from the sixth to the twelfth month and 60 per cent from the twelfth to the twenty-fourth month (see Jesús Martín and Martí 1994). A high effective marginal tax rate in low and average income brackets means that, in some cases, employment benefits are higher than incomes (Franks 1994).

The 1992 reforms therefore sought to reduce these disincentives by increasing the minimum period of work to qualify for benefits from six months to one year, lowering the average duration of benefits from twenty to twelve months, and delaying the beginning of benefits until the exhaustion of severance payments. Whether this will have any real impact on unemployment, however, is unclear: as Dolado and Jimeno (1995:13–14) point out, the duration and coverage of Spanish unemployment benefits is not excessive compared with other European countries; long-term unemployment is concentrated among young people and women with no work experience and therefore having no entitlement to unemployment benefits. There may, however, be a case for the reform of Spanish social assistance benefits which may have a disincentive effect (Jimeno and Toharia 1992:103).

Reduction of working time

Although up to now work-sharing has been virtually non-existent in Spain, it has been advocated in various forms by the labour movement and occasionally by the government. Some work-sharing measures have even been introduced, although with little effect, and even part-time work (arguably a form of work-sharing) has been very limited in extent.

Early retirement

Spain has for some time had a system of early retirement which companies use for rejuvenating and restructuring their work force. Thus workers receive 60 per cent of their state pension entitlement at 60, 68 per cent at 61, 76 per cent at 62, 84 per cent at 63 and 92 per cent at 64. But there have been no measures to make early retirement conditional on replacement by a new worker, so it is unlikely that this has done much to create new employment. As part of a rationalisation process, however, it undoubtedly allows expensive permanent workers to be replaced by cheaper fixed-term workers.

In addition, since 1984, employers who retire workers early on a partial basis have been given incentives for their replacement with a new recruit. These *contratos de relevo* (relief contracts) allow workers to retire between the ages of 62 and 64 and work half time while receiving half of their state pension. Employers receive a 50 per cent reduction in their social security contributions if the part-time replacement is retained after the full-time retirement of the partial pensioner. However, as elsewhere, this option has not been greatly used: such contracts accounted for 0.04 per cent of all contracts in 1985 and 0.03 per cent in 1992. In fact, they have not been especially attractive for either employers or employees: while the former incur less costs and have greater freedom to reorganise work if they fully retire workers, the vacancies opened have been too poorly paid (often below benefit levels) to attract anyone except untrained young people and married women with no previous work record. Abreu and Costa (1994:62) have recently recommended the relaunch of these contracts with more flexible rules on when partial retirement begins and the possibility of instigating temporary work alongside the part-time regime, although this is not part of the official employment policy agenda.

Part-time work

Part of the problem of the current regime is a general antipathy towards part-time work in Spain which prevents its use as a more general form of work-sharing. Although facilitated by the 1984 employment reforms, part-time work has been rigidly defined as less than two-thirds of a standard day, week, month or year and, more importantly, has incurred the same social security costs for employers as full-time work. In 1993 only 6.3 per cent of workers were on part-time contracts, the majority of whom would have preferred a full-time post (Grubb and Wells 1993:31).

Under the December 1993 reform package, three innovations have been made which are designed to boost part-time work as a means of employment creation: part-time work is redefined as that considered less than normal for the activity concerned; social security protection – and therefore employers' contributions – for part-time workers employed for less than 12 hours a week or 48 hours a month is limited to industrial accidents, work-related illnesses and guaranteed payment of wages (they are not covered for ordinary sickness and receive no unemployment benefits); and part-time contracts can be concluded for a fixed-term or indefinite period (EIRR 1994).

Restrictions on overtime

Restricting overtime has long been advocated by the unions as a means of job creation, and average annual overtime hours have been bargained down over the years, although with no obvious impact on the rate of unemployment. The government, however, seems to think that it may help and in December 1993 introduced measures to make overtime less attractive to employees: the statutory obligation to pay premium rates for overtime equivalent to no less than 75 per cent above ordinary rates was removed and replaced by standard rates.

Shorter standard working hours

In late 1993 the government announced a vague proposal to save jobs by reducing hours of work, which was welcomed by the unions, who had been advocating a standard 35-hour week for some time. This proposal seems to have since disappeared, and the Spanish government opposed the policy of shorter working hours in EU-level negotiations. The proposal, inspired by the idea of a four-day week then under negotiation at Volkswagen in Germany, was rejected as 'absurd' by both the president of the employers association, José Maria Cuevas, and by the chief executive of General Motor's Spanish subsidiary, Juan José Sanz. Only the chief executive of Nissan, Spain, Juan Echevaria Puig, appeared receptive to the idea. However, SEAT (VW's Spanish subsidiary) has since suggested a VW work-sharing solution in its dispute over redundancies with the unions, although this has done little to moderate their opposition to workforce reductions (EIRR 1993b)

Institutional reform

Two types of institutional reform have been undertaken in Spain in an effort to improve the formulation and implementation of employment policy: decentralising the administration of employment policy and stimulating dialogue between employers and unions at the national and regional levels.

Decentralisation of employment policy administration

In 1993 a National Programme of Professional Training covering the period 1993–1996 was approved which seeks to improve coordination of the three basic Spanish training bodies; the Foundation for Vocational Training (FORCEM), the Ministry of Education and the Public Employment Office (INEM). In line with this reform, many training activities are being transferred to the regions, continuing a process which is already well under way. Administrative decentralisation in Spain has been a critical step in helping create the basis for local development strategies by giving regions important powers in economic, social and territorial matters, and by the early 1980s local economic development strategies already affected around 10 per cent of the active industrial population. These were assisted after 1986 by the Employment Promotion

Programmes, one of which was specifically aimed at the promotion of local economic initiatives (Granados Cabezas 1992). This has had some effect on an otherwise deficient national vocational training system and some regions – the Basque country and Valencia, for example – have flexible and effective training structures. But in those regions with the highest rates of unemployment, such as Andalusia and Exremadura, the institutional infrastructure remains highly inadequate (Rhodes 1995).

Concertation

The process of reform sketched above has been assisted by dialogue at the national level: the reorganisation of the training system, for example, has the backing of a tripartite agreement. But going beyond to other more sensitive employment issues has been difficult. A tripartite forum for dialogue, the Economic and Social Committee (CES), was established in 1989; tripartite consultative committees on employment, social security and health policies have been established at both national and regional levels; and workers' participation has been established on the boards of public sector companies with more than 1,000 employees. Since 1990 the Socialist government has been seeking to revive the neo-corporatist social pacts of the early 1980s as a means of forging a consensus on labour market reform. However, the extreme politicisation of labour market issues already referred to has prevented any accord on the more sensitive regulatory questions.

POLITICAL DYNAMICS

The key question to be answered in the Spanish context is why one particular variety of radical unemployment policy – the deregulation of contractual arrangements for new recruits –has been prioritised above all others. Although it is only part of the story, a brief survey of Spanish political and economic development reveals how Spain's labour market – and its responses to unemployment – have been shaped by the exigencies of the democratic transition.

Until the mid 1970s there was little problem with unemployment. The economy was sheltered and heavily protected, jobs were generally permanent and protected by the state, and there was always the safety-valve of emigration: one million people left Spain in the decade after 1964. This was to change dramatically in the decade after Franco's death in 1975. During that period, Spain's democracy was consolidated and its economy opened to the outside world. As far as the labour market is concerned, this was a period of tumultuous change. Tensions bottled up under Franco exploded in industrial conflict in the late 1970s at a time when Spain's traditional system of industrial relations was collapsing and political control of the economy was being shaken by the impact of the two oil price shocks. At the same time, rapid modernisation of the economy was destroying hundreds of thousands of jobs in both agriculture and industry. A wages-price spiral produced inflation of 30 per cent by 1977 accompanied by steadily rising unemployment, and workers' grievances over losses in purchasing power and unfairly distributed tax increases became hard to contain (Fina 1987). Meanwhile, labour market actors were still in the process of constituting themselves: the CCOO was established as a national organisation in 1976 and the employers' CEOE in 1977 – which was also the year of the first democratic elections. The new centre-right government had to bring some order to the economy and the industrial relations system in general while also defusing social conflict and consolidating Spain's fragile democratic structures.

The response was a form of 'strategic neo-corporatism' in which the government conceded a substantial narrowing of wage differentials and the maintenance of Francoist employment protection, in return for wage moderation and an 'implicit pact' between workers and economic managers under which the costs of economic modernisation would be accepted. This was buttressed by a massive increase in public spending, from 25 to 38 per cent of GDP between 1976 and 1983.

Despite this, between 1970 and 1982 the real cost of labour increased by about 40 per cent over productivity (Pérez-Díaz 1993:226). The process of political exchange inaugurated by the Moncloa Pacts of 1977 and terminating with the 1984 Economic and Social Agreement (Acuerdo Económico y Social) produced what Pérez-Díaz (1993:229) has called a 'gradual maladjustment to crisis': a series of *ad hoc*, improvised solutions that have succeeded only in creating a profound dualism and segmentation in the labour market alongside an underground economy of major proportions. Neo-corporatism in these circumstances was not only compatible with dualism but reinforced it. Until the mid 1980s everyone had something to gain from concertation: the unions legitimised themselves as social actors and achieved an extension of welfare provision; employers were rewarded with wage moderation and an institutional framework for labour relations; and the state was able to use this process – albeit at high budgetary cost – to promote social peace and controlled modernisation. All benefited from the consolidation of democracy. But at the same time, the number of 'outsiders' was growing rapidly: between 1977 and 1985 the rate of unemployment rose steadily from 5.1 to 21 per cent, the consequence largely of the collapse of formerly-protected inefficient firms faced with higher wage and non-wage costs and open competition (Fina 1987:30)

Thus, as part and parcel of its democratic transition, the adaption of Spain's system of employment regulation and industrial relations system created structures, expectations and obligations that would subsequently prove hard to reform. This is partly why the Spanish authorities opted for a 'safety-valve' approach to the employment crisis after 1984, the 'safety-valve' being low-cost, fixed-term contracts sought not especially by employers (who actually criticised them for discriminating in favour of new firms with little dead-weight permanent employment) but by policy-makers influenced by neo-liberal ideas and faced with a potentially explosive increase in the numbers out of work. Nonetheless the unions were still vital for political stability and existing regulations had to be preserved. Thus the new measures were introduced with the consent of the labour movement, due to the depth of the recession and by pressure from various groups of workers, especially the young. At the same time, these contracts were initially seen by the unions as a *quid pro quo* for their demands for a reduction of overtime as a means of employment creation (Fina *et al.* 1989:122–4; Bentolila and Dolado 1994:85).

At that point they could not have foreseen that the consequent casualisation of employment would prove highly detrimental to their future strength, the desperate defence of which explains their subsequent opposition to any further liberalisation of the labour market. Their loss of influence after the mid 1980s was due to several developments. The first and most important has undoubtedly been the collapse of membership from 20–25 per cent in 1980 to around 10 per cent ten years later, producing a consequent crisis of organisation and strategy (see Rigby and Lawlor 1994). While they remain an important force through their much wider support in workplace elections and their capacity for strike mobilisation, after 1985 they ceased to be a critical partner for either the state or employers. By the end of 1984, the state had much less need of the corporatist, democratic stabiliser of concertation, and in any case embarked on an era of strict economic and monetary discipline which produced a schism in the 'Socialist family', pushing the UGT further left and much closer to the CCOO (Gillespie 1990). Meanwhile, the employers felt less need to compromise with a weakened labour movement (at least in the national arena) and now rejected policymaking by consensus, one result of which had been an expansion in the welfare budget and an increase in their own social costs.

Henceforth the unions were forced to fall back on the defence of their own interests, which became increasingly narrow. Solidaristic policies proved much less easy to pursue in a highly fragmented labour market (Estivill and de la Hoz 1990; Lucio and Blyton 1995). While trade unions have continued to advocate alternative solutions to the unemployment crisis, such as a shorter working week, and have even tried to create federations for the unemployed, and women's rights committees, they have been unable to make any impression on a state apparatus from which they are now effectively excluded. Nor have they been able to brook any dismantling of the protective apparatus surrounding permanent employees inherited from the Franco regime. After all, this is the guarantee, in the last resort, of their own survival. But it has also meant a growing alienation of much of the work force – female, young, precarious and unemployed – from the predominantly male, blue-collar culture of the labour movement.

In turn, the unions' unwillingness to compromise on the dismissals issue has provoked the employers into a similarly rigid position on labour market reform. Unless dismissal regulations for permanent employees are relaxed, then no other solutions to the unemployment crisis will be given serious consideration. But the trade unions would only consider a re-regulation of open-ended contracts if their currently weak rights to representation in the workplace were enhanced, thereby allowing them to participate in redundancy procedures and monitor company-level social plans. But this, in turn, is anathema to employers, among whom an authoritarian/paternalist conception of power in the workplace still tends to prevail. When in 1990 the unions reached an agreement with the government on the monitoring of contracts – requiring employers to show contracts to unions, to check their legality, before passing them on to the state employment authorities – José María Cuevas, the president of the CEOE, declared that this represented 'the most serious attack on the market economy and freedom of enterprise since the transition to democracy' and paved the way towards the 'sovietisation' of industrial relations! (EIRR 1990).

The failure of attempts to introduce such solutions since the late 1980s illustrates the scale of the problem. The union's most recent 'success' was in 1988 when they forced the government to back down on a controversial plan for youth employment. Aimed at the then 1.5 million unemployed people under 25 years of age, the plan sought to put 800,000 young people into work over a three year period by reducing employers' social security contributions and fixing payment at the level of the statutory minimum wage. As Gillespie (1990:45) points out, the unions reaction to the plan was ill-considered and extreme: the plan was denounced for discriminating on the basis of age, for subsidising a low standard of employment out of public funds and for being unconstitutional in undermining the principle of 'equal pay for equal work'. Yet this reaction was quite understandable given the predicament in which the unions now found themselves. Given the massive casualisation of the workforce since 1984 – contributing to their own loss of members – any further reform of a deregulatory kind had to be resisted. Their response, contained in the joint CCOO/UGT Propuesta Sindical Prioritaria of 1989, was a proposal for job creation via a shorter working week, earlier retirement and the control and elimination of overtime, and greater investment in education and training. They also advocated tighter controls on temporary employment contracts to promote job security; given that Spain was at that point near the peak of a boom – with unemployment down to 17.0 per cent from 21.0 per cent four years earlier – they felt that this could be achieved without too much damage to job prospects. But neither the employers nor the state showed any interest.

Nor were the unions assisted by any explosion of social unrest as unemployment increased again in the early 1990s. The fact that unemployment in Spain has not been concentrated among heads of households, the role of the Catholic extended family in taking care of the jobless, and the safety-valve of work in the informal economy, all reduce the pressure that even the current 24 per cent rate of unemployment places on the government.

However, the increasingly dysfunctional character of the Spanish labour market, and the slump in economic growth of the early 1990s, clearly warrant a concerted approach to labour market strategy. For the unions were not the only ones to be affected by the increasing casualisation of labour and the new rise in unemployment after the peak of the boom in 1990. Alongside the growing numbers out of work, the increase in labour turnover caused by the expansion of fixed-term contracts was also exacting a high cost from the state budget in terms of unemployment benefit and social assistance. As for employers, what they have gained in flexibility in labour use they have lost in terms of higher wage growth. With one-third of the workforce employed on such contracts, the 'insider' bargaining power of the permanent workers has increased: since fixed-term workers will bear the brunt of any competitive shocks to the firm, permanent workers are 'buffered' from the market and can raise their wage demands (Bentolila and Dolado 1993; Jimeno and Toharia 1993). Compounded by the absence of centralised pay bargaining in Spain and the predominance of sectoral contracts with extension clauses (agreed wage rates are extended even to firms that do not participate), this may help explain why wage growth has not responded to the increase in unemployment (Abreu and Costa 1994; Franks 1994). As for the economy as a whole, fixed-term contracts, labour market segmentation and high labour volatility have had a detrimental impact on training, innovation and productivity by discouraging investment by firms in human capital formation and promoting a short-term, price-based response to competitiveness (see Alvarez Aledo 1994).

The 1990s have seen an attempt to revive concertation on the government's terms, but this continues to be blocked by the issue of labour market reform. This explains the failure of the 'pact on competitiveness' sought by the then minister of the economy, Carlos Solchaga, in 1991 and 1992, in which union support was solicited in return for the creation of an investment fund made up from 'excess profits': although the Spanish profit rate is currently the highest in the OECD, levels of investment are well below the G7, EU or OECD averages (Dolado and Jimeno 1995:6). It also accounts for the collapse in 1993, after just one round of discussions, of negotiations for a social pact designed to ease the introduction of the government's most recent unemployment measures. At that point, the Socialists had just lost their absolute majority in parliament and were keen to proceed on a consensual basis. Once again the plan was rejected by the unions, and elements of the package – modifications of dismissals regulations, the reform of part-time contracts, the introduction of new youth and training contracts – were introduced unilaterally by the government. More radical and far-reaching measures than these are ruled out both by the current degree of antagonism between the social partners and by divisions in the government itself. Perhaps most importantly, as the Spanish prime minister, Felipe González has admitted, the government presently has nothing to exchange with the unions in return for labour market concessions (EIRR 1994). In the past they could be wooed with promises – and policies – of welfare state expansion. But in an era in which employers' social costs are already high, and tight budgetary restrictions are the order of the day, this is no longer possible.

OUTLOOK

In assessing the prospects for innovation in unemployment policy, two dimensions of the labour market need to be considered: the future political dynamics, and the technical/economic feasibility of alternative solutions.

Firstly, it is clear that the main sticking point in the reform process in Spain is the highly-charged issue of dismissals. This has now achieved such symbolic dimensions, both for employers and unions, that it risks blocking anything other than a pragmatic process of tinkering with existing labour market rules. There is a wide-spread consensus among policymakers and experts that reform must occur in the regulation of open-ended contracts if the present imbalances in the labour market are to be alleviated and a wider variety of other reforms are to be placed on the employment policy agenda. But it is unlikely that major alterations to the existing costs and procedures that protect the core, unionised workforce could be achieved by government fiat. And it is unlikely that this would be attempted, even by the right-wing Popular Party that is almost certain to enter government after the next general elections. Union agreement to such a reform is essential: their membership density level may be low but they still have a significant veto power based on their much greater support via workplace elections and a capacity, albeit diminished since the late 1980s, for strike mobilisation. Although it did not deter the government from its path in 1993, the unions were able to bring industry to an almost complete standstill in January 1994 following the introduction of the most recent reforms.

But how can union support for radical reform be gained? One theory is that in a dual labour market such as Spain, the political prerequisite of radical reform in favour of the unemployed requires the core of 'insiders' to shrink to the point where a coalition in favour of deregulation becomes too large for the unions to fight (see Saint-Paul 1993; Bentolila and Dolado 1994). But this idea is politically naive: to date, the expansion of the army of 'outsiders', which in Spain includes the precariously employed as well as the unemployed, has only made the unions more intransigent. What is required is a process of negotiation in which the reasons for union hostility to reform are also tackled: the weakness of union representation in the workplace, the low level of investment in training and education, and the lack of serious consideration given to alternatives to deregulation. At the same time, other issues need to be confronted, including the incoherent system of collective bargaining in Spain which, neither centralised nor decentralised, is itself inimical to employment creation: wages are set rigidly on a sectoral basis, taking no account of firm performance and, in consequence, those companies most exposed to competition cut their costs by shedding labour (Bushell and Salaverria 1992; Garcia Perea and Gómez 1993).

But a successful new approach hinges on one key change: a return to employment-creating growth, requiring a more expansionary monetary stance than the most recent one which, by seeking disinflation through pegging the exchange rate and 'importing credibility' through the ERM, has only produced a very gradual disinflation process. It has also created an immense pool of unemployed (see Dolado and Jimeno 1995). Unless this occurs, the government will have nothing to offer the unions in return for their agreement to labour market reform.

Of course, this begs the question of what sort of radical reform would be appropriate and feasible in the contemporary Spanish context. This is more than a technical issue: the pursuit of unworkable or fruitless policies in a difficult political environment will only produce disappointment and new frustrations. Some of the most recent policies will help correct the imbalances created by an overwhelming concentration in the past on fixed-term contracts as the mechanism for job creation. Positive results should be achieved by limiting the use of such contracts, by relaxing restrictions on part-time work and by encouraging employers to train young workers via fiscal incentives and by replacing the *ordenanzas laborales* with collective agreements. But these policies amount to little more than tinkering at the margin: they are not going to solve Spain's unemployment crisis. What, then, of the alternatives?

The obvious alternative – and one that unions (and some members of the government) want considered – is a strategy of work-sharing, based on a combination of measures. The unions have long advocated a reduction in working hours and both the standard working week and the use of overtime have been curtailed over the years. New disincentives for overtime were introduced in the 1993–4 reform package. But employers, especially in a recession, will not expand employment as a result: the most logical step is to intensify work during the standard working day. Shorter hours will induce additional hirings only in those firms which are already hiring. Unions are also pushing for shorter working weeks as a response to job-shedding in large companies, most notably multinationals in the automobile sector. But at its best, this will only allow job preservation among the permanently employed (in Spain those on temporary contracts are easily shed); it will do nothing to assist the 'outsiders' in the labour market.

Apart from the more general critique that the idea of work-sharing is based on a 'lump-of-labour fallacy' – the view that the amount of work in the economy is fixed and should be redistributed more equitably (see Snower 1995) – there are also practical problems. Shorter working hours will only have a positive impact in sectors where plants are operated on a permanent basis; they will have a negative impact on unit labour costs, and produce no employment gains, if hours of plant use are governed by the working week (Drèze 1987:173). In Spain, where large companies that operate on this basis are relatively few (only 8 per cent of the work force is in firms with more than 100 employees), the impact would be limited and sectorally specific, even if the removal of the labour regulations facilitates this option. As for early retirement schemes, although there may be some scope for improving the prospects for young workers if such schemes also involve fiscal incentives linked to mandatory replacements, the costs for employers are usually dissuasive. A more general, society-wide shift to a shorter working week (or a programme, Danish-style, of job rotation and sabbaticals) is impractical, not so much because of fiscal problems as because of the highly 'disorganised' nature of the Spanish labour market and the very large number of low-paid workers. Segmentation, multiple forms of employment, a large micro-firm sector and an enormous informal economy are as inimical to the state's quest for solidarity as they are to that of the unions. Furthermore, the introduction of a more generalised shorter working week would clearly reduce incomes – and this would be fiercely resisted in a low-wage economy such as Spain's.

In sum, the current alternatives are not especially promising from the point of view of job creation, although they may have a role to play in limited circumstances alongside a much larger package of reforms. A social pact that tackled the unemployment problem on all fronts, based on a recognition that there is a strong 'Keynesian' element in Spanish unemployment that can only be helped by an expansionary monetary policy, would be much more beneficial (Sebastián 1995; Dolado and Jimeno 1995). For if growth is also to be job creating, then some of the rigidities in the labour market must also be confronted, alongside an increased investment in human capital, policies to boost currently low levels of investment and a serious reconsideration of innovation and industrial policies. The alternative is a stagnant approach to policymaking that parallels the stagnation of Spanish employment.

REFERENCES

Abreu, O. and Costa, C. (1994) 'The labour market: rigidities and reform', *European Economy*, 7 (Special Issue on 'The Economic and Financial Situation in Spain'): 25–72.

Alvarez Aledo, C. (1994) 'La segmentación laboral en el sistema productivo español: estructura y evolución', *Información Comercial Española*, 730:165–77.

Antolín, P. (1994) *Labour Mobility, Unemployment Flows, Vacancies and Job Search Behaviour in the Spanish Labour Market*, Barcelona, Institut d'Anàlisi Econòmica, Working Paper 276/94.

Bentolila, S. and Blanchard, O. J. (1990) 'Spanish unemployment', *Economic Policy*, 10:234–81.

Bentolila, S. and Dolado, J. J. (1993) 'Fixed-term contracts and wage setting in Spanish manufacturing firms' in Banco de España, *Economic Bulletin*, January: 59–64.

—— (1994) 'Labour flexibility and wages: lessons from Spain', *Economic Policy*, 18:55–99.

Bushell, R. and Salaverria, J. M. (1992) 'Proceso de formación de precios y salarios y limitaciónes del mercado laboral', *Papeles de Economía Española*, 52/53: 108–25.

Dolado, J. J. and Jimeno, J. F. (1995) *Why is Spanish Unemployment so High?*, Centre for Economic Policy Research, Working Paper No. 1184, London: CEPR.

Drèze, J. H. (1987) 'Work sharing: why? how? how not?' in Layard, R. and Calmfors, L. (eds), *The Fight Against Unemployment*, Cambridge, Mass., MIT Press: 139–79.

EIRR (1990) 'Spain: government-union agreement on contracts', *European Industrial Relations Review*, 195:9.

—— (1992) 'Spain: radical labour market reform', *European Industrial Relations Review*, 220:12–14.

—— (1993a) 'Spain: dismissals and the politics of flexibility', *European Industrial Relations Review*, 236:24–6.

—— (1993b) 'Spain: government considers shorter hours to save jobs', *European Industrial Relations Review*, 239:13.

—— (1994) 'Spain: labour market reform', *European Industrial Relations Review*, 242:21–4.

—— (1995) 'Spain: the development of labour flexibility', *European Industrial Relations Review*, 252:15–17.

Estivill, J. and de la Hoz, J. M. (1990) 'Transition and crisis: the complexity of Spanish industrial relations' in Baglioni, G. and Crouch, C. (eds) *European Industrial Relations: The Challenge of Flexibility*, London: Sage:265–99.

Fina, L. (1987) 'Unemployment in Spain: its causes and the policy response', *Labour*, 1 (2):29–69.

Fina, L., Meixide, A. and Toharia, L. (1989) 'Reregulating the labor market amid an economic and political crisis: Spain, 1975–1986' in Rosenberg, S. (ed.) *The State and the Labour Market*, New York and London, Plenum Press: 107–25.

Franks, J. R. (1994) *Explaining Unemployment in Spain: Structural Change, Cyclical Fluctuations and Labor Market Rigidities*, International Monetary Fund Working Paper, No. 94/102, Washington, IMF.

García Perea, P. and Gómez, R. (1993) 'Institutional aspects of the Spanish labour market compared with other community countries' in Banco de España, *Economic Bulletin*, October: 65–81.

Gillespie, R. (1990) 'The break-up of the "Socialist family": party-union relations in Spain', 1982–89', *West European Politics*, 13 (1):47–26.

Granados Cabezas, V. (1992) 'Autonomous development as a strategy for regional policy: a balance-sheet of Spanish experience with special reference to Andalusia' in Garofoli, G. (ed.) *Endogenous Development and Southern Europe*, Aldershot, Avebury.

Grubb, D., and Wells, W. (1993) 'Employment regulation and patterns of work in EC countries', *OECD Economic Studies*, 21, Winter 1993.

Jimeno, J. F. and Toharia, L. (1992) 'El mercado de trabajo español en el proceso de convergencia hacia la unión económica y monetaria europea', *Papeles de Economía Española*, 52/53:78–107.

—— (1993) 'The effects of fixed-term employment on wages: theory and evidence from Spain', *Investigaciones Economicas*, 17 (3):475–94.

Lucio, M. M. (1991) 'Employer identity and the politics of the labour market in Spain', *West European Politics*, 14 (1):41–55.

Lucio, M. M. and Blyton, P. (1995) 'Constructing the post-Fordist state? The politics of labour market flexibility in Spain', *West European Politics*, 18 (2):340–60.

Martín, Jesús Mª and Martí, F. (1994) 'Unemployment benefits in Spain' in Banco de España, *Economic Bulletin*, April: 63–74.

Pérez-Díaz, V. M. (1993) *The Return of Civil Society: The Emergence of Democratic Spain*, Cambridge, MA, Harvard University Press.

Rhodes, M. (1995) 'Regional development and employment in Europe's southern and western peripheries' in Rhodes, M. (ed.) *The Regions and the New Europe: Patterns in Core and Periphery Development*, Manchester, Manchester University Press: 273–328.

Rigby, M. and Lawlor, T. (1994) 'Spanish trade unions 1986–1994: life after national agreements', *Industrial Relations Journal*, 25 (4): 258–71.

Rojo Torrecilla, E. (1994) 'Politicas de empleo y de inserción: tendencias actuales y perspectivas de futuro' in Instituto Sindical de Estudios, *Evolucion Social en España*, Madrid, ISE: 173–97.

Saint-Paul, G. (1993) *On the Political Economy of Labour Market Flexibility*, Centre for Economic Policy Research, London, Working Paper No. 803.

Sebastián, C. (1995) 'El disequilibrio en el mercado de trabajo', *Papeles de Economía Española*, 62:344–60.

Snower, D. (1995) *Evaluating Unemployment Policies: What do the Underlying Theories Tell Us?*, International Monetary Fund Working Paper, No. 95/7, Washington, IMF.

Toharia, L. (1988) 'Partial Fordism: Spain between political transition and economic crisis' in Boyer, R. (ed.) *The Search for Labour Market Flexibility: The European Economies in Transition*, Oxford, Clarendon Press: 119–39.

7 Denmark

Jørn Loftager and Per Kongshøj Madsen[1]

INTRODUCTION

Since the early 1970s a range of unemployment policies has been applied in Denmark: public job creation, job training in public and private enterprises, targeted educational programmes etc. They have all shared the feature of being targeted directly at the long-term unemployed. The persistence of unemployment, and especially its drastic increase in the early 1990s, led to increased political interest in unconventional measures to combat unemployment, such as paid leave arrangements. Such arrangements were often introduced under the label 'job-rotation' because their aim was to make employed persons take leave for education, child care or simply a sabbatical, while the vacancies were filled by people previously unemployed. Thus the schemes were labelled as 'pull-strategies' because their aim was to create job vacancies for the unemployed, in contrast to the traditional 'push-strategies' which focus on improving the qualifications of the unemployed.

A second aspect of the paid leave arrangements is their element of citizens' income, in the sense that the schemes allow a temporary withdrawal from the labour market financed by public funds. The introduction of the schemes has therefore given new life to the classical debate on the practical relevance of the idea of a citizens' income.

In this chapter the paid leave arrangements and proposals for a citizens' income are described and the pressures and barriers relating to them analysed. The chapter concludes with a discussion of the future relevance of paid leave arrangements and citizens' income to the Danish labour market.

CONTEXT

With regard to unemployment, Denmark is no different to the rest of Europe. Figure 7.1 shows the unemployment rate for the period 1970 to 1995. The effects of the oil-crisis in 1974 and again in the late 1970s are clearly shown. So is the tendency to hysteresis: during upswings, unemployment diminishes somewhat, but never down to the previous level. There is a clear ratchet-effect.

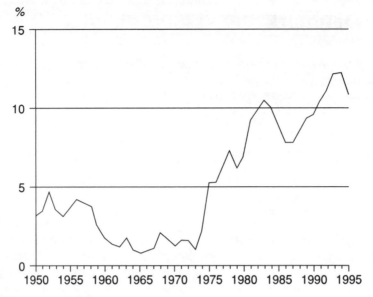

Figure 7.1 Unemployment in Denmark, 1950–1995

Source: ADAM's data bank and Economic Council

Given this background, Denmark has a long history of programmes to fight unemployment, and its expenditure on labour market policy measured as a share of GDP is a European record of more than 6 per cent, as can be seen from Figure 7.2. Most of the expenditure is, however, on passive measures such as unemployment benefits and early retirement pensions. Unemployment benefits are paid to all insured wage-earners provided they have worked for at least six months. These benefits amount to 90 per cent of the previous wage up to a maximum of about £16,000 per year, for a period of up to seven years.

Between 1979 and 1993 the main pillar of active policy towards long-term unemployment was a programme of job-offers, training, and support to unemployed people setting themselves up as self-employed, but this approach yielded meagre dividends, enabling only a minority of partici-pants to become employed on the open labour market. This, together with a sharp new increase in unemployment from 1990, increased the political pressure to find new measures to break the vicious circle of long-term unemployment. The result was a general labour-market reform imple-mented from 1 January 1994, which had as its main characteristics:

- Changing assistance to the long-term unemployed from a rule-based system to a system based on an assessment of the needs of the individual unemployed person.
- Decentralising policy implementation to regional labour-market author-

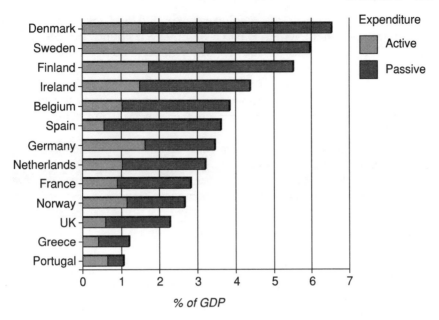

Figure 7.2 Expenditure on labour market policy in the EU, 1990, 1991 or 1992

Source: OECD *Employment Outlook*

ities, which were empowered to adjust programme design to fit local needs.

- Cutting the connection between job training and the unemployment benefit system, so that participating in job training no longer gave a right to unemployment benefits should the participant become unemployed again after the training period.
- Introducing a number of paid leave arrangements to encourage both employed and unemployed people to take leave from the labour market.

Three final points are important to keep in mind when looking at Danish labour market policies in the 1980s and 1990s. First, the institutional background for the formulation of labour market policy is a long tradition of corporatist decision-making in which trade unions and employers' organisations are heavily involved, in a labour market where around 80 per cent of wage earners are members of trade unions. Labour market policy at the national level is the responsibility of the Ministry of Labour and is strongly influenced by the National Labour Market Board, a corporatist body with representatives from trade unions, employers organisations and local government. At the regional level the implementation of policy is controlled by regional labour market boards, which are also composed of representatives from unions, employer groups and local government. The unemployment benefit system is based on private insurance organisations controlled by the trade unions. To call Danish labour market policy corporatist is almost an understatement.

Second, labour market policy has been developed against the background of a general shift from Keynesian demand-management to a tighter fiscal policy and increased emphasis on the structural problems of the Danish economy.

Finally, the period has shown a dramatic decrease in wage inflation and the development of close ties between the Danish krone and the German mark, which made it more difficult to use exchange rate changes to solve economic imbalances than it had been in the 1970s.

RADICAL UNEMPLOYMENT POLICIES

Parallel to the development of mainstream policy, a number of individuals and organisations have fed more radical proposals for combatting unemployment into the debate. These proposals have been put forward mainly by left-wing political parties, trade unionists and semi-professional organisations such as the Socialist Economists. Not surprisingly, the list of proposals contains mainly elements that are also found in the international debate, such as demands for more active labour market policies, more public investment in areas such as the environment and urban renewal, and generally more public involvement in managing the economy. On the right, employers regularly call for unemployment benefits to be cut. There are also vigorous debates at present on whether participation in training should be a condition for receiving benefits, and whether those working on public employment projects should receive benefits or a standard wage.

However, it is noteworthy that attitudes towards work-sharing and reduced working time among Danish radicals have been mixed. Individuals and organisations with close links to the trade unions have been especially reluctant to accept such 'defensive' measures as elements in a radical strategy for lowering unemployment.

The same has been true of attitudes towards citizens' income, which furthermore lacks support from the political establishment. Not only is the idea absent from the agendas of the Danish political parties of any influence, it is rejected outright. However the very fact of this explicit rejection of citizens' income demonstrates that the idea has become a recurrent issue in the Danish debate concerning social and labour market problems.

An interesting question therefore arises: how was it possible that paid leave arrangements not only became included in the list of radical measures for fighting unemployment, but also became part of actual labour market policy in the 1990s, while the idea of a citizens' income is still intensely debated?

Table 7.1 Danish paid leave arrangements, 1994

	Education leave	*Sabbatical leave*	*Childminding leave*
Target group	Employed Unemployed Self-employed	Employed	Employed Unemployed Self-employed
Applicant must be eligible for unemployment benefits?	Yes	Yes	No
Maximum duration	1 year	1 year	26 weeks/1 year
Right for the applicant?	No	No	Yes (up to 26 weeks)
Mandatory substitute?	No	Yes	No
Amount paid as share of unemployment benefit	100%	80%	80%

Note: The benefits for sabbatical leave and childminding leave were reduced to 70% of unemployment benefits in 1995, and will be further reduced to 60% in April 1997

Source: Ministry of Labour

Before taking a closer look at the political dynamics behind paid leave arrangements and the idea of a citizens' income, the following sections describe the main elements in the two strategies.

Paid leave arrangements

The common feature of Danish arrangements for paid leave is that they enable wage-earners, and in some cases also the self-employed, to leave their job for a limited period and then return to work. Some of the paid leave arrangements also include the unemployed, who during the leave are not subject to the usual requirement of being at the disposal of the labour exchange. The discussion in this section is, however, mainly directed at paid leave arrangements for the employed. Table 7.1 gives an overview of the three main forms of paid leave arrangements presently existing in Denmark.

To the information in the table can be added the point that applicants for education leave and sabbatical leave must be more than 25 years of age and have been on the labour market for more than three years. These criteria do not apply to childminding leave.

The paid leave arrangements have three main objectives. First, they aim at improving the quality of life of the individual by creating opportunities for further education, a richer family and social life, or the pursuit of other self-defined purposes.

Second, from the point of view of employers and society as a whole, paid leave for education is designed to improve the qualifications of the labour force, which is especially important at a time when technology is changing rapidly and the ageing of the workforce means that an increasing number of skilled workers are retiring and need to be replaced.

Finally, one may argue the need for paid leave arrangements in order to effectively fight unemployment, in a number of ways. First, one may emphasise the element of work-sharing in paid leave arrangements and view them as means of distributing the burden of unemployment more evenly over the workforce. In its simple form, where the amount of work is seen as a given number of working hours that can be distributed more or less evenly over a (homogeneous) workforce, the argument is not accepted by most labour market researchers because changing the number of people doing the work changes the amount of work done.

Instead the tendency to hysteresis in unemployment has stimulated the view that it is important to reduce the risk of unemployed people becoming locked into long-term unemployment. At the same time policymakers have focused on the barriers that hamper the long-term unemployed from becoming re-employed. One important factor seems to be unemployment itself, in the sense that a long period of unemployment acts as a signal to potential employers that something is wrong with a person, even if the employer cannot spot the particular reason during a job interview or from studying his or her formal educational qualifications. To improve the person's chances of becoming employed, one must therefore establish incentives for employers to give the applicant a temporary job offer in order to allow the opportunity to reassure the employer. From this point of view, programmes directed solely at educating the unemployed will only have minor effects, because this important re-employment barrier is not overcome.

For this reason, emphasis is put on the element of increased job-rotation that may follow paid leave arrangements. Job-rotation is mandatory for sabbatical leave, in that the employer must employ an unemployed substitute during the leave of the employee, but for education leave and childminding leave job-rotation is stimulated in various ways without being a formal requirement. The intention is that those employed as substitutes will drastically improve their chances of getting stable employment.

Right from the start in 1994, the paid leave arrangements proved to be very popular. The number of persons on leave increased from 22,400 in the first quarter of 1994 to 41,600 in the second quarter. The total number of persons taking leave in 1994 was approximately 140,000. The distribution of persons getting leave in 1994 by type of paid leave arrangement and sex is set out in Figure 7.3 which shows a clear disproportion in the share of women and men taking leave, especially childminding leave.

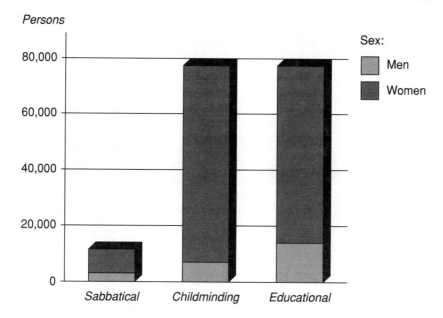

Figure 7.3 Number of paid leaves granted in first three quarters of 1994 in Denmark

Source: Ministry of Labour

Almost half of those taking childminding leave, and two-thirds of those taking education leave, are unemployed. Among the employed, public sector employees dominate for all three types of paid leave. This reflects the gender bias mentioned above not only in the sense that the public sector employs a majority of female labour, but also because of the greater barriers to taking leave that exist in the private sector.

Of the 45,000 persons granted education leave during the first three quarters of 1994, the largest group (41 per cent) planned to attend some form of short-term general course that would not lead to any formal qualifications, while 20 per cent wanted to take some kind of preparatory courses that would lead to formal qualifications. The third largest group (15 per cent) followed a number of (shorter) courses, while the rest were spread over a large number of educational activities. For all three paid leave arrangements, the duration of the leave was long: just short of the one year maximum.

Survey research on the number of employers asking the labour exchange for substitutes for employees taking leave indicate that the replacement rate for education and childminding leave is approximately 50 per cent, while the rate for sabbatical leave is by definition 100 per cent. The replacement rate is substantially higher for public than for private sector employees. One should note, however, that these figures underestimate the use of substitutes because they only refer to cases where the employer hires the substitute through the public labour exchange office. Other surveys indicate that the share of substitutes to persons on leave is around 70–75 per cent.

In most cases job-rotation is the result of decisions taken by individual employers and employees, but in a growing number of cases job-rotation schemes are set up by firms and labour market offices acting in concert; trade unions may also be involved. These joint schemes are genuine education and training programmes under which employed workers are sent on various courses while the labour market office takes the responsibility of providing qualified unemployed people to replace them. They may also be financed by other subsidies for the training of employed personnel, and are seen by both the labour market authorities and the labour market organisations as very useful ways of combining an upgrading of the skills of the employed with job training for the unemployed.

The prospects for 1995 of the paid leave arrangements will be influenced by two factors. First, the large number of participants in 1994 to some extent seems to have been influenced by needs held back over the previous year, during which the paid leave arrangements were announced but not put into operation. Second, the compensation for childminding and sabbatical leave was reduced in 1995 from 80 per cent to 70 per cent of maximum unemployment benefits.

Preliminary statistics indicate an increase in the total number of persons on leave from 57,200 in August 1994 to 67,400 in August 1995. There is a significant increase in the number of persons on education leave (from 12,300 to 25,100), while the number of persons on childminding leave has fallen from 41,500 to 37,800. The number on sabbatical leave was 4,500 in August 1995 compared to 3,400 in August 1994. These figures leave no doubt that paid leave arrangements will play an important and probably increasing role in the Danish labour market in the years ahead.

Citizens' income

A national citizens' income scheme can be defined as a universal state-guaranteed sum for each individual citizen that is enough to meet basic needs but is not conditional on marital or employment status and is not means-tested (Jordan 1988:115; Walter 1989:18). Such a citizens' income scheme would replace most of the existing complex system of benefits and tax deductions, such as unemployment benefits, pensions and child allowances. According to supporters of the idea, a citizens' income scheme offers two major advantages over existing arrangements: it would be a simpler and more effective instrument to combat unemployment and marginalisation, and it would reduce undesirable side-effects of current welfare schemes such as moral hazard, fraud, patronisation and stigmatisation.

Because of its unconditional character, a citizens' income would not produce the same serious work disincentives as income-based social security payments which, by withdrawing benefits as work income increases, discourage recipients from taking a job, since with a citizens' income people would always be better off with a job than without one. In addition, a citizens' income scheme, by supplementing work income, would be a weapon against poverty among people in low-paid jobs – the so-called working poor – which is perceived as a desirable (European) alternative to the (American) workfare strategy (Brittan and Webb 1990).

Furthermore, it is argued that a citizens' income scheme would generate a considerable number of new jobs, because by supplementing work income it would enable people to take jobs paying below the existing minimum wage. On the other hand, the provision of a citizens' income would make it possible for individuals either to reduce working hours or to quit paid work periodically. That is, to a certain degree 'involuntary unemployment would be replaced by voluntary unemployment' (Walter 1989:53).

After a long period during which Danish discussions of citizens' income were by and large limited to small fora within different green groups and movements, the issue has in recent years come to play quite a prominent role in public debate. This has been fuelled not only by citizens' income sympathisers but also by opponents of the idea, who have made frequent use of citizens' income as a threat, in particular by warning against 'the danger' that existing arrangements will in practice lead to a citizens' income situation – an introduction of citizens' income 'by the back door' (Ølgaard 1995). This risk of a *de facto* citizens' income has been used as a general argument for making structural changes in labour market policies. By contrast, individuals and organisations favourably disposed to the idea have referred to the parallels between existing schemes and a citizens' income as an argument for the introduction of such a scheme.

POLITICAL DYNAMICS

We now turn to the more analytical question of the political dynamics of the two radical proposals. More specifically, the problem is to explain why paid leave arrangements were suddenly adopted and implemented by the government in the early 1990s, and why the idea of a citizens' income scheme has become a political issue of some importance despite strong opposition to it.

Paid leave arrangements

The Danish paid leave arrangements have goals and consequences of both economic as well as social and political character. In this section these are examined on a number of levels of analysis: the individual level, the level of the labour market, the level of the public sector and the level of society as a whole. This is supplemented by a distinction between their short and longer-term effects. It is then argued that the paid leave arrangements entered government policy through a 'window of opportunity'.

Individual level

For the employee, the question of applying for paid leave will be answered on the basis of a number of economic and non-economic considerations, including:

- The economic conditions of the paid leave arrangement.
- The extent to which paid leave is a formal right.
- His or her motivation for using the paid leave (education, childminding etc.).
- The anticipated reactions of employer and colleagues.

For unemployed people taking leave, the difference between the conditions that apply during the leave period and the conditions for obtaining unemployment benefits will of course be of central importance. By taking leave, an unemployed person is relieved of the obligation to stand at the disposal of the labour exchange office. At the same time 'the clock is stopped' in the sense that the period on leave is not counted as part of

Table 7.2 Costs and benefits of paid leave arrangements in Denmark

	Benefits	Costs and risks
Employee		
Economic factors	Wage increase (e)	Income loss during leave (e/s/c)
	Increased job security (e)	Cost of education (e)
	No costs for childcare (c)	
Non-economic factors	Personal development (e/s/c)	Risk of career stop (e/s/c)
	Improved qualifications (e)	Loss of social contact (e/s/c)
	Improved job quality (e)	Change of environment (e)
	More leisure time (s/c)	
Employer		
Economic factors	Increased productivity (e)	Training of substitute (e/s/c)
	Increased flexibility (e)	Wage costs of substitute (e/s/c). Cost of education of employee (e)
Non-economic factors	Employee well-being (e/s/c)	Potential loss of employees (e/s/c)
	Stronger employee commitment to firm (e)	

Notes: (1) The table is inspired by Csonka *et al.* (1994) ch3
(2) e = education leave; s = sabbatical leave; c = childminding leave

the maximum duration of unemployment benefits. For childminding leave the unemployed person must then weigh these benefits against the fact that the payment level is less than that of unemployment benefit (for education leave there is no difference, and the unemployed are not eligible for sabbatical leave).

Employers' attitudes towards paid leave arrangements are also the result of a number of considerations, including:

- Their regard for the personal wants and motivations of their employees.
- Their evaluation of the usefulness to the firm of the activities performed by the employee during the leave period.
- The rules and economic conditions for hiring and training substitutes.

The increase in the number of persons on leave during 1994 clearly indicates that a large proportion of both the employed and unemployed population has been attracted by the paid leave arrangements. Childminding leave has been the most popular, but education leave also has a large and growing number of participants, probably stimulated by the removal on 1 January 1994 of the formal obligation to take in a substitute. The majority of those taking education leave are still public employees, but the intake from the private sector is growing, stimulated by a number of job-rotation arrangements organised by firms, in conjunction with the labour market authorities.

This suggests that a number of barriers for both individuals and firms to paid leave arrangements were removed by the labour market reform of 1994, in particular the removal of the obligation to take in substitutes and the institution of a formal right for employees to take childminding leave.

The level of the labour market

The short-term effects of paid leave arrangements on the labour market are undisputed:

- The number of registered unemployed decreases by one person every time an unemployed person takes leave.
- If an employee takes leave, the decrease in registered unemployment is related to the share of vacancies being filled with substitutes.
- Total employment falls when employed persons take leave except in the case where all vacancies are filled by substitutes.

Overall evaluations of the paid leave arrangements in relation to the functioning of the labour market yield ambiguous results. On the one hand they imply a general reduction in labour supply. In the light of the high level of unemployment in Denmark this can, in the short run, be seen as a positive effect: the same can be said of the increased possibilities for unemployed people to become substitutes for employees who take leave. Furthermore, in the longer run education leave will improve the qualifications of the workforce.

The risk of paid leave arrangements is, however, that the lowering of the labour supply in the longer run stimulates wage pressure and erodes cost-competitiveness. This risk is of course increased if the paid leave arrangements lead to bottlenecks in specific parts of the labour market. One should note, however, that such risks are not related to paid leave arrangements in particular, but to all active labour market policies that reduce open unemployment.

The level of the public sector

For the budgets of the public sector, publicly financed paid leave arrangements are, in the short run, a limited net burden because there are savings in expenditure on unemployment benefits. The magnitude of the net costs will depend on (1) the relation between leave compensation and unemployment benefits, and (2) the degree to which substitutes are taken in. Thus total public expenditure on unemployment benefits and compensation to persons on leave will fall every time an unemployed person takes childminding leave since, as we have seen, the level of compensation is lower than that of unemployment benefits.

For employed persons taking leave, the effects on public budgets will depend on the relationship between the replacement rate and the level of compensation relative to unemployment benefits. More precisely, if the replacement rate is higher than the rate of compensation relative to unemployment benefits, there will be net public savings (Kongshøj Madsen 1995). This means that although savings cannot be made for education leave, since the rate of compensation is 100 per cent of unemployment benefit, the government must save money on sabbatical leave, since replacement is mandatory while the level of compensation for those on leave is less than unemployment benefit, and will also save money on childminding leave provided that the replacement rate exceeds the compensation rate, which in 1995 was 70 per cent of unemployment benefit.

In addition, there may also be savings in other areas, for example by reducing the need to provide public childcare places.

The overall evaluation of the burden on public budgets in the longer run depends on the specification of the future scenario for the labour market. If this is high unemployment, so that the alternative to leave is open unemployment, then the net costs of the public sector and society as a whole will be limited. This is most clearly the case where the paid leave arrangements involve a high rate of substitution for employees on leave by people hitherto unemployed.

However, assuming the alternative scenario, a return to high (full) employment, the costs of paid leave arrangements must be estimated to be considerably higher. Here the alternative to leave is no longer open unemployment, but employment and the tax income and increased production that stem from this. The real economic costs of the publicly financed paid leave arrangements, especially childminding and sabbatical leave, would equal the transfer income of the persons on leave. Only for education leave would this cost have to be balanced against the gain in productivity stemming from its positive effects on labour market flexibility and workforce qualifications.

The societal level

At the macro-level, the paid leave arrangements will furthermore have effects of a social and political nature. These will in the short run be related to the lowering of registered unemployment that is a consequence of paid leave arrangements, as this implies a step to solve an important social and political problem: there will also be an improvement in quality of life both for the persons on leave and for the unemployed who become employed as substitutes. In the longer run, the macro-effects work in several directions. On the one hand, there is the possibility of bottle-necks and wage pressure. On the other, leave for educational purposes will improve the qualifications of the workforce and the growth potential of the economy.

The paid leave arrangements entering through the problem window

Understanding the reasons why the paid leave arrangements became political reality in Denmark in the early 1990s involves combining a number of factors.

First, after some years of stable unemployment there was a dramatic increase in registered unemployment from 1991 to 1993, when the number of unemployed reached an all-time record of 350,000 persons, or 12.4 per cent of the labour force. In January 1993 the long-serving Conservative-Liberal Government resigned over an immigration scandal and was replaced by a new government under Social Democratic leadership. Fighting unemployment was declared the prime political target, and the new Prime Minister, Poul Rasmussen, strongly committed himself to 'break the curve of unemployment'.

Second, there were positive experiences with the small-scale paid leave arrangements introduced as experiments by the previous government in 1992: the schemes seemed popular, and were in line with a popular sentiment of having to 'share the available work' with the unemployed. Furthermore, the paid leave arrangements not only fulfilled specific needs for working parents, but also enabled employees to get new experiences outside the workplace. Changing attitudes towards work in general were probably also involved. In addition, employers were positive, especially towards the idea of combining paid leave arrangements with education and training for their employees, and the whole scheme fitted well with the catchphrase of 'life-long education'.

Finally, for the elites involved in policy formulation the paid leave scheme to a large degree fulfilled the need to invent something new. The established instruments of labour market policy were under heavy attack, evaluations of job training and training of the unemployed having found little effect on unemployment levels, and the paid leave arrangements were in line with new ideas of focusing education and training towards those already employed. In addition, from the point of view of public finance the scheme seemed like a 'free lunch' in the sense that it would largely be financed by savings on unemployment benefits; at the same time the number of registered unemployed would rapidly fall.

In summary, all the different interests and attitudes for once pointed in the same direction, which helps to explain why the paid leave arrangements were implemented as part of the labour market reform of January 1994.

Citizens' income

The fact that citizens' income has become an issue in Danish political debate in recent years demonstrates that public political deliberations are not controlled entirely by the members of the policy elite in this area – the political leadership, state bureaucracy, interest organisations of the labour market, professional economic experts at universities and business schools, and the press – who have to a very large extent agreed to reject the idea. How has it been possible for the idea to get through? In order to explain this, several factors have to be considered. Below, we will briefly mention some politico-ideological factors of clear and immediate importance for the appearance of citizens' income on the agenda. Subsequently, we will concentrate on basic socio-economic developments and the politico-institutional settings as important background factors, and outline some of the principal arguments from the debate.

Political origins and support

The idea of citizens' income has often been associated with the green, post-materialist and post-industrial politics which has emerged during the last three decades (Frankl 1987). This green trend has manifested itself rather strongly in Danish politics. Among the political parties, the Radical Liberal Party has been influenced, and circles within the party have kept the idea of a citizens' income alive over the years. This fact is important because the Radical Liberal Party generally holds the balance of power in the Folketing (Parliament). It was therefore a breakthrough when the Radical Liberal Party conference in 1994 decided to recommend that the party work towards a national citizens' income scheme.

Economic and employment aspects

A standard argument against citizens' income has been that it lacks any economic foundation. In order to assess this, the Minister of Economic Affairs, Marianne Jelved, initiated an examination of the implications of introducing one. The results appeared to be catastrophic for anyone with the slightest sympathy for the idea:

> Chapter 4 demonstrates that a citizens' income scheme (a fixed basic payment to every citizen from the government) might simplify the welfare system substantially, increase employment of marginal groups, and provide better incentives to participate in the work force, but such a scheme is impossible to finance by taxes (marginal tax would exceed 100 per cent in some cases). Modified citizens' income schemes would not have the same inviting properties as a 'pure' scheme.
>
> (Økonomiministeriet 1993:242)

However the ministerial analysis was not left unchallenged. For instance, it has been argued that the analysis is based on misconceived premises (Loftager 1994b; Panduro 1995). First and foremost, it does not pay any attention at all to the tax system and fails to acknowledge that citizens' income has to be seen as an integrated part of a new system of both taxes and benefits (Atkinson 1995).

In addition, the analysis fails to address simple but important questions regarding the economic consequences of a citizens' income scheme. Thus it does not offer figures on the number of persons who have no income or whose income is below a certain citizens' income level. This sum is interesting for two reasons: first, because it might give a good indication of the net deficit that would have to be financed, and second because the number of people in this category is rapidly decreasing. Because of a steady growth in female employment, Denmark has become a society of individual income receivers. In 1994, 97 per cent of all adult Danish women were gainfully employed or publicly supported; less than 3 per cent were housewives (Goul Andersen 1995b:5). The evident trend is that any adult person who does not earn his or her income is assigned some sort of transfer income, and today no more than about 50,000 people are not entitled to an income of their own. In the age group 18–59 about 40 per cent receive some sort of social benefit, and about 20 per cent of Danes in the age group 19–66 get their main livelihood from public transfer payments (Viby Mogensen 1993:66). Against this background it is quite understandable why a phrase like 'citizens' income by the back door' has been coined. By implication it seems hard to see why the introduction of a 'real' citizens' income would necessarily result in an economic catastrophe.

Nonetheless, according to the critics of citizens' income and 'the support state' in general, this huge amount of transfers is not sustainable in the long run. Referring to a growing polarisation between 'the draught animals' – employed persons not dependent on public transfers – and publicly supported groups, it has become a standard item to demand reductions in the burden of transfers. Without such reductions, so the argument goes, it will not be possible to secure continuing solidarity and avoid further polarisation (cf. Goul Andersen 1995b).

However, recent research clearly disproves the existence of this kind of polarisation. It concludes that:

> the unemployed remain integrated in the political system, and ... even though a huge majority of the population are more or less dependent on the public sector for their incomes, welfare state support has largely been maintained also by the minority who are entirely independent of transfers or wages from the public sector.
>
> (Goul Andersen 1995b:35).

Furthermore, it is worth noticing that although the number of people supported by the public has grown tremendously, in the same period the proportion of the population who are employed has been remarkably constant. That is, what has happened is not that the burden of support has increased, but that private support within the framework of the family has to a large extent been replaced by public support within the framework of the welfare state (CASA, 1995).

In addition, and in support of the claim that a citizens' income scheme would not involve the drastic reduction in the supply of labour feared by many economists, research on the Danish labour market shows that the very high marginal tax rates and the generous system of unemployment benefits have only very small supply effects (Pedersen 1993). It was also found that many single women breadwinners work 'too much', that is, more than theoretically expected, precisely because they have extremely high real marginal tax rates (Viby Mogensen 1993:68). Furthermore, to the extent that a citizens' income creates jobs, by enabling people to accept jobs at lower pay levels than at present, it will be at least partly self-financing.

Moral aspects and political settings

Another part of the debate on citizens' income has concentrated on – broadly speaking – moral considerations. Former Minister for Social Affairs and former Chairman of the Social Commission, Aase Olesen, has strongly opposed the idea on moral grounds (Loftager 1994a). Referring to autonomy and self-reliance, that is the capacity to take care of and look after oneself, Olesen claims that a citizens' income would imply a dependency on the state which was detrimental to these values. The paradox is, however, that advocates of citizens' income refer to precisely the same values of autonomy and self-reliance in support of a citizens' income scheme. In their argument, the central assumption is that modern society has developed in such a way that money income has become a precondition for taking care of oneself.

It is not denied that meeting this condition by means of a citizens' income will in fact involve a relationship of dependence on the state. But it is questioned whether this should be of such concern, as the same objection can be raised against all possible rights which only exist as long as they are guaranteed by the state and supported by the citizenry. Moreover, it is argued that what really deserve critical attention are the kind of dependencies which are involved in existing unemployment benefit and social assistance systems (Loftager 1994a).

The reason why this kind of reasoning on the issue of citizens' income has become part of the public agenda has undoubtedly to do with the fact that a citizens' income scheme would be in good accordance with a number of basic features of the Danish welfare state. As an example of what Esping-Andersen calls a 'social democratic' regime-type (Esping-Andersen 1990), the Danish welfare state is characterised by a high degree of universality and by tax-financed social benefits instead of private insurance arrangements. The Danes have long ago, so to speak, got used to appreciating the provision of goods on universalistic terms. In general, people find it fair that everyone has the right to an old age pension and that the services of the education system and the health system are provided for the whole population irrespective of financial capacity.

Moreover, in a situation in which it is a largely accepted institutional fact that the state supports a substantial proportion of the population, it is not surprising that it is relatively easy to evoke responses to discussions of a citizens' income. Of course, the present transfer system differs from a citizens' income system on a crucial point, namely that – apart from pensioners – most receivers of publicly financed income today do not get it unconditionally: in the case of unemployment benefit the fundamental condition is that beneficiaries are available to the labour market. At the same time, however, it is interesting to observe several circumstances which tend to erode this condition in practice.

First, as a consequence of long-term mass unemployment the obligation to be available for work has in many cases become more formal than real. Second, different schemes have made it possible for elderly people to leave the labour market before pension age. At present, if you are 50 or above and if you have been unemployed for at least twelve months you are entitled to a so-called transitional benefit until pension age. Moreover, and perhaps most importantly, there are the paid leave arrangements, which entitle people belonging to the labour force to an income from the state without being available to the labour market.

In summary, the idea of a citizens' income has remained on the political agenda despite elite opposition due to its firm roots in the strategically-placed Radical Liberal Party, plus its consistency with Denmark's large, tax-financed and universalistic welfare state, which means that the step from present arrangements to a citizens' income is not as far as it might seem at first glance.

OUTLOOK

Paid leave arrangements

The debate on the paid leave arrangements exemplifies the classical conflicts in policies to combat unemployment:

- Should unemployment be reduced by creating more jobs or by reducing the supply of labour?
- Will the positive short-term effects on unemployment be overtaken by the negative impacts of wage-inflation and deteriorating cost-competitiveness?
- What should be given the highest priority: more production or more spare time, family time and/or time for education?

In regard to the macro-political level, it is worth pointing to the significant popular support for the paid leave arrangements. The exact reason for this is not yet clear, but it seems likely that the main cause is their element of work-sharing, as this is easy to explain in simple terms. On the other hand, a number of experts, political parties and labour market organisations have expressed great scepticism towards the paid leave arrangements (Det Økonomiske Råd 1994, Dansk Arbejdsgiverforening 1993, LO 1994). There is thus a remarkable parallel to the Danish Maastricht referendum, except that this time the population is for, and the experts and politicians are against.

Now that paid leave arrangements have become an established institution of the Danish labour market, the question becomes one of how present barriers to its extension can be minimised, and what its prospects are in the long run.

Barriers relating to employees

As set out in Table 7.3, the potential target group for the three paid leave schemes is very large: 60 per cent of the adult population is eligible for at least one kind of leave, and 75 per cent of this group express an interest in taking paid leave.

But at the same time there are a number of important barriers to taking leave. First, the economic conditions applying during the leave period mean that persons in the middle and high-income brackets will find it very difficult to survive economically while on leave; the lowering of the rates of compensation in 1995 has further increased this problem.

Second, many employees – especially in the private sector – experience high non-economic barriers to taking leave. In a number of cases these

Table 7.3 Attitudes towards paid leave arrangements in Denmark

	Childminding leave	Sabbatical leave	Education leave	At least one sort of paid leave
Number eligible	816,000	1,658,000	2,210,000	2,391,000
As % of adult population	20	41	55	60
% eligible population wanting to apply:				
Yes (or already had leave)	52	42	39	59
Maybe	14	19	17	15
No	35	38	44	25

Source: Bacher *et al.* (1994) Table 8

barriers are related to a fear of an erosion in job conditions on returning to work, or that the leave will be taken as a excuse for dismissal. There is an obvious need to improve the job security of people on leave.

For unemployed persons taking leave, both the economic and non-economic barriers are lower but there is a risk that the leave, if not given relevant educational content, will further marginalise them. However whether this is actually the case is not yet known.

In a scenario of low unemployment, in which there are less obvious gains from a macro-economic or macro-political perspective than in the present situation of high unemployment, it may be reasonable to establish more flexible possibilities for individual financing of paid leave arrangements. One way of doing this would be to make it possible to transfer taxable income from years with high income to years with lower income in order to avoid the asymmetries in a progressive system of income taxation in which a fluctuating stream of income is sometimes taxed more heavily than a stable stream.

Another possibility would be to increase the flexibility of rules relating to drawing funds from private or public pension funds. Today such flexibility is solely related to early retirement, but if one respects the freedom of the individual to plan his or her working time over his or her entire working life, then there is a case for allowing people to use pension funds to finance paid leave.

Barriers relating to employers

One important asset for a modern public or private employer is a motivated, stable and skilled workforce. From this, one cannot however deduce a generally positive attitude towards paid leave arrangements.

For education leave, one would expect the employer to be positive due to the potential improvement in the qualifications of the person on leave. However, a survey of employers revealed a number of barriers from the firm's point of view (Csonka *et al.* 1994):

- Lack of information, especially among small firms.
- Insufficient economic incentives, from the point of view of both employers and employees.
- Difficulties in giving the employee a guarantee of a return to the same job following the paid leave period.
- Lack of interest in further education on the part of employees.
- Difficulties in finding qualified substitutes.

This means that to generate a generally positive attitude among employers and to transform that into practical action, a number of conditions need to be met:

- The content of the education must correspond to the actual demand for qualifications in the specific firm.
- There must be qualified substitutes available.
- The expected increase in productivity must at least equal the short-term costs of having to do without the usual employees during the leave period.
- Appropriate economic subsidies must be available.

For childminding and sabbatical leave the employer will find it harder to locate economic gains to the firm, except in cases where the firm for other reasons needs to reduce its workforce. Generally the problem is to develop arrangements which balance the wishes of the employee with the employer's needs for a stable workforce and for substitutes. Relevant considerations for the employer will therefore include:

- The notice given by the employee wanting to take leave.
- The flexibility concerning use of substitutes and re-employing the person on leave.
- The availability of substitutes.

Paid leave arrangements in the perspective of the long run

The Danish debate on the paid leave arrangements has been very much influenced by the specific labour-market situation in which they were introduced. The paradox here is that while the decision to introduce them was taken during a period of high and increasing unemployment, they were implemented during the most powerful economic boom since the mid 1980s.

Therefore it is important, as a final remark, to emphasise that in the longer perspective the most interesting aspect of the paid leave arrangements is that they represent a new way to realise the underlying tendency towards shorter working time that has been seen during the whole post-war period. This trend has traditionally expressed itself as lower daily working hours, longer vacations and lower retirement ages. Here the paid leave arrangements represent a further possibility whereby the individual employee steps back from working life, but only for a limited period of time. The Danish experience with paid leave arrangements indicates that this flexible reduction of working time fits the preferences of large parts of the population. In the long-term this might be the most significant result of Denmark's full-scale experiment with new forms of paid leave.

Citizens' income

Is the implementation of a national citizens' income scheme in Denmark a realistic possibility? On the one hand, the same factors that explain how citizens' income became an issue on the public political agenda can also be said to speak in favour of a realisation of the idea: on the other, very widespread elite opposition to it makes the prospects rather poor, at least in the short run. In the longer run, things might turn out otherwise, depending on both structural socio-economic developments and the policy measures the decision-makers adopt in response to these developments. Assuming, first, that we are unlikely to return to a situation of 'normal' full employment and, second, that the process by which family support has been replaced by a situation in which practically all of the adult population are individual income receivers is irreversible, one might say that a basic precondition for the introduction of a citizens' income scheme has already been met.

Given this, the next question is whether the idea of citizens' income is likely to become 'operational' at the level of political decision-making. In this respect, much will depend on the electoral support for the idea and the politicians' responsiveness to popular ideas.

Recent research on popular attitudes toward 'How unemployment should be combatted' (Goul Andersen 1995a) shows that a tremendous gap exists between the attitudes at the policy elite level and at the voter level. In general, voters' trust in current policies and policy suggestions is rather limited, one of the few exceptions being the introduction of paid leave arrangements, which ironically enjoys rather ambiguous support in the policy elite. Conversely, the voters support strategies to which the policy elite is opposed. Work-sharing strategies in particular receive strong popular support, and the single strategy which gets the most positive appraisal among the voters is the so-called 'dustman model' of paid leave arrangement whereby employees share the paid leave: 83 per cent of respondents were in favour of this (Goul Andersen 1995a:28).

Furthermore 40 per cent of respondents consider the proposal for a citizens' income to be 'good', 46 per cent consider it 'bad', and 14 per cent 'don't know'. Compared to the support for the 'dustman model' this may seem rather weak backing, but compared to the very massive and outspoken rejection of the idea at the policy-elite level and in the press it is surprisingly strong. Therefore although one ought to interpret such data very cautiously, it seems fair to conclude that – other things being equal – the outlook for a national citizens' income scheme is improved in the light of these findings.

Thus much depends on the degree of responsiveness among the decision-makers – and, as just indicated, their responsiveness tends to be very weak in these matters. Whether this picture will change in the future no one can tell for sure. But recent political history shows that new ideas, for example the 'green' policies of post-materialist politics, can break through outside conventional political channels despite the opposition of the political elite.

NOTE

1 Prime responsibility for the sections on citizens' income is taken by Jørn Loftager, and for paid leave arrangements by Per Kongshøj Madsen.

REFERENCES

Andreasen, Karin, Hansen, Helen and Vedel, Gitte (1993) *Uddannelses- og jobro-tationsprojekter. En analyse af omfang, karakter og perspektiver*, Delrapport 1 og 2, CASA, København.
Arbejdsministeriet (1992) *Arbejdsmarkedspolitisk Årbog 1992*, København.
—— (1993) *Arbejdsmarkedspolitisk Årbog 1993*, København.
—— (1994) *Arbejdsmarkedspolitisk Årbog 1994*, København.
Atkinson, A.B. (1995) *Public Economics in Action*, Oxford, Clarendon Press.
Atkinson, A.B., and Mogensen, G.V. (eds) (1993) *Welfare and Work Incentives*, Oxford, Clarendon Press.
Bacher, Peter, Clemmensen, Niels, Løvgreen, Peter and Wandall, Jakob (1994) *Notat om orlovsordninger*, Udviklingscenteret for folkeoplysning og voksenun-dervisning, København.
Brittan, S. and Webb, S. (1990) *Beyond the Welfare State. An Examination of Basic Incomes in a Market Economy*, Aberdeen, Aberdeen University Press..
CASA (1995) *Velfærd eller forsørgelse*, Copenhagen, Centre for Alternative Social Analysis.
Csonka, Agi, Jepsen, Anne Mette, Christensen, Birgit and Friis, Berit (1994) *Virksomhederne og uddannelsesorloven*, Arbejdsnotat 1994, 1, Socialforsknings-instituttet, København.
Dansk Arbejdsgiverforening (1993) *Vækst og beskæftigelse*, København.
Det Økonomiske Råd, Formandskabet (1993) *Dansk Økonomi November 1993*, København.
—— (1994) *Dansk Økonomi Juni 1994*, København.
Esping-Andersen, G. (1990) *The Three Worlds of the Welfare Capitalism*, Oxford, Polity Press.
Finansministeriet (1993) *Finansredegørelse 93*, Finansministeriet, København, 1993.
—— (1994) *Finansredegørelse 94*, Finansministeriet, København, 1994.

Frankl, B. (1987) *The Post Industrial Utopians*, Cambridge, Polity Press.

Goul Andersen, J. (1995a) *Hvordan skal arbejdsløsheden bekæmpes?*, Arbejdspapir nr. 5 fra det danske valgprojekt.

—— (1995b) *Welfare State Legitimacy in a One-third Society. Attitudes Towards the Welfare State among Public Employees, Public Supported, and the State Non-dependent Minority*, Aarhus University, Department of Political Science.

Heising, Kjeld (1994) *Arbejdsmarkedsreformen*, Frydenlund.

Høgelund, Jan, and Rosdahl, Anders (1992) *De nye rotationsordninger – nogle foreløbige erfaringer*, Arbejdsnotat 1992, 5, Socialforskningsinstituttet, København.

Ingerslev, Olaf (1993) *Arbejdsformidling, løntilskud og orlovsordninger – En analyse af virksomhederne i Høje-Tåstrup Kommune*, AKF Forlaget, København.

Jordan, B. (1988) 'The prospects for basic income', *Social Policy and Administration*, 22, (2):115–23.

Krog, Ole (1994) 'Arbejdsmarkedsreformen – et bedre arbejdsmarked', *Samfundsøkonomen*, 1994, 1:15–21.

LO/Landsorganisationen i Danmark (1994) *Fuld beskæftigelse i Danmark*, København.

Loftager, J. (1994) *Citizens Income and the Crisis of the Welfare State*, Aarhus University, Department of Political Science.

—— (1994a) 'Borgerløn og marginalisering', *Salt*, 2.

—— (1994b) 'Borgerløn og talmagi', *Salt*, 2.

Madsen, Per Kongshøj (1995) 'Orlovsordningerne – Gode nok eller for meget af det gode?', *Samfundsøkonomen*, 1995, 1:21–8.

Panduro, B. (1995) *Borgerløn*, Aarhus University, Department of Political Science.

Pedersen, P.J. (1993) 'The Welfare State and taxation in Denmark' in Atkinson, A.B. and Mogensen, G.V. (eds) *Welfare and Work Incentives*, Oxford, Clarendon Press.

Walter, T. (1989) *Basic Income*, London, Boyars.

Viby Mogensen, G. (1993) *Arbejdslyst og velfærd – en umulig cocktail?*, København, Spektrum.

Ølgaard, A. (1995) 'Borgerløn ad bagdøren', *Berlinske Tidende*, 2 February 1995.

Økonomiministeriet (1993) *Økonomisk Oversigt December 1993*, København, J.H. Schultz Information A/S.

8 Norway

Thore K. Karlsen

INTRODUCTION

The year 1987 has been called the craziest year in the post-war economic development of Norway. Despite the sharp fall in crude oil prices during the spring of 1986, leading to a decline in value corresponding to 7.2 per cent of GNP (Central Bureau of Statistics 1991), credit-fuelled consumption continued to rise steeply and weekly working hours were reduced from 40 to 37.5 hours with full wage compensation. During the summer of 1987 unemployment reached a historic low of 1.3 per cent, but the general wage rise, including the compensation for shorter weekly working hours, amounted to between 16 per cent and 18 per cent depending on the industry. This meant that the growth in prices and inflation accelerated, leaving the country at the beginning of 1988 with the highest aggregate costs per industrial worker in the OECD area (NHO 1995).

Someone had to put on the brakes, and the government, the Trade Union Confederation (LO) and the Employers' Association (NHO) agreed on a long-term austerity plan to improve the Norwegian economy's competitiveness. In 1988 and 1989 wage rises were determined by law, leading to a reduction in real income for Norwegian wage-earners in these years. By 1995 the austerity policy had brought Norway from first to sixth place with regard to aggregate costs per industrial worker (NHO 1995), but the policy will have to be continued for some years in order to produce a more fundamental improvement in the country's competitive position.

However, the austerity policy had a price: from the autumn of 1988 unemployment rose continously from 3.4 per cent to 9.0 per cent during the first quarter of 1994, and between 1988 and 1992 total employment sank by about 3 per cent. Since then employment has risen by 1.6 per cent and by March 1995 unemployment had been reduced to 7.2 per cent, but despite continuing growth – 4.7 per cent in 1994 – the reduction in the number of unemployed has now come to a standstill (National Employment Agency 1988–95, Central Bureau of Statistics 1995).

Not surprisingly, the continuation of austerity politics gets more difficult each year. During the wage negotiations of spring 1995 important groups of wage-earners tried to break out of the austerity coalition. No wonder,

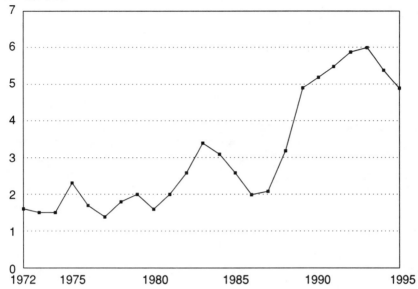

Figure 8.1 Unemployment in Norway, 1972–1995

Source: OECD 1992 (1972–87) OECD 1995 (1988–95)

because in 1994 the press had almost daily reported all kinds of firms and companies paying record dividends to stockholders. Under such circumstances the employees had difficulty understanding why they should follow the appeal of moderation, and important groups of industrial workers in many cases succeeded in getting wage increases above the stipulated increase in prices of 2.5 per cent (Central Bureau of Statistics 1995). Even heavier pressure came from unions organising predominantly female labour within the public sector, such as nurses, auxiliary nurses, nursery nurses and teachers, who, backed by a Law on Equal Wages and a pronounced LO policy in favour of equal pay and various statistical wage surveys, demanded considerable wage increases to fill in the gap between male and female wages. Only by means of compulsory arbitration was the government able to prevent the nurses from succeeding, and the nursery nurses were defeated only after a long strike.

If the LO, NHO and government do lose control of wage increases, parts of the competitive improvements during the past few years will be surrendered before they have had the desired effects in the labour market. This setting would also reduce the economic surplus for radical unemployment policies.

In this chapter, after an examination of the broad political and economic context of radical unemployment policies in Norway, a number of recent radical unemployment policy proposals are described, and then analysed using a paradigmatic approach. The chapter closes with a diagnosis of the outlook for radical unemployment policies in Norway.

CONTEXT

To understand the setting for radical policy initiatives in Norway it is necessary to understand the Norwegian regulatory regime and paradigm. This description is followed by a brief sketch of recent economic developments, the development of unemployment, the strategic response to unemployment by the regulatory regime, current mainstream passive and active unemployment policies, and the role of part-time work and public sector employment.

The regulatory regime and paradigm

The Labour movement came to power in Norway at the end of the Second World War, and has, with short interruptions, governed the country ever since. Its central actors are the Labour Party (Arbeiderpartiet), the LO and some unions. The relationship between the LO and the Labour Party – the first two of the four major actors in economic policy – has been especially close; in public debate they have been called the 'two faces of Janus'. For example, there are regular meetings of a central committee for political cooperation between the two which are attended by highly ranked members of both organisations. The leader of the LO is, according to custom, always a member of the party secretariat (board), and members of the LO secretariat invariably either hold government office or are at least ministerial deputies.

The third member of the central power quadrilateral consists of the national economists. Inspired by the Soviet five-year plans and Keynes, labour intellectuals after the war installed an economic discipline at university level directed at central steering and coordination of the economy. Concentrated in the planning and budget divisions of the Ministry of Finance, and employed in substantial numbers by the Employers' Association and to a lesser degree by the LO, this profession laid the foundations for the post-war economic governance of Norway. As a profession it has a certain range of basic theories and instruments at its disposal to explain and solve the problem of unemployment. Its members are strong adherents of detailed and centralised economic steering, equilibrium theories, and Keynesian deficit-spending in times of low conjunctures.

The main paradigmatic values and reality perceptions of this regulatory regime are: continuous economic growth, economic equalisation, continuous structural rationalisation of the economy (equal pay for equal work set via central wage negotiations leads to the eradication of weaker companies, thus freeing labour and capital for new activities); extensive public welfare with strong elements of economic redistribution, and public control of the bulk of the GNP.

Taxes and fees, tax exemptions, strongly progressive taxation of individuals, a variety of subsidies and welfare arrangements, and centrally controlled wage increases are the main means of realising the paradigmatic values. Common combinations of policies include higher taxes and new or higher consumer subsidies, small wage increases and tax relief, and high wage increases and increased public subsidies to companies. This easy coordination of economic measures across sectors illustrates how closely the actors of the regulating regime are coupled.

Including oil revenues, the public sector pulled in 69 per cent of GNP in 1994 (Central Bureau of Statistics 1995). However the high level of taxation has made necessary many subsidies for politically accepted or desired economic activities. In 1991 subsidies to economic activities amounted to 6.2 per cent of the GNP, or eight times the total investment of private, non-personal companies (Central Bureau of Statistics 1993).

The fourth major player, the NHO, was until the 1980s a constant but less important actor in the regulatory regime. Although always represented in corporative committees, it was usually overruled in all important matters of conflict with the Labour movement until the advent of a Conservative Government in the early 1980s. Since then the position of the NHO has strengthened, and now the Labour Government needs its cooperation for its strategies to modernise the mainland (non-oil) economy.

Recent economic developments

Since the 1970s the Norwegian economy has become increasingly dependent on the surplus from the oil activities in the North Sea. It was the shock of falling oil prices in 1986, combined with the decreasing production volume of the export-oriented and home-competing industries, that made the government opt for a long-term austerity policy to improve the international competitive capacity of the mainland industries. This was regarded as positive by the LO because LO-affiliated unions have a near-monopoly on organising workers in the industries producing material commodities. But the precondition for a future harvest of more members via growth in industrial employment was the disciplining of LO members to small wage raises for many years to come, so the LO supported the government's legislative enforcement of wage limits in 1988 and 1989.

In 1988 the GNP decreased by 0.5 per cent, and between 1989 and 1991 it increased by 0.6–1.6 per cent annually, but in 1994 it finally took off with growth of 4.7 per cent (Central Bureau of Statistics 1993, 1995). It remains to be seen if such high growth is favourable to further years of austerity politics.

The development of unemployment

As mentioned earlier, from the last quarter of 1988 to the first quarter of 1994 unemployment grew from 3.4 per cent to 9.0 per cent (National Employment Agency 1988–1994). However the official statistics differentiate between totally unemployed people and people occupied in labour market programmes, and only the statistics for the totally unemployed are delivered to the OECD. For Norway, this leads to a particularly warped picture since the government, in line with its agreement with the LO, continually keeps about a third of the unemployed in so-called active labour market programmes.

Whereas export industry has been continuously rationalising, and is planning further lay-offs in 1995, import-competing industries pose a structural problem. In this sector, where important industries are relatively labour-intensive, labour costs had grown to a level where they could no longer compete with imports. Thus it is mainly in this sector that austerity policies may have positive employment consequences, if they are allowed to continue long enough.

Even though employment in 1994 again rose to the level of 1991, it is an open question whether this will lead to the forecast reduction in unemployment. Recent employment growth of about 36,000 has only reduced unemployment by about 20,000. This is because unemployment is more pervasive and widespread than can be concluded from the public unemployment statistics. There are a number of reasons for this. First, an unknown number of young people between 20 and 30 years of age have fled from the labour market into educational institutions. At some stage they will return equipped with better qualifications for working life. Second, the workforce will continue to grow until 2011, and future female participation in the labour market has probably been underestimated. Third, about 5 per cent of all wage-earners – and 15 per cent of part-time working women – report themselves to be currently underemployed. Fourth, recent changes in the law have severely narrowed the criteria for disability pensions, leading to a quadrupling of the number of persons in occupational rehabilitation programmes; sooner or later a high proportion of these people will be forced back into the labour market. Fifth, in some private industries and public sub-sectors, such as banking, private insurance, telecommunications, postal services, the railroad and some public administrations, technological rationalisation has now reached the systemic stage at which profits can be reaped in the form of extensive lay-offs, which are expected to amount to 20–35 per cent of employees. Finally, between 1988 and 1991 the number of recipients of municipal welfare grew by about 30 per cent. Since the right to unemployment benefit is attached to employment, the age group 20–24 years of age, which has the highest proportion of persons entering the labour market for the first time, is overrepresented in the group of social welfare recipients by 10 per cent, compared with an average of 5 per cent in the total population (Central Bureau of Statistics, National Employment Agency).

The solution of the regulating regime: a decade of austerity policies

To solve the unemployment problem, in 1993 the government, LO and NHO jointly formulated the so-called 'Solidarity 2000' policy, which aims at a reduction of unemployment to a state of equilibrium by the year 2000 (Ministry of Finance and Customs 1994). This equilibrium state is currently calculated to be about 3.5 per cent with a rising tendency. The constituent elements of the 'Solidarity 2000' policy are the following:

1 Annual wage increases below those in other industrialised countries.
2 Continuation of active labour market programmes at the present level, which means they should at all times include at least a third of the unemployed.
3 Balanced public budgets. The effort to balance the state budget has up to now been directed at cutting subsidies to private industries and a reassessment of welfare benefits. In both respects results have hitherto been very modest, but there is now consideration of further measures, such as making the childrens benefit means-tested or taxable.
4 A less precise commitment by employers to modernise the economy and to restrict dismissals.
5 No changes in taxes, revenues or prices of public services.
6 Government loans for new economic activities.

One can hardly describe the above policy package as radical, at any rate not in Norway. Ever since the Second World War Norway has developed and used sophisticated tools for macro-economic steering, and tripartite agreements and cooperation have a post-war tradition as a means of managing national crises. The costs of the active labour market programmes have to a large degree been financed by public deficit spending in the best Keynesian tradition.

The critique against the 'Solidarity 2000' policy can be summarised under two main headings.

First, there are some risks that it will not succeed. On the one hand, economic growth may not reach the prescribed level of at least 3 per cent, which is an important condition for the functioning of the policy, since it takes 1 per cent economic growth to absorb 7,500 persons in the Norwegian labour market at the present level of economic productivity, while the annual number of newcomers to the labour market has been calculated at between 13,000 and 15,000 for the period 1993–99 (NOU 1993:11). On the other hand, the LO may not be able to discipline either its own members or, even more importantly, the members of other union confederations, over such a long period of time.

Second, the very long-term nature of the policy arouses criticism that it leads to intolerably high human and social costs due to unemployment remaining high for so long: individual lives are destroyed and high proportions of the young are not properly integrated into the society and community.

Passive unemployment policies

Unemployment benefits in Norway are non-contributory and the individual right to benefits is attached to former employment. As non-contributory benefits they are financed directly by taxes in the government budget. This facilitates flexibility in unemployment policy since the government in deciding new measures and changing existing ones is not bound by insurance-based rights of employees. With the entire government budget at its disposal, it is also relatively easy to redirect funds from other items to measures against unemployment.

The attachment of benefits to former employment can, however, be regarded as a disadvantage in some respects. First, it is a disadvantage for debutants in the labour market who are not able to find a job; their only alternative is the means-tested social welfare allowance of the municipalities. Second, with no claims for monetary support and scarce chances of being found a job, an unknown proportion of new entrants do not bother to register at employment offices, so they do not show up in unemployment statistics and may easily slide into long-term unemployment.

Active unemployment policies

Active unemployment measures can be divided into individually and company-directed programmes. Those directed at individuals comprise work training and education, other programmes finance the wages, or parts of the wages, of employees in companies that are reorganising, introducing new technology, etc.

Programmes for individuals are usually directed at specific groups in the labour market such as young people, long-term unemployed, women, and people between 20 and 25 years of age who lack a complete, publicly certified education. Unemployment has hit different educational and age groups with varying force, depending on the the functioning of the labour market and labour market programmes. As in most other West European countries young people, people over 50 and people without formally certified qualifications above the obligatory minimum level of lower secondary school are considerably overrepresented. But for people under 20, the government has issued a so-called 'Youth Guarantee', instructing the Labour Market Administration to provide them with places either in educational institutions or in work training programmes. Consequently there is practically no unemployment in this age group. But because of high minimum wages for young employees and the fact that the segment of young people profiting from the Guarantee consists, to a large degree, of people with broken school careers or a minimum of education, the Guarantee has had as a side effect a concentration of youth unemployment in the age group 20 to 25 years, which now has the highest proportion of unemployed of all age groups.

Since 1988 there have been a number of important changes in the regulations relating to programmes. In 1989 work training programmes were opened to persons on municipal social welfare, that is, to persons without a right to unemployment benefit; and persons without former employment were made eligible for educational programmes and educational benefit.

In 1993 educational leave for municipal employees was introduced. Employees are entitled to one year's leave on full wages, and their substitutes are paid by the National Employment Agency 85 per cent of full wages, with one day a week on-the-job training.

Also in 1993 the maximum period of unemployment benefit was prolonged beyond eighty weeks, and combined with an obligatory work training period of at least six months or an educational period of varying length.

During the unemployment period starting in 1988 the work training programmes for youth and long-term unemployed underwent a process of goal substitution. Whereas the original aim of these programmes was not only to give work training but also to make the trainees 'stick' on the jobs, that is, to get them employed as well, they soon developed into pure training programmes. This was due to the high number of training jobs needed and the clearance procedures: every training job had to be cleared with the local shop stewards to prevent the substitution of permanent jobs by training jobs. Finding new training jobs and operating the clearance procedures proved to be so work-intensive that the National Employment Agency was forced to maximise the throughput of unemployed on the available training jobs, so the goal was reformulated into 'maintainance of working ability'. At present the National Employment Agency provides continuous financing of jobs in the public sector on condition that the persons in them are exchanged every six or ten months. This has doubtless had exactly those substitutive effects which the clearance procedures were designed to prevent.

Whereas unemployment benefit is a legal right of the unemployed, the active programmes are steered by a central budget, the funds of which are distributed to local Employment Offices according to a set of qualitative and quantitative criteria. This has led to a queuing of clients waiting for training and education. In one local office the waiting-time amounted to seventy weeks for a training period of eighty weeks (Karlsen 1994). For many individuals the active programmes therefore worked as a perverse incentive: for fear of losing their position in the queues, they did not venture to accept jobs which might give them a chance but did not imply a guarantee of permanence.

Evaluations of these schemes yield mixed results. One year after the training measure, former trainees had 14–21 per cent higher rates of employment or education attendance than unemployed people in the same age groups who had not been exposed to training (National Employment Agency 1989, 1992). For educational courses the result was more negative: according to two independent evaluations, attendees had a slightly lower employment rate six months later than persons who had been unemployed for the same period of time (National Employment Agency 1992). This was because the persons who did not attend courses had more time for job-seeking.

During the first few years of the crisis, long-term unemployment (over twenty-six weeks) increased to about 40 per cent, but it is now stable at around 30 per cent (National Employment Agency 1989, 1995). One explanation for this may be that after participation in an active labour market measure the unemployed are registered in the public statistics as new unemployed, and their former careers are erased from the system.

Part-time work

Over the past twenty years there has been extensive use of part-time work in the economy. In fact this was how the fast-growing participation of women in working life was absorbed. With a present female participation rate of about 75 per cent, the proportion of female employees working part-time currently amounts to about 47 per cent (National Employment Agency 1994). However at the end of 1993 15.2 per cent of part-time working women reported themselves to be underemployed (Central Bureau of Statistics 1994, National Employment Agency 1995). Male part-time work amounted to only about 9 per cent, but there are strong cultural barriers to men working part-time: for these reasons part-time work as a strategy to reduce unemployment in Norway can be regarded as more than exhausted.

Public sector employment

Although not currently a major unemployment strategy, the public sector was used to absorb the relatively high rate of unemployment during the years 1984–85 and, more generally, to absorb the vast increase in female participation in the labour market between 1979 and 1990.

RADICAL UNEMPLOYMENT POLICIES

As a consequence of the critique of the 'Solidarity 2000' policy, different and radical proposals for a faster and more comprehensive solution of the unemployment problem have been put forward, mostly by individuals with little or no basis in political parties, unions or employer organisations.

Table 8.1 Radical unemployment policies in Norway

Strategy	Measures
Public sector solution	Public sector employment
Work-sharing	6-hour working day with full compensation
	Work-sharing without compensation

Often these are academics with a relatively independent status in research institutes, nevertheless, some of the proposals have been adopted by trade unions and/or political parties.

The public sector solution

One proposal was raised by the research leader of the Norwegian Institute for Municipal and Regional Development Research. This is based on a calculation of the total costs of unemployment and the number of jobs this amount of money might finance in municipal and other public services. The proposal is to accept the current level of public spending and employ 200,000 persons, which amounts to practically all the unemployed persons in Norway, mainly in municipal personal services. With the growing number of people above 80 years of age who need care, the much-criticised lack of capacity in existing services for the aged, the extension in 1994 of obligatory schooling from 9 to 11 years, and the need for more pre-school facilities due to the growing proportion of women participating in the labour market, employment in the personal services sector will in any case have to be significantly increased during the next few years. By thus expanding the capacity of public personal services and not allowing privatisation one would also maintain the social-democratic claim of equality or zero differentiation in the quality of welfare services. The proposal does not imply any reduction of weekly working time, but instead a considerable increase in the supply of labour. However it would imply an unprecedented expansion of the Norwegian welfare state and lead to an obliteration of the distinction between producers and consumers of welfare services.

The proposal has received support from unions organising municipal workers, teachers, nurses and auxiliary nurses; for the unions the rationale is, of course, the possibility of increasing their membership, their members also envisage shorter weekly working hours and reduced workloads. The proposal has also gained some support from the Socialist People's Party, a non-marxist party to the left of the Labour Party which usually obtains its largest vote from women occupied in the public sector, especially professionals and semi-professionals in personal services. It is also at present the most important representative of egalitarian ideals in Norwegian politics.

Opposing the proposal are the Labour Government, the majority of political parties, and the leadership of the LO and NHO. The government and the other political parties have one obvious reason in common: at some stage the new jobs would have to be tax-financed, since deficit-spending to finance labour market policies cannot be continued indefinitely, but no party is willing to take the responsibility for introducing new taxation on top of the already high level in Norway. In addition, the government has acknowledged the importance of the export-oriented, on-shore private industries for the future post-oil economy of the country and is trying at least not to increase the size of a public sector that is already quite large by international comparison. The removal of all unemployment over a short period of time might also, given the dynamics between the labour market and industrial relations, lead to steering problems, bottlenecks, and local or sectoral lack of manpower, which would lead to wage pressure and higher inflation.

The 6-hour working day with full compensation

Since 1991 Oslo has been governed by a leftist coalition of which the Socialists and the Labour Party are the constituent parts. The Socialists for some time pressed hard to launch an experiment of a 6-hour working day with full compensation (that is, a cut in hours without a commensurate cut in wages) among care personnel in nursing homes and in ambulant home-care services for elderly people. The experiment finally began on 1 June 1995. It encompasses about 100 employees and will be evaluated by the Institute for Applied Social Science (FAFO). The Oslo municipal administration had applied to the Ministry for Employment and Municipal Affairs for funding of the evaluation research, but this was refused. Thus two attempts by the Socialist People's Party to have different but expensive versions of work-sharing made part of the agenda of the social sciences and the media have been determinedly rejected by the government. However the municipal government of Oslo decided to perform the experiment anyway.

The hope of the initiators of the proposal is that it will lead to a reduction in absenteeism, which is notoriously high in these sectors, and in the incidence of long-term occupational diseases, which is also very high and causes a relatively high rate of disability retirement. In Norway the employer is required by law to continue the payment of full wages to sick employees for the first fortnight of each illness, and to hire stand-ins to do the work that cannot be performed by the regular staff. If absenteeism can be extensively reduced, the employer will save the costs of stand-ins, and the reduced workload may lead to a lower rate of disability retirements. The consequent municipal and state savings are supposed to exceed the extra wage costs stemming from the effective 20 per cent increase in the hourly wage rates of workers participating in the experiment.

This is a proposal leading in the direction of weekly working hours differentiated according to the principle of workload, according to which groups of employees with a high workload should have shorter weekly working hours than groups with easier and more interesting work.

However, the government, the LO and the NHO all oppose it. Work-sharing with full compensation is regarded as being both too expensive and a threat to the gains in competitiveness attained by six years of austerity policies. The LO has expressed a preference for a lowering of the old age pension threshold and opposes the use of community resources for other reforms of working time.

Work-sharing without full compensation

In Norway work-sharing has been tacitly practised since the start of the 1970s: the number of manhours worked in 1994, at 2,877 million, was only slightly more than the 2,829 million worked in 1972, yet the number of employed persons increased from 1,661,000 in 1972 to 2,040,000 in 1994 (Ministry of Finance and Customs 1994). Between these years weekly working hours were reduced by five hours and the yearly vacation was prolonged by one week. In addition, female employment increased by over 30 per cent, most of which was part-time work: this might be regarded as the historical evidence of the employment effects of work-sharing.

Under the impression of rising unemployment rates and the spectacular events in the Volkswagen company during the autumn of 1993, I myself launched a proposal to significantly reduce unemployment based on a 10 per cent cut in working hours without wage compensation but with tax reductions for lower-income earners. The plan had eight main provisions:

1 A reduction in weekly working hours of 10 per cent for all persons occupied in firms with more than four employees. An exception or deduction was made for the 15 per cent of jobs that were considered to consist of indivisible management functions or to require specialist education. Also excluded were all part-time workers. If enough extra labour was hired to to ensure that the total number of manhours worked remained the same – a 100 per cent substitution rate – 100,000 new full-time jobs would be created. Official unemployment at that time ran at about 180,000 persons, so that the measure, if implemented, would still have left about 4 per cent unemployed, which was, and is, well above the estimated equilibrium level. French, Belgian and Dutch experiences during the 1980s demonstrated that the employment effects of small reductions in working time are easily frittered away by measures of rationalisation, but at the time the proposal was made many Norwegian companies had been through a five year period of reorganisations and lay-offs, so that a reduction in working time of 10 per cent would for most of them represent a functional coercion to hire new employees.

2　No wage compensation: wages, like hours, would be cut by 10 per cent, since the object was to reduce unemployment without impairing the competitive capacities of the economy and annihilating the results of the austerity policies. For middle incomes this would in most cases mean a net wage reduction of 5 per cent because of progressive taxation.

3　Individual tax reductions for low incomes or for all incomes up to a certain amount. There is already computer software in the market which is able to perform such reductions individually, adding them and transferring them over from the employers' systems to the Inland Revenue Administration. The intention was that the lower income groups participating in the arrangement should have zero wage reduction. (This provision might also offer part-time employees an incentive to participate.)

4　The refunding of tax losses to the municipalities from the state, after savings due to reduced expenses for social welfare were subtracted.

5　An extension of opening hours and operating times of machines and factories, combined with a flexibilisation of work-time arrangements. Greater flexibility is the price employees must pay for the increase in leisure time. This is, however, in harmony with employee preferences in regard to work-time organisation as identified by the Public Work-Time Committee in 1987: most employees prefer to perform the necessary work concentrated in time, and to concentrate leisure similarly in continuous time-blocks.

6　No compensation for any additional costs incurred by employers participating in the arrangement. To begin with they might experience additional communication and organisational costs, but in the longer run these would probably be more than counterbalanced by savings due to reduced absenteeism, extended opening and operating hours, and better performance by employees.

7　Institutionalisation of the scheme by a binding tri-partite agreement between the trade union confederations, the employers associations and the government. Norway has a law for the generalisation of wage agreements, which might be used, but additional legislation would be necessary to commit the state agencies involved. The agreement would have to be a framework agreement leaving the details of application to local negotiations. Because of the experimental nature of the proposal, the agreement would be limited to two years. This would reassure both the sceptics, who fear it cannot function, and the optimists, who expect that the labour market will absorb the unemployed without radical policies and that the proposed arrangement would therefore create strong pressure in the labour market. To reassure employees, full protection would be given against dismissals for the duration of the agreement.

8　For democratic and motivational reasons the general introduction of the proposed measures would be preceded by a national campaign, and perhaps by some smaller and limited experiments.

Despite revenue losses due to the tax reduction leaving incomes up to about £20,000 a year without net income loss, the cost of the proposal for the government would be offset by its savings due to the accompanying reduction in unemployment and by the existence of the upper income limit for the tax reductions. Thus the scheme would be cost neutral to the government, implying only a shift in policy from financing unemployment to financing employment. Technically, the tax relief might also be regarded as a retransfer of a part of GNP from the public sector to the private sector of the economy (Karlsen 1994).

The proposal at once attracted great interest in the press and was discussed twice on the National Television Network. It was supported by local shop stewards, regional representatives of the LO, the Union of the Auxiliary Nurses, parts of the Labour press, the Socialist Peoples' Party, the Liberal Party, some 'green' alternative future organisations, and a number of independent academics. A round of lectures and discussions followed in various trade unions, and the National Research Council arranged an academic discussion of it in June 1994.

But the government, LO, NHO and big unions all rejected it. The government argued that it might create a shortage of manpower in specialised occupations and sectors, and that even more people than today would take on a second job. According to the level of living survey, the proportion of employees with two jobs has already grown from 9 per cent in 1980 to 15 per cent in 1991 (National Bureau of Statistics).

However it is strange that the argument of sectoral manpower shortages does not also apply in reverse: if shorter working hours leads to more people becoming available to take second jobs, then there will be more people available to make up any skill shortages that result from shorter hours.

Sectoral shortages of labour are in any case highly improbable, as there has been an explosion in participation rates in university, college, and higher secondary school education (Central Bureau of Statistics 1988, 1994). A survey conducted by FAFO in March 1993 showed that in the age group 20–24 years, 17.5 per cent of males and 12.5 per cent of females would quit education tomorrow if offered a job. Shortages of specialists have been registered only in nursing, but this is no real shortage since the nurses, by means of a strong union have succeeded in monopolising many jobs that functionally can be just as well executed by auxiliary nurses, among whom there is a considerable rate of unemployment.

From the NHO came the same arguments plus the idea that work-sharing was not the way to go because of the demographic development of the population with an increasing proportion of people over 70 years of age. Therefore Norwegians ought to work more, not less. To increase employment, it would be preferable to stimulate the demand for services in the private sector of the economy by means of a reduction of wages at least for labour market newcomers.

The LO stuck to the austerity agreement with the government, arguing that a reduction of weekly working hours might jeopardise the favourable effects of this policy. During some of the austerity years inflation was down well below 2 per cent, and rates of interest for housing loans sank from about 16 per cent in 1989 to about 7.5 per cent in 1994. The LO also repeated the argument brought by the government against the public employment proposal, namely that it would annihilate the gains in competitive power of 11 per cent accomplished through the austerity policy. Finally, the Labour Government and the LO jointly announced that new jobs should come in the production of new goods and services; shorter weekly working hours would only contribute to freezing employment in the production of today's products, thus impeding the necessary dynamics in the future labour market. However, every reduction of working hours in the post-war period, from 48 hours a week in 1945 to 37.5 hours a week in 1987, has had a lock-in effect on labour, and anyway the proposal was not directed at the complete eradication of unemployment but instead aimed at leaving 4 per cent of the labour force in active labour market measures designed to render them eligible for new jobs in new kinds of production.

Finally, the national economists argued that a reduction in working hours now would lead to inflationary pressure in the labour market in the year 2011, when the growth of the labour force is forecast to halt.

However in many arenas they chose to attack the proposal as if it implied a reduction of working hours with full wage compensation. This was the case in one TV discussion and at a conference arranged by the Norwegian Research Council. Their strategy was to confuse the public and the participants in the conference by overlooking the nature of the work-sharing proposal, and to discredit it with all the negative qualities and consequences of a full wage compensation proposal.

POLITICAL DYNAMICS

In the following section I intend to analyse the labour market policies in Norway as the output of a closely-coupled system with a specific paradigm for macro-economic regulation. Its specificity rests on its central beliefs as to regulation, the particular structure of cooperation and alliances between its central carriers, their interests, and their standard modes of operation in coping with regulatory problems.

The paradigmatic approach to political analysis seems to be particularly well suited for regulatory regimes that can be described as relatively closely coupled. Above all this is because the central concept of the paradigm presupposes a distinct hierarchy of actors: its core profession, the high priests of reality-description and the supreme judges of right or false action (MacDonald 1985); the institutions and organisations that have most closely attached their actions, prestige and survival to it; the executive bodies that profit to a smaller degree from it; and the external interests that for various reasons are excluded from any influence. Norway fits the three criteria for a closely-coupled system: continuity of interaction between the units, vital common interests against units outside the system, and strong mutual interdependencies for survival.

Given this, my working hypothesis is that radical proposals to solve the unemployment problem which conflict with the interests, models of reality and standard modes of operation of the central actors of the paradigm will be rejected. Conversely, only proposals compatible with the interests and the reality-conceptions of these actors will have a chance of being accepted. But then they will no longer be radical, because they will either imply the repetition of previously established procedures on a different scale than formerly, or consist of an adaption of these procedures to situations defined as exceptional and unique. After these situations have been coped with, the actors may then return to paradigmatically acceptable procedures.

If this line of argument is followed, one conclusion must be that similar unemployment policies in different countries will, depending on their regulatory regimes, be designated as radical or not radical, and that their chances of becoming accepted and practised will vary accordingly.

The public sector proposal and the proposal for the 6-hour working day with full compensation are regarded by most people as being both too expensive and ineffective as a means for reaching full employment. One important reason for this is that the last few years of low inflation and low rates of interest have taught the population that moderation and balanced budgets mean increased purchasing power. During the inflation-ridden years of the 1970s and 1980s many employees doubted the value of wage settlements, because in many years wage rises were quickly eaten up by inflation. Very few want to jeopardise the stabilising effects of the austerity policies.

On the other hand, the population at large does not accept the present level of unemployment either. A survey conducted by the organisation 'Alternative Future' in January 1994 found that 44 per cent of employed people were willing to accept work-sharing with a net income loss if it could be guaranteed that this would lead to a reduction of unemployment. Another survey in the AKER corporation showed that 82 per cent of shop stewards were willing to accept work-sharing and a net wage reduction on the same conditions; similar signals also came from the lower echelon of shop stewards in the press discussion. Thus the proposal for work-sharing combined with wage and tax reductions seems to have widespread support in the population and among the shop stewards closest to the shop floor or the 'grass-roots'.

But the power elites and their organisations are still, for various reasons, against it. One common reason for this may be that the government, employers' associations and union confederations are all heavily reliant on the national economists for professional advice in economic matters. Until recently this brought important advantages. First, the paradigm – growth, equality, rationalisation, welfare and a large public sector – did function. Second, identical models of economic analysis and a common professional language have generated a culture of common perspectives and values that has doubtless facilitated compromises in economic policy during the post-war period.

On the other hand, this dependence has also led to a comfortable conservatism among all these actors, not least among the economists themselves, who are criticised for dogmatism, excessive disciplinarity and a lack of orientation towards the application of their science. Their attacks on the work-sharing proposal, as if this implied the 6-hour working day with full compensation, also demonstrate either an inability to think in new terms or a mendacious professional interest in keeping their positions as the prime architects of economic and labour policy.

The present Labour Government has set out to modernise the country economically and politically. For this purpose it is necessary to curb the power of organised interests, because corporative structures are so strong that in many respects rational political decisions are not possible. The recent attempt to join the EU can be regarded as an attempt to crush corporatism with the assistance of the European Commission, but years of buying voters have left so many interest groups with a suction pipe into the public purse that a majority in the referendum was impossible.

Therefore the strategy of disciplining the population by means of an austerity policy has to be continued, and unemployment is the major means of creating a crisis consciousness in a population in order to render unpopular decisions possible and motivate citizens to take their share of additional burdens and adapt more actively to new requirements in working life. This has to be understood against the traumatic background of 1987 when, due to an overheated economy, the government and the LO lost control of the unions, and the unions lost control of their members. Every proposal which seems to threaten the basis of austerity and discipline must therefore be kept out of central policy processes. Thus government arguments should be understood as being mainly of a tactical nature, in part produced to conceal the real arguments behind the prevailing policy.

The arguments of discipline and control also apply to the LO. If the LO loses control of its members, this might strengthen a perceived trend towards local agreements. In addition, control of its members is what makes the LO an interesting cooperation partner for the government and the employers: furthermore, the LO is not only disciplining its own members but also the members of the other union confederations and unorganised employees as well.

But the LO is also caught in another and more difficult plight. Up to now it has stuck to the austerity agreement, but with consequences which

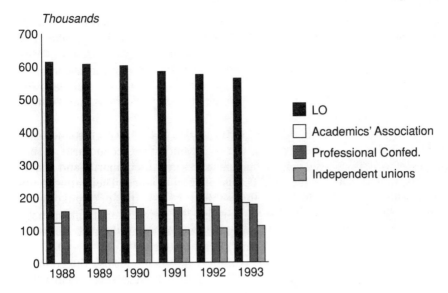

Figure 8.2 Trade union membership in Norway, 1988–1993
Source: Stokke 1994

it cannot put up with for much longer. As mentioned, there are three trade union confederations plus a number of independent unions in Norway. The LO has traditionally had most members and been the most powerful, organising the core sectors and industries of the country. However, these sectors have been the ones hardest hit by unemployment, and it is clear that unemployed people tend not to renew their membership after a period of unemployment (Stokke 1994). Therefore the LO is continually losing members, whereas the other confederations, organising other sectors and academic employees, are experiencing continous growth in their membership (see Figure 8.2).

According to calculations conducted by FAFO, non-LO unions combined will overtake the LO in membership in 1998. They have already demanded representation in the very important Technical Calculation Committee, a body with representatives from the most important interest groups in the country, which is charged with the task of calculating and deciding the volume of economic growth each year. The results of the discussions in the committee serve as the point of departure for the annual wage negotiations in the whole economy. Through its monopoly as a representative of the employees on this committee, the LO has had a strategic advantage over the other confederations, so that the policies of the LO often had to become their policies. With a seat on the committee, the competing confederations might be able to develop more efficient strategies to attract members from the LO.

Within the LO itself there is also a critical balance between unions organising employees in the private and public sectors. Although just over 60 per cent of jobs in the Norwegian economy are still in the private sector, the rate of unionisation in many private industries is much lower than in the public sector. Thus the balance between the public and the private sector really is critical, and might become tilted in favour of the public sector by a growth in employment here corresponding to about 11 per cent of all employed persons in the labour force (K. Nergård 1993).

One consequence of this, ironically, is that the LO might actually gain by the realisation of the work-sharing proposal because it would secure or enhance employment in its core sectors and contribute to keeping the balance between public and private sector unions in the LO.

On the other hand, to support the proposal would come close to admitting errors in its present labour market policy, and no trade union would yet dare to break the tradition of negotiating only for higher wages. There is within the LO a widespread fear that shifting the paradigm from negotiations for higher wages to negotiations for a combination of lower wages and more leisure time would lead to even greater membership losses than today.

This analysis of the LO's position is supported by the way the LO has treated the continuous growth in the use of overtime in the economy since 1988. In the autumn of 1988 the volume of overtime totalled about 42,000 full-time jobs. Currently, it amounts to about 100,000 full-time jobs (Central Bureau of Statistics 1988, 1995), but the LO has not dared to intervene, knowing that overtime is widely regarded as a fringe benefit among its members. Although the LO did recently launch a campaign to convert overtime into permanent jobs, this has only the status of an appeal to its members, and forms no official part of the wage negotiations taking place in the private sector.

For the Employers' Association, as for the government and the LO, 1986 and 1987 were traumatic years. In 1986 they lost the battle about the reduction of weekly working hours, which had involved strikes as well as a lock-out. The following year the shortage of manpower led to substantial wage drift: from 1988 the number of bankruptcies started to rise, reaching a peak in 1993 of about 180 per cent above the 1988 level (Central Bureau of Statistics 1994).

Therefore, the employers do not support any measures that threaten to create even the least pressure in the labour market. They also share the philosophy of the government and the LO about the healthy and disciplining effects of unemployment and the austerity policy. Besides, unlike the German employers, who since 1985 have successfully demanded extended operating hours and flexibilisation in return for granting shorter individual working hours, the Norwegian employers lost the first round of this battle in 1987, when the reduction in working time in almost all firms led to a reduction in operating hours as well (Karlsen 1989). In subsequent years they have not developed the necessary competence in matters of flexibilisation and working time policies to be able to manage a new reduction in weekly working hours. Apart from this, the Employers' Association has tried to put the reduction of wages for labour market debutants on the political agenda, but with little success.

In a political system, the functioning of which Stein Rokkan described with the phrase 'Votes count, but resources decide' – that is, a political system with strong corporative structures – the NHO may have good reasons to fear a further growth of the unions in the public sector. If 50 per cent of new employees became union members, public sector unions would soon outweigh the unions in the private sector in numbers and influence, thus becoming capable of directing still more taxpayers' money to their own sector.

Common to all three of the major institutional actors – the government, the NHO and the LO – is the desire not to share power with actors outside the triangle, since they gain important advantages through monopolising the strategic decisions on economic policy, and do not have to relate to actors whom they do not know and whose actions therefore are incalculable.

Compared to other West European countries there have been relatively few proposals for, and few experiments on, work-sharing in Norway. Whereas governments and unions in countries like France, Belgium, Denmark and Finland, and employers and unions in Germany, have been open to agreements and experiments, these have been rejected in Norway, and also in Sweden. One explanation may be the tight connection between the Labour parties and the trade union confederations in these countries, combined with the position of national economists within the labour parties. During the post-war period, the parties in both countries have quite similarly relied heavily on national economist expertise for economic steering. The supremacy of their models has not been seriously questioned by economic developments until now, but their political cultures are completely pervaded by the models of national economists, which in many cases have reached the status of dogmatic beliefs instead of tools for empirical economic analysis and pragmatic policies.

Another explanation may be that the labour market crisis is younger in these countries than on the continent. In most continental countries it started around 1980, but in Norway and Sweden it did not begin until towards the end of the 1980s, thus the belief is still held that Keynesian measures will solve it. On the continent all kinds of traditional measures have already been tried, but with scant effect. The consciousness that the best way to secure one's own job is not to participate in a devastating competition for scarce jobs but to create more jobs by work-sharing takes time to spread in a population. In Norway and Sweden the populations have not yet had enough time to arrive at this recognition.

OUTLOOK

Without support from the most powerful bodies of interest-accumulation in the country, the proposal to employ all unemployed in the public sector has little chance of being realised. It has been blocked in the political process at various stages and excluded from the political agenda by the government, the LO and the NHO; expansion of the public sector would threaten the economic austerity politics of these bodies. Not only is the public sector already administering 70 per cent of the GNP for consumption, public savings and investments and redistribution to all kinds of industries and client groups, but there are the power implications within the LO as well. The only imaginable scenario under which these proposals might become official policy would be a situation in which (a) union membership in the public sector already outnumbered union membership in the private sector and (b) the unions in the public sector united in a single confederation. However public sector expansion might also develop more gradually as a consequence of a stepwise and necessary expansion of personal services in the welfare sector.

For the time being the proposal for work-sharing without wage compensation is excluded from all important political arenas. It was discussed in the committee of the Deputy Ministers in December 1993, but turned down by a majority of deputies with an education as national economists. After the first heated discussions in the press, government representatives stopped answering critical attacks. From the summer of 1994 employment started to grow and unemployment to decrease, enabling the political elites to maintain that their policy has started to work. Until unemployment starts to increase again it will be impossible to achieve a breakthrough for work-sharing.

Unlike the other proposals, however, this one is well known, has widespread if latent support in the population and among shop stewards, and meets the important functional and political requirements of being cost-neutral to firms, and of not threatening to tilt the balance of power between the private and public sectors of the economy. Another advantage is its neutrality towards the wages of lower-income groups.

For the above reasons, the scenario under which this proposal would become politically acceptable is simply, increasing unemployment.

In addition, however, there is also a long-term development that might lead to at least partial acceptance of the proposal. Younger officials of two LO unions have managed to put work-sharing on the agenda of these unions. This has partly been done for idealistic reasons, but also because young parents, according to the 1992 Level of Living Survey, have the longest weekly working hours and find it increasingly difficult to combine childraising and family life with the requirements of working life. Their time-budgets do not go around. Many of them would therefore prefer shorter working hours to higher wages, but to achieve a breakthrough for this preference in the LO system will undoubtedly take some years.

There seems to be a growing consensus among social scientists that work-sharing in whatever form or shape is the only means to restore approximately full employment. This points to the necessity of international comparative research on (a) the regime constellations that allow different types of unemployment policy, (b) the relationship between the human and social consequences of the labour market crisis and the readiness of a regulatory regime to try radical policies, and (c) the processes leading to, and the mechanisms used by, various types of actors to bring about paradigmatic changes.

REFERENCES

Alternativ fremtid (1994) *Survey om arbeidsdeling*, Oslo.
Central Bureau of Statistics (1988–94) *Educational Statistics 1988–94*, Oslo.
—— (1993) *National Accounts Statistics 1991*, Oslo.
—— (1989–95) *Statistical Monthly Review 1989–95*, Oslo.
—— (1981–95) *Statistical Yearbooks 1980–94*, Oslo.
—— (1981–92) *Survey of the Level of Living 1980–91*, Oslo.
—— (1988–94) *Wage Statistics 1988–94*, Oslo.
—— (1988–95) *Work Force Inquiry 1988–95*, Oslo.
FAFO/MMI (1993) *Ungdomsundersøkelsen 1993*, Oslo.
Karlsen, T. K. (1989) *Arbeidstid og fleksibilitet i arbeidslivet*, FAFO, Oslo.
—— (1991) *Arbeidsmarkedspolitikken i en brytningstid*, FAFO, Oslo.
—— (1994) 'Modell for arbeidsdeling', in *Folkevett*, 28 February 1994
MacDonald, D. (1985) *Industrikulturen fra dannelse til krise*, Oslo.
Ministry of Finance and Customs (1994) *National Budget 1995*, Oslo.
LO (1994–95) *Blikk på arbeidsmarkedet 1994–95*, Oslo.
National Employment Agency (1987–95) *Statistical Reviews 1987–95*, Oslo.
—— (1994) *Evaluering av AMO–kurs*, Report (2) 1994, Oslo.
—— (1992) *Evaluering av praksisplasser*, Report (5) 1992, Oslo.
—— (1995) *Mot et mer fleksibelt arbeidsmarked*, Oslo.
National Insurance Institution (1993) *Social Insurance Statistics 1993*, Oslo.
Nergaard, K. (1993) *Samarbeid og selvstendighet*, FAFO, Oslo.
NHO (1988–95) *Lønns- og fraværsstatistikk 1988–95*, Oslo.
NOU (1987) 9A and 9B, *Arbeidstidsundersøkelsen*, Oslo.
—— (1988) 21, *Økonomisk utvikling*, Oslo.
—— (1988) 3, *Om grunnlaget for inntekstoppgjøret*, Oslo.
—— (1993) 11, *Mindre til overføringer – mer sysselsetting*, Oslo.
—— (1993) 12, *Tid for barna*, Oslo.
Stokke, T. (1994) *Organisasjonsgraden i Norge 1956–93*, FAFO, Oslo.

9 Switzerland

Kermit Blank

INTRODUCTION

While most OECD economies have encountered high jobless rates since the oil shock of the 1970s, Switzerland has often been considered a special case due to its successful maintenance of full employment. Between 1940 and 1990 the average yearly unemployment rate exceeded the 1 per cent mark only once, a 1.1 per cent rate resulting from the recession of 1982–84 (see Figure 9.1). More recently, however, Switzerland's special status has come into question. The recession of the early 1990s brought with it a five-fold increase in the unemployment rate, from less than 1 per cent to an unfamiliar high of 5.2 per cent (January 1994). With unemployment levels not seen since the 1930s, Swiss authorities have faced a necessary re-evaluation of existing labour market policy.

The policy response has thus far been quite cautious. Given the limited size and scope of federal spending and the strong commitment to monetary stability, aggressive demand-stimulus through fiscal and monetary expansion has not been undertaken. And although funding for active labour market measures has increased dramatically, total expenditures are still the among the lowest in the OECD. More radical options, such as state legislated work time reductions, expansion of public employment, or extension of welfare state exit options (early retirement), have not had enough support to be implemented. In short, neither full utilisation of standard labour market policy measures nor dramatic policy innovation has been forthcoming. Instead, policymakers have tended to look for the next economic upswing to return Switzerland's unemployment rate to a more desirable level.

Despite its relatively conservative response to increased unemployment, Switzerland still presents an interesting case for those interested in radical unemployment policies. This is true not because of recent innovations, but because of ongoing policies that are unconventional in the European context. Rather than stimulating labour demand or pursuing active labour market policy, Swiss policymakers have emphasised the cyclical manipulation of labour supply, particularly through use of foreign worker policy

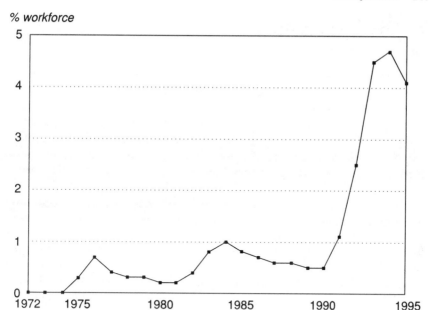

% workforce

Figure 9.1 Unemployment in Switzerland, 1972–1995
Source: OECD 1992 (1972–87) OECD 1995 (1988–95)

and short-time work. These approaches are relevant both to comparative discussion of radical unemployment policies and to any analysis of Switzerland's future labour market prospects.

This chapter analyses Swiss foreign worker policy and short-time work in the broader economic and political context of the Swiss response to recent unemployment increases. Are these policies still effective, and if not, how much does their ineffectiveness account for jobless growth? What explains the conservatism of the Swiss response to higher unemployment, and how politically viable are unemployment policy innovations that go beyond these traditional approaches? After an overview of Swiss labour market institutions, standard employment policies, and unemployment insurance, the subsequent section describes and evaluates Swiss radical unemployment policies, namely the regulation of foreign labour and use of short-time work. This is followed by an analysis of the political dynamics of unemployment policymaking in Switzerland, focusing on the causes of recent unemployment and the possibility of reform in the context of a consensus-oriented political system. The chapter concludes by discussing the outlook for the future.

CONTEXT

Labour market institutions

Although Katzenstein (1984) characterised Switzerland as a liberal variant of democratic corporatism, in many ways the Swiss political economy is more liberal than corporatist. Peak-level bargaining and state-mediated class compromise are not features of Swiss economic policymaking. Rather, private business is in a strong position to control both employment and (together with the financial sector) investment decisions with relatively little interference by either labour or the government. The Swiss Labour movement is comparatively weak and the state plays a relatively minor role in relations between the social partners and in the economy as a whole. In 1990, government expenditures as a percentage of GDP were only 30.7 per cent, compared to 49.6 per cent in Austria, 61.4 per cent in Sweden, and 43.4 per cent in the OECD countries on average (OECD 1994a). It is obvious from these figures that full employment in Switzerland until 1991 cannot be explained as a nationalisation of employment problems through public employment increases, as in Sweden for example. In general, policymakers and social partners exhibit a strong belief in the efficiency of the market-place and attribute much of Switzerland's economic success to the efforts of Swiss firms.

Business interests in Switzerland are both politically strong and highly centralised. The two major associations of business, the Federation of Swiss Industry (Vorort) and the Central Federation of Swiss Employers' Organisations (ZSA), have overlapping memberships and, by mutual agreement, serve different functions. Comprised of the largest and most internationally-oriented firms in Switzerland, Vorort acts as political spokesperson for business regarding issues affecting Switzerland's overall economic position, and generally takes a economically liberal and internationalist stance on issues of domestic and foreign economic policy (Katzenstein 1984). The ZSA has a narrower role, representing a wide range of business interests in matters of collective bargaining and social policy (Schweizerische Bankgesellschaft 1987).

Trade unions in Switzerland, on the other hand, are both decentralised and comparatively weak. There are many reasons for this weakness. First, Switzerland's decentralised manufacturing base, small plant size, and increasing movement towards a service-based economy have proved to be obstacles to greater trade union density (Katzenstein 1984). Between 1960 and 1985, only about 30 per cent of the labour force was unionised, falling to just 26.6 per cent in 1990 (OECD 1994c). Second, the openness of the Swiss economy and the high degree of foreign direct investment of Swiss multinational corporations impose certain limitations on trade union strategy. The need for exporters to maintain competitive prices and quality services, and the implicit threat by them to withdraw operations from Switzerland, tend to moderate union demands (Katzenstein 1984).

The weakness of the trade union movement is also the result of decentralisation and internal social and political divisions; there is no centralised and monolithic trade union or trade union confederation. Trade unions are organised by industry, and they remain independent within the several national trade union confederations. The largest organisation of trade unions and the most dominant politically is the Swiss Trade Union Federation (SGB), which comprises fifteen individual trade unions with about 441,000 members, or about 13 per cent of the total work force.[1] In addition to the SGB, there is a confessional trade union federation (CNG) with about 106,000 members, and a white-collar union federation (VSA) with almost 148,000 members. The trade union movement also suffers from lack of political cohesion: positions taken by the more moderate metalworkers and watchmakers unions often vary considerably from those of the more radical public employees union and the construction, chemical and textiles unions (Katzenstein 1984:99–100).

Institutionalised links between trade unions and their affiliated political parties – the SGB with the Social Democratic Party (SP) and the CNG with the Christian People's Party (CVP) – provide some measure of compensating political power, but unions are both legally and financially independent of political parties and are often at odds with their political partners. The SP, for example, tends to offer public-sector solutions to labour issues, whereas the unions more often prefer a private-sector strategy (Katzenstein 1984:100). Nevertheless, the links between parties and unions provide an implicit guarantee of free collective bargaining and ensure that governmental interference in the affairs of the unions and their federations is minimal. With unions and employers both preferring to regulate working conditions through private negotiation, it is no surprise that incomes policies have thus far played no role in Swiss economic policymaking.

Industrial relations in Switzerland are relatively uncoordinated and often quite decentralised. Bargaining is a matter for individual unions, taking place at either the sectoral or the company level (or even plant level), with little if any involvement by either employers' organisations or trade union confederations. These umbrella organisations focus their efforts on more political activities, dealing with the federal government and attempting to influence its economic and social policies to their advantage. As a matter of principle the state does not intervene directly in the relationship between unions and employers, although collective agreements are legally binding for their signatory parties.

Despite the weakness of labour and state non-intervention, the Swiss labour market is exceptionally peaceful. Post-war industrial relations have been characterised by a gradual buildup of voluntary cooperation between business and labour, giving Switzerland one of the lowest strike rates in the OECD. An important feature of Swiss collective agreements are their clauses on industrial peace, in many ways the origin of this distinctive 'ideology of consensus'. Such a peace agreement was concluded for the first time in 1937 by the metal and machinery industries, and stated that disputes over application and interpretation of collective agreements were to be resolved without recourse to strikes or lock-outs. More than 90 per cent of workers in the private sector are now covered by peace agreements.

Unemployment policymaking

The use of demand-oriented labour market measures in Switzerland has always been relatively weak, for both political and economic reasons. Politically, Keynesian demand-management does not accord well with the pro-market commitment of Swiss economic policymakers, a policy stance broadly in line with the dominance of business in the political economy (Katzenstein 1984). In fact, policymakers have explicitly stated that the state has no responsibility to compensate for deficient demand during economic downswings (Blaas 1992:369). Economically, the openness of the Swiss economy and the importance of Swiss banking make price stability a top priority. Consequently, monetary policy is generally restrictive, with emphasis given to meeting monetary supply targets (Danthine and Lambelet 1987, Schmidt 1985, OECD 1994b). Fiscal policy is similarly confined, given the small size and scope of national government spending in a relatively decentralised federal institutional structure (OECD 1994b). In addition, the Swiss public frequently defeats fiscal policy proposals which the Federal Council puts on the political agenda by means of referenda.

It is also consistent with the general principle of state non-intervention that active labour market policy has traditionally been rather under-developed in Switzerland, at least in comparison to other European countries. Part of this, of course, is the result of extremely low unem-ployment rates prior to 1991, but even at the height of the recession in 1993 no more than 0.38 per cent of Swiss GDP was spent on active labour market measures, compared to 1.58 per cent in Germany, 2.56 per cent in Sweden, and 0.56 per cent in the OECD as a whole (OECD 1994c).

Active labour market policy in Switzerland, under the rubric 'Preven-tative Measures', is executed by cantonal labour offices and financed by the federal unemployment insurance system. There are three general instruments. First, cantonal labour exchanges provide counselling and serve as information networks which match vacancies and job-seekers. Second, identified discrepancies between the abilities of job-seekers and actual job vacancies are dealt with through educational measures – basic training, training in specific skills, and retraining (Grossen 1994). Finally, employment for those who are difficult to place, particularly the disabled, is facilitated by vocational rehabilitation, by grants-in-aid for initial training periods, and through craft-based, technical or administrative activities as transitional employment programmes.

Unemployment insurance

Changes in the system of unemployment insurance in Switzerland over the years have greatly affected both how unemployment statistics are recorded and how businesses calculate the costs of employment. Prior to 1977 unemployment insurance in Switzerland was strictly voluntary and, because of historically low rates of unemployment, not widely used. When recession struck Switzerland in 1974 after the oil shock, only 22 per cent of Swiss workers were insured against loss of income (Schmidt 1985:112). After calls for reform and a successful referendum vote, a compulsory, nationwide unemployment insurance system was created which first came into effect in April 1977 and became fully functional in 1984. This change has had several important repercussions.

First of all, the severe bias downward in official unemployment statistics has been eliminated by the new unemployment insurance regime. Since most workers laid off during the mid 1970s recession were not insured, most also had no incentive to officially register as unemployed in the cantonal labour exchange. The almost non-existent unemployment rates prior to 1977 thus reflect in part the lack of compulsory unemployment insurance. Evidence of significant under-reporting is provided by survey-based unemployment statistics originating from census figures. The ratio between census statistics and official unemployment figures was 8:1 in 1976, the year prior to the introduction of mandatory insurance, compared to 2.75:1 in 1987 (Schmid *et al.* 1993:11). The fact that this latter ratio is still quite high may be the result of stringent proof requirements demanded by the labour offices of an insured individual's inability to find work. Since 1991 a more accurate yearly survey has been done by the Federal Office for Statistics, using guidelines set forth by the International Labour Office. While the survey's reported numbers were almost twice as high as official figures in 1991, they were only slightly higher in 1992 and were actually less in 1993. With unemployment insurance providing the incentive for the jobless to register, unemployment figures have risen in part simply because they have become more accurate.

The transition to compulsory unemployment insurance has had more direct effects on unemployment as well. As Schmidt (1995) argues, the high benefit levels of the new system have given firms in Switzerland greater incentive to externalise employment problems, and have given unemployed workers greater incentive to extend the length of their work search. While both of these factors have contributed to unemployment increases, the former is the greater problem in Schmidt's view. Firms have reacted to the increased social wage and the newfound social safety net by retrenching and restructuring their use of labour. Many have found that dismissal costs, combined with the costs of hiring and training when demand picks up, provide insufficient incentive to retain labour during times of recession. Swiss firms, he argues, resorted to lay-offs much more quickly and to a greater degree in the early 1990s than in previous recessions even though the decline in total demand was comparatively mild.

RADICAL UNEMPLOYMENT POLICIES

Labour supply as a policy instrument[2]

A bias downward in reported unemployment is not, of course, the only reason for Switzerland's observed success in maintaining low unemployment rates. Even if the above estimates of bias are correct, Switzerland has still sustained unemployment levels of less than 5 per cent from the 1970s to the present, an enviable record. Given the reluctance of policy-makers to engage in either aggressive demand management or active labour market measures, what other factors account for Switzerland's success?

According to the predominant view, a major reason for the Swiss employment record is the existence of a strong and adaptable market economy with a low degree of state intervention. Since similar conditions exist in other liberal economies, like the US, with not nearly the same record of success, one must look for other explanations. The most prominent alternative is the ability of the Swiss political economy to regulate its labour supply. In periods of economic recession, full employment has historically depended on a rapid downward adjustment in the supply of labour (Schmidt 1985). The extent to which this has occurred is unique to Switzerland and contrasts sharply with the labour market experience of other full employment countries such as Sweden, Norway, and Austria, where low rates of unemployment have coexisted with an increase in the total number of jobs.

For example, Switzerland was hit much harder by the world recession in the mid 1970s than other European countries and the OECD on average (Danthine and Lambelet 1987). The sharp decline in output which corresponded with the oil-shock induced recession also corresponded with a sharp drop in employment: Switzerland lost almost 330,000 jobs from 1974 to 1976, almost 10 per cent of the labour force (Blaas 1992). Yet the unemployment rate never exceeded 1 per cent in part because labour force participation also contracted precipitously: 245,000 foreign workers and 60,000 Swiss workers (mainly women) withdrew from the market, leaving only 25,000 unemployed persons still in the market and an unemployment rate of no more than 0.8 per cent (Blaas 1992). Thus despite a deep employment crisis there was almost no unemployment. While this had a lot to do with the lack of unemployment insurance for most workers,

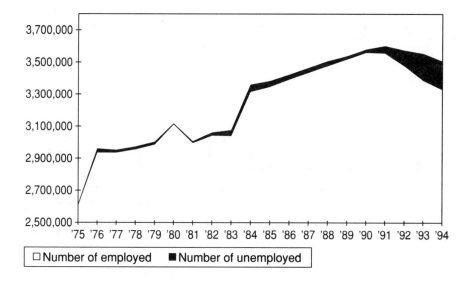

Figure 9.2 Total Swiss labour force, 1975–1994

Source: Die Volkwirtschaft (various issues)

adjustment of labour supply through foreign worker policy was particularly effective.

During the economic recovery of 1976–80, employment recovered strongly. A total of 125,000 new jobs were created, eliminating unemployment almost entirely and providing almost 100,000 jobs for foreign workers. However the 1981–83 recession again resulted in sharp job losses; during this period, some 65,000 people lost their jobs. But since 20,000 Swiss workers and 20,000 foreign workers withdrew from the labour market, only 25,000 workers were unemployed, again giving rise to an unemployment rate of around 0.8 per cent (Blaas 1992). Thus an extremely high elasticity of labour supply was responsible for a swift adjustment to rapidly changing labour demands, equilibrating the Swiss labour market rather smoothly.

The recovery from 1984–91 produced even stronger job growth, with over 238,000 new jobs and an unemployment rate of less than 1 per cent. But when recession returned in 1991, this time labour supply contraction did not mirror the drop in labour demand: over 230,000 jobs were lost, but instead of large-scale labour market withdrawals, as before, only 45,000 foreign workers and 15,000 Swiss workers left the market, and the number of unemployed rose to around 170,000. The effectiveness of labour supply manipulation as a tool of employment policy seems to have diminished considerably.

Table 9.1 Radical unemployment policies in Switzerland

Strategy	Measures
Labour supply adjustment	Foreign worker policy
	Short-time work

The policy most responsible for the labour supply adjustment of the 1970s and 1980s, foreign worker policy, will be discussed next in more detail. While Switzerland's policy toward foreign labour is probably inimitable and, for obvious reasons, of dubious ethical value as an unemployment measure, it is nonetheless considered here as a radical unemployment policy in the European context. A second labour supply measure will then be examined, short-time work, which does not produce contractions in labour force numbers but, by allowing workers to reduce their work time, maintains jobs and thus reduces unemployment rates.

Foreign worker policy

Like most other Northern European countries, Switzerland had to deal with labour shortages during the post-war economic boom of the 1950s and 1960s and sought foreign guest workers to meet the demand, mainly from southern Europe. In comparison with other labour importers, however, the degree of this foreign work force expansion was extremely high. In 1965 the share of foreigners in the labour force was 23.7 per cent in Switzerland, compared to 5.7 per cent in Germany, 6.5 per cent in Belgium, and 4.6 per cent in Sweden (Blaas 1992). With over 946,000 foreign workers, this ratio reached 28 per cent in 1994 (*Die Volkwirtschaft* 1995). These numbers have traditionally made foreign worker policy the most important element of labour market policy in Switzerland.

How has foreign worker policy been used? Two kinds of work permit allow a foreign worker to be legally employed in Switzerland. Temporary permits are issued for a maximum of one year and are subject to annual renewal. Permanent work permits, on the other hand, are valid indefinitely, allowing permanent residency rights in Switzerland. Temporary work permits are differentiated into three categories: permits for border commuters; seasonal permits; and annual permits. A seasonal worker becomes eligible for an annual permit after having worked for four consecutive nine-month seasons. After five years work in the country, annual permit holders from most western European nations can apply for permanent residency status. All others must wait an additional five years.

Federal authorities limit the number of seasonal and annual permits issued in any given year. While quotas, first introduced in 1963 to stabilise the size of the foreign population, place upper limits on the number of permits, they are not decisive in controlling the overall size of the foreign

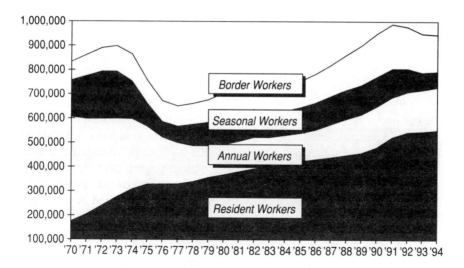

Figure 9.3 Foreign labour force adjustment in Switzerland (by category)

Source: Die Volkwirtschaft (various issues)

labour force. Instead, the number of new permits is mostly determined by the labour market itself, since finding a job is a prerequisite for obtaining a permit, foreign workers with jobs do not have their permits revoked. Nevertheless, because of the frequency with which temporary permits must be renewed, the size of the temporary foreign work force is forced to adjust to declines in labour demand.

The elasticity of foreign labour supply has declined, however, At the beginning of the 1970s, the major part of the foreign labour force consisted of annual and seasonal workers, so the inflow of foreign workers could be managed quite easily by controlling the renewal of annual and seasonal permits. Today foreign workers with resident status take up the dominant share of the labour force, so the options for foreign worker policy have become quite limited. It is for this reason that the increase in unemployment rates in the 1990s has a lot to do with the changing picture of foreign labour in Switzerland.

Short-time work

The policy of short-time work is another unconventional form of unemployment policy which manipulates labour supply to meet demand. Used extensively in Switzerland for over twenty years, short-work policy is thought of as temporary, stopgap relief designed to provide security for jobs which are considered competitive in the long term but are endangered in the short term by a transitory reduction in labour demand. Short-time

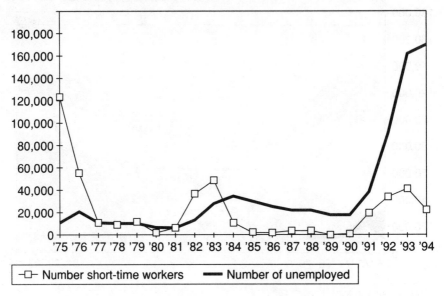

Figure 9.4 Use of short-time workers in Switzerland, 1975–1994

Source: Die Volkwirtschaft (various issues)

work regulations allow employers to reduce working hours in order to maintain jobs during cyclical downturns in economic activity, with workers in turn receiving benefits from the federal unemployment insurance system at a level equivalent to 80 per cent of their wage rate for the hours reduced. In principle, an involuntary temporary reduction in hours is treated by Swiss labour market authorities as 'partial unemployment', workers receive unemployment benefits for lost hours, but retain their positions.

The advantages are obvious for all participants involved. For the affected employee, their position is preserved and although total pay is marginally reduced, a more severe income loss is avoided. In addition, skills and work habits are maintained. For firms, experienced employees are maintained during a downturn, and the costs of dismissal and later rehiring are avoided. State authorities also benefit, because the costs of short-time work for the unemployment system are lower than would be the case if the affected workers were dismissed (Flechsenhar 1978). Furthermore, short-time work regulations prevent – or at least conceal – large increases in the unemployment rate.

The short-time work regulations have been used consistently in Switzerland (see Figure 9.4), and, as is intended by the programme, the incidence of partial unemployment is strongly cyclical. During the recession years of the mid 1970s and early 1980s, the number of short-time workers greatly exceeded the number of total unemployed. The use

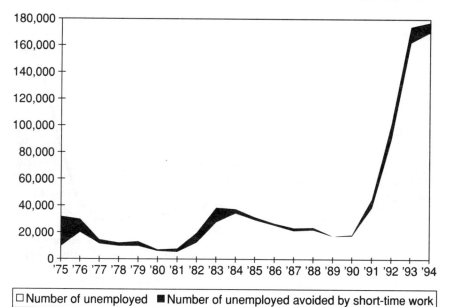

Figure 9.5 Contribution of short-time work to employment in Switzerland, 1975–1994

Source: Die Volkwirtschaft, (various issues), own calculations

of short-time work by economic sector has traditionally followed the same pattern as that of job reduction, being found mainly in highly labour-intensive industries such as metal and machine-tool production, as well as the watch industry.

What does short-time work contribute to the reduction in unemployment and the unemployment rate? One method of estimation was provided by the Federal Office for Industry, Commerce and Labour (see Schmidt 1985). According to this method, the total number of lost hours claimed for compensation due to reduced work time is converted into a weekly average of lost hours. Dividing this through by the average number of hours worked per week per employee, an estimate of the number of employees retained through use of short-time work can be obtained. Figure 9.5 shows that these numbers are considerable. For 1975 the contribution of short-time work to the reduction in unemployment figures is estimated to have been 21,581 persons, which reduced the unemployment rate by 0.8 percentage points. For the peak recession years 1983 and 1993 the reduction in unemployment was about 10,000 persons, for a reduction of 0.3 percentage points.

Recourse to shorter work hours in the 1990s, however, decreased significantly relative to previous recession periods as firms have tended to lay off workers rather than make use of short-time work (see Figure 9.4). While there were 163,000 people unemployed in 1993, for example, workers participating in short work only totalled 42,000. While unemployment numbers in the period between 1991 and 1992 more than doubled, the corresponding number of short-time workers only increased by around a third over the prior year.

There are two main reasons for this. First and most importantly, lay-offs appeared to be for many employers the less expensive alternative. This applied especially to firms whose personnel had relatively little job-specific knowledge and generally low qualifications, for example firms in the tourist industry, who found that the hoarding of personnel through short-time work produced more costs than the alternative of dismissing surplus labour and rehiring as and when required. This was because the conditions for compensation for partial unemployment became less attractive to firms as the new unemployment insurance system was extended. After the recession of the early 1980s, policymakers observed that many firms were using short-time work to avoid needed rationalisation (Schaad and Schellenbauer 1994). Many sectors that used short-time work the most, for example clothing and textiles firms, had structural competitiveness problems which required permanent capacity reduction. Their use of short-time work was therefore seen as an abuse of the programme, so controls were tightened. Compensation was limited to a maximum period of eighteen months spread over two years (extended to twenty-one months in April 1993). In addition, firms were required to pay one half-day's wage for every month a worker was on short-time work, as well as the employer's share of social insurance contributions calculated on the entire wage, including payments for unemployment insurance.

The second reason for the reduction in the use of short-time work was that many firms in the 1990's chose, for reasons not connected with the financial conditions of short-time work, to begin structural retrenchment programmes which involved permanent reductions in the size of the work-force (Schaad and Schellenbauer 1994).

It has now become obvious to many observers, especially when comparing the number of unemployed persons with the number on short-time work, that reform of short-time work regulations has left this measure under-utilised. A new model suggested by the Heinrich Landert corporation, called SOFLEX (Solidaristic and Flexible part-time work), attempts to improve the current system by making changes which would maintain the cost-neutrality for firms of short-time work, while still limiting its use to temporary reductions in labour demand (Schaad and Schellenbauer 1994). The model provides for voluntary agreements between employer and employee which allow the employer to reduce work time by up to a maximum of 20 per cent of normal hours during temporary slack periods. The essential difference is cost-neutrality for the firm, which Landert has calculated to be 1.2 per cent for every 1 per cent reduction in work time.

Thus for every five people working at 80 per cent, one 100 per cent job is saved, as well as 120 per cent in wage costs. The 20 per cent saving in comparison to dismissal is calculated to be sufficient to offset the cost of necessary reorganisation of the business. For employees the wages lost due to shorter hours are compensated for by unemployment insurance as is currently the system, although Landert suggests that compensation rates remain flexible. So that structural change is not hindered, the availability of SOFLEX benefits decreases over time. Although Landert's idea has not been widely used, it illustrates the degree to which firms and their employees are willing to innovate within the framework of current policies.

POLITICAL DYNAMICS

The sources of unemployment growth in Switzerland

Labour market policymaking in Switzerland has entered a period of transition, as unemployment rates have climbed during the 1990s to unaccustomed high levels and traditional policy options no longer seem to be effective. What is the cause of this transition? One obvious reason is the downturn in economic growth. The number of jobless began to rise as GDP stagnated in 1991 and then increased dramatically as GDP contracted in 1992 and 1993. Regression estimates of the association between change in unemployment and change in yearly average GDP for the twenty-three OECD countries show Switzerland to be almost exactly on the trendline (Schmidt 1995). The fact that unemployment rates have dropped as economic growth has recovered is one reason why more activist labour market intervention has been rejected: but if Switzerland is now a 'normal' case in this regard, why did its 'special' case status exist for so long, allowing it to maintain full employment even during recessions in the 1970s and 1980s? Something else must be added to the explanation.

As argued above, three additional factors seem to be of importance. First, the change in the unemployment insurance regime has meant that unemployment is no longer hidden by involuntary exit from the labour force. Recent estimates suggest that with full implementation of compulsory unemployment insurance, the downward bias in official unemployment rates has been reduced if not eliminated. The new insurance regime has also led to increases in the 'true' rate of unemployment by giving Swiss firms more flexibility in laying off workers, something dramatically in evidence during the 1990s recession. Second, as illustrated above, the traditional source of labour supply manipulation, foreign worker policy, has become attenuated over the years as more and more foreign workers have become permanent residents with the same working rights as Swiss citizens. Finally, short-time work benefits have become more restrictive, giving business less incentive to retain workers on part-time when demand is reduced: all of these things have conspired to increase recorded unemployment in Switzerland.

One interesting aspect of this account is that these developments are primarily internal and unique to Switzerland. Indeed, standard explanations of unemployment performance in the comparative political-economy literature do not seem to accord well with the Swiss experience. One hypothesis about recent unemployment increases in the OECD is that global economic integration has reduced governmental capacity to utilise counter-cyclical demand-management to achieve full employment (Hall 1994; Garrett 1995). This theory fails to explain variation in Swiss unemployment performance not only because trade openness and capital mobility are nothing new to Switzerland, but also because Keynesian policies have never played a central role in Swiss employment success in the past. Another hypothesis about variation in unemployment levels is that full employment is associated with the electoral strength and participation in government of parties of the left (Korpi 1989). However because of its 'consociational' system, Switzerland has had grand coalition governments since 1959, with two Social Democratic representatives on the seven member Federal Council. There has been little variation in the participation and strength of the Left, which means that explanations of recent unemployment increases based on shifts in domestic social coalitions or party-political competition do not apply.

The politics of policy innovation: the importance of Swiss consensus-building

Given higher unemployment rates and greater limitations on traditional labour market measures, why has the unemployment policy response in Switzerland been so tentative? From the above discussion of labour market institutions, the answer is not surprising. The pro-market orientation of Swiss policymakers, the historically limited role of the state in economic policymaking, the institutional strength of business interests, and the weakness of the trade unions all place formidable political barriers in the path of radical employment policy innovation in Switzerland.

The particularities of Swiss policymaking institutions also provide an extremely important, but perhaps less obvious, part of this explanation. In particular, the institutional necessity of building widespread consensus among various political actors and interest groups before moving new policies forward places significant structural limitations on innovation. The importance of this context for future labour market legislation, such as work time reduction or work-sharing, makes Swiss consensus politics worthy of further elaboration.

Swiss legislative initiatives require consensus-building because of the dispersion of institutional power. The Swiss parliament is divided into two chambers, the Nationalrat, elected by proportional representation, and the Ständerat, elected by the cantons. The executive is composed of a seven member council, the Bundesrat, whose members are chosen by the parliament in proportion to party strength. Since 1959 a grand coalition of the four largest parties have combined to share executive power in the Bundesrat. This is the so-called 'magic formula' of two representatives from the Christian Democrats, two from the Social Democrats, two from the Free Democrats, and one from the Swiss People's Party. In addition, Switzerland is strongly federal, with national-level jurisdiction limited to areas specifically set out in the constitution. Finally, all legislation is subject to direct electoral veto through the referendum process. Each of these institutional provisions tends to engage a variety of competing interests in the policymaking process, thus slowing decision making and requiring constant bargaining and consensus-building to change the status quo.

In practice, however, it is the referendum that constitutes the critical veto point (Immergut 1992). Even if proponents of more activist labour market policy were to successfully pass legislation expanding federal authority in this area, reforms could still be blocked by a subsequent successful referendum challenge. Thus the referendum effectively moves decision-making from the executive and parliamentary arenas into the electoral arena, where reforms are often much harder to sustain. In referendum voting, the Swiss tend both to ignore partisan loyalties and to vote against the legislation being challenged rather than for it. Furthermore, high rates of participation (which averages 40 per cent) tend to be correlated with higher incomes and higher levels of educational attainment (Immergut 1992), and it is precisely voters of higher socio-economic status who are least likely to benefit from more extensive (and expensive) use of labour market measures.

The referendum process gives organised interest groups significant political power. Although they cannot control the outcome of referendum votes, interest groups have sufficient resources to collect the necessary 50,000 signatures to mount a referendum campaign. As the gatekeepers to the referendum they demand the attention of Swiss policymakers, who prefer to avoid the risk of having legislation defeated after a lengthy process of executive and parliamentary deliberation. The most effective means for policymakers to prevent a possible veto is to address interest-group concerns early in legislative preparations. Given that any one group can credibly threaten a referendum challenge, agreement on legislation has to be close to unanimous; it is thus the concern to avoid referendum campaigns that accounts for much of the compromise character of a large part of federal legislation.

This consensus-building process gives trade unions in Switzerland more political power and involvement in economic decision-making than perhaps would be predicted by looking at their organisational strength. They are in fact heavily involved at every stage of the legislative process

(Compston 1994). Their power, however, tends to be more negative than positive in the sense that although their ability to veto legislation, through threats of a referendum campaign, allows them concessions at the bargaining table, it does not allow them to force through proposals unacceptable to other actors who have the same veto power, especially business interests. Expensive or highly interventionist employment policy proposals are thus unlikely to make it make it very far in the legislative process.

Besides the referendum, Swiss voters may also participate directly in policymaking through use of the initiative process, which enables organisations that can collect 100,000 signatures to put legislative proposals directly to the people: such proposals become law if accepted by a majority of the voters and a majority of cantons. This is another way for trade unions, the Social Democrats, or other interested groups to propose more far-reaching policy reforms, and is one way of circumventing the veto of powerful business interests both in the legislative process and in the course of bargaining between the social partners. However, although a number of initiatives targeted at reducing unemployment through work time reductions have been put to the people in recent years, all have been heavily defeated (see Table 9.1).

This demonstrates how difficult it is to pass initiatives without the full support of the various political interests in Swiss society, especially those of the business sector, and illustrates the continuing necessity of consensus building if policy reform is to succeed. It also shows the prevailing support for market mechanisms and management decision-making, as opposed to state legislated workplace intervention. In the most recent initiative, 84 per cent of those who voted against the reduction in working time initiative believed that 'increases in the costs of production' was an important reason for voting no, and 82 per cent of those who voted no also believed that the issue was better resolved at the sectoral or firm level (Vox 1989).

OUTLOOK

Given that consensus between the political parties and between the social partners seems necessary for a more activist labour market policy to succeed, a short review of the labour market policy positions of the most important of these actors would seem appropriate. Agreement appears to exist, at least for some measures, such as continued education and retraining, although not in areas which appear to be particularly innovative. For more radical measures, there is very little agreement.[3]

Positions on the role of the state in using fiscal and monetary policy to relieve unemployment bifurcate politically along the left-right axis. Employers and parties of the right tend to support the status quo, that is, little intervention, while Swiss trade unions, as well as the Social Demo-

Table 9.2 Recent Swiss initiatives on reducing working time

Date	Initiative	% voting yes
2 February 1976	Limited reductions in retirement age to 60	21%
2 December 1976	Reduction in working week to 40 hours	22%
10 March 1985	Longer vacations	35%
12 June 1987	Limited reduction in retirement age to 60	35%
4 December 1988	Reduction in working week to 40 hours	34%

Source: Vox 1989

cratic Party, have renewed their call for anticyclical stimulus of the economy For the Swiss Trade Union Federation (SGB) and the Social Democrats, this means encouragement of investment through measures such as investment bonuses for communities and promotion of housing construction, as well as assistance in technology development and venture capital subsidies. For the confessional CNG, budget deficits and employment programmes should be used, if needed, to stimulate the economy during a recession; both unions and the Social Democrats agree that the national bank should pursue the goal of full employment as well as monetary stability.

Employers and parties of the right, on the other hand, have tended to support more conservative, pro-business approaches. Their position is articulated well in a recent report of the Commission for Economic Issues, an expert committee of professors, business and trade union representatives, and policymakers (Kommission für Konjunkturfrage 1992), which argues that employment in the future will depend mostly on supply-side, structural economic conditions that are best facilitated by the encouragement of competition, selective deregulation, tax cuts, greater labour market flexibility and the elimination of various work restrictions on industry. Fiscal intervention through state employment programmes, they argue, should be rejected. The Swiss employers association argues that in addition to these measures, Swiss competitiveness should be encouraged both by restructuring and technological adjustment and by fiscal relief for firms, as well as by wage reductions if necessary.

With regard to conventional, active labour market measures, there is some consensus among trade unions and parties of both left and right that education and retraining should be strongly encouraged in the fight against unemployment, although whether or not current programmes should be expanded is a matter of debate.

For more radical unemployment measures, there is less agreement. The trade unions and Social Democrats are in favour of work time shortening as an important measure against unemployment. For the SGB this means that the average weekly work time should be reduced progressively from 40 to 38, 36, and finally 34 hours (30 hours for the CNG). In addition, earlier retirement and pension availability should be available, for men at age 62 and women at 59 years. To encourage further shortening of work times, the SGB argues that overtime work should be penalised by doubling contributions to unemployment insurance. However all major parties of the right have come out against work time shortening as a means of reducing unemployment, although the employer's federation is less negative, arguing that work time shortening could be taken into consideration as long as it was cost-neutral for firms.

Conclusion

Given the degree of consensus necessary for policy reform to succeed, the outlook for radical innovation in Swiss labour market policy seems quite limited. There is some agreement that education and retraining should be facilitated and labour mobility encouraged, but measures in these areas are already in place. Foreign worker policy and short-time work are still politically viable, but as discussed above, they are much less effective than before. Significant work time reductions or job-sharing provisions that are initiated at the legislative level would almost certainly be vetoed by business interests, and initiatives to do so at the electoral level, via initiatives, have proven to be unsuccessful in the past. On the other hand, proposals for radical deregulation, wage reductions, or unemployment insurance cutbacks would almost surely be vetoed by the trade unions. Given that by 1995 the unemployment rate was falling again with the recovery of GDP, and the fact that Switzerland still has one of the lowest levels of unemployment in the OECD, the status quo in labour market policy is likely to prevail into the foreseeable future.

NOTES

1 The most comprehensive resource on Swiss trade unions, from which the statistics in the text of this chapter were taken, is Fluder *et al.* (1991). In English see Hotz-Hart (1992).
2 See OECD 1986, 1993 for general overviews of Swiss unemployment policy.
3 Discussion of the positions of the social partners and political parties can be found in Schaad and Schellenbauer (1994), from which this review is largely taken, except where indicated by other sources.

REFERENCES

Blaas, Wolfgang (1992) 'The Swiss model: corporatism or liberal capitalism?' in Pekkarinen *et al.* (eds), *Social Corporatism: A Superior Economic System?*, Oxford: Clarendon Press.

Compston, Hugh (1994) 'Union participation in economic policy-making in Austria, Switzerland, The Netherlands, Belgium and Ireland, 1970–1992', *West European Politics*, 17 (1):123–45.

Danthine, J.P., and Lambelet, J. C. (1987) 'The Swiss recipe: conservative policies ain't enough', *Economic Policy*, 5:149–79.

Die Volkwirtschaft, various issues.

Flechsenhar, Hans Rolf (1978) 'Kurzarbeit – Kosten und Finanzierung', *Mitteilungen aus der Arbeitsmarkt- und Berufsforschung*, 11(4):443–56.

Fluder *et al.* (1991) *Gewerkschaften und Angestelltenverbände in der schweizerischen Privatwirtschaft*, Zurich: Seismo.

Garrett, Geoffrey (1995) 'Capital mobility, trade, and the domestic politics of economic policy', *International Organization*, 49(4):657–87.

Grossen, G. (1994) 'Arbeitsmarktpolitik in der Schweiz', *Die Volkswirtschaft*, 1/94.

Hall, Peter (1994) 'The comparative political economy of Europe in an era of interdependence', paper prepared for presentation to the conference, *Politics and Political Economy of Contemporary Capitalism*, Berlin, May 26–7 1995.

Hotz-Hart, Beat (1992) 'Switzerland: still as smooth as clockwork?', in Anthony Ferner and Richard Hyman (eds) *Industrial Relations in the New Europe*, Oxford: Basil Blackwell.

Immergut, Ellen (1992) *The Political Construction of Interests: National Health Insurance Politics in Switzerland, France and Sweden, 1930–1970*, New York: Cambridge University Press.

Katzenstein, Peter J. (1984) *Corporatism and Change: Austria, Switzerland, and the Politics of Industry*, Ithaca, New York: Cornell University Press.

Kommission für Konjunkturfragen (1992) 'Die Wirtschaftslage', *Die Volkwirtschaft* 9(92).

Korpi, Walter (1989) 'Political and economic explanations for unemployment: a cross-national and long-term analysis', *British Journal of Policy Studies*, 21: 315–48.

OECD (1994a) *Economic Outlook*, Paris.

—— (1986, 1993, 1994b) *Economic Survey of Switzerland*, Paris.

—— (1994c) *Employment Outlook*, Paris.

Schaad, Jakob and Schellenbauer, Patrik (1994) 'Beschäftigung and Arbeitszeiten. Ökonomische Aspekte', in Ruh, Hans *et al.* (eds) *Arbeitszeit and Arbeitslosigkeit. Zure Diskussion der Beschäftigungspolitik in der Schweiz*, Zürich: Verlag der Fachvereine.

Schmid, Hans *et al.* (1993) *Vollbeschäftigungspolitik: Der Wille zum Erfolg*, Bern: Verlag Paul Haupt.

Schmidt, Manfred G. (1985) *Der schweizer Weg zure Vollbeschäftigung: eine Bilanz der Beschäftigund, der Arbeitslosigkeit and der Arbeitsmarktpolitik*, Frankfurt: Campus Verlag.

—— (1995) 'Vollbeschäftigung und Arbeitslosigkeit in der Schweiz. Vom Sonderweg zum Normalfall', *Politische Vierteljahresschrift*, 36 (1):35–48.

Schweizerische Bankgesellschaft (1987) (ed.), *Die Schweizer Wirtschaft 1946–1986: Daten, Fakten, Analysen*, Zürich.

Vox Analysen Eidgenössischer Urnengänge (1989) 35 (13):23.

10 Comparisons and conclusions

Hugh Compston

INTRODUCTION

This book is predicated on the view that as current policies to control unemployment appear to have failed, new ones need to be tried. For such policies to work, they need to be politically feasible as well as economically sound. Our investigation into the political dynamics of radical unemployment policies is designed to improve our understanding of the political opportunities and barriers that exist in the area of unemployment policy innovation.

This means a perspective in which economic considerations are just one factor among many that influence political decisions on whether to adopt new unemployment policies. That is, the political and economic questions are analytically distinct, and one must admit both the possibility of governments implementing economically foolish policies as well as the possibility of economically realistic policies being rejected for political reasons. We take the view that there is room for a study of the political feasibility of radical unemployment policies that does not subordinate itself to previously determined judgements concerning the economic efficacy of these policies. This economic question can be debated elsewhere: as political scientists we are interested in a purely political perspective that disregards economic arguments except insofar as they are at the same time political factors that influence governmental decisions about whether to adopt new unemployment policies.

The purpose of this final chapter is to draw together the findings of the nine case studies that comprise the bulk of this book in order to present some summary results and conclusions concerning, first, the range and nature of radical unemployment policies in Western Europe today; second, the political dynamics of radical unemployment policies in general and of work-sharing in particular, this being the policy selected to be analysed in depth by all contributors; and, finally, the conditions that facilitate the acceptance of radical unemployment policies, once again concentrating on work-sharing.

RADICAL UNEMPLOYMENT POLICIES IN WESTERN EUROPE

Table 10.1 sets out the radical unemployment policies identified by the authors of the case studies on the basis of the definition set out in the Introduction, which is that radical unemployment policies are those that are (a) plausibly asserted by proponents as being capable of significantly reducing unemployment and (b) either qualitatively innovative and new in the 1990s at the national level or outside the mainstream of West European economic policy as defined by the economic policy agreed at EU level by all member states at the end of 1992. This definition includes not only policies that were accepted or implemented during the early 1990s, but also policies that were not accepted but were nevertheless on the political agenda and being discussed. The list of policies set out in Table 10.1 is not exhaustive, since only eight countries and the EU are covered and it is not certain that all radical policies from all cases are included, but it does cover most of the major radical unemployment policies and policy proposals current during the early 1990s, and it is fairly comprehensive in regard to work-sharing.

As indicated in the Table, the three most common types of radical unemployment policies current in Western Europe during the early 1990s were deregulation, concertation and work-sharing.

Deregulation

Although to some extent deregulation is already part of mainstream economic policy, it remains radical insofar as it is extended into new areas; it is thus particularly important in countries where labour markets have hitherto been heavily regulated, such as Spain. The four forms of deregulation most often identified as unemployment policies were relaxation of hiring and dismissals regulations, introduction of more flexible working time, wage reductions, and reduction of statutory charges on labour.

The rationale for relaxing restrictions on who employers can hire (Italy) is that employers will be more likely to take on new employees if they themselves can choose them. Similarly, the perceived advantage of making it easier for employers to dismiss employees (Italy and Spain) is that employers will be quicker to hire people if they know that they can get rid of them if necessary. In general, relaxation of dismissals regulations is a policy supported by employers but opposed by trade unions, since it implies reduced job security for their members.

The idea behind introducing more flexible working time (Germany) is to reduce labour costs by reducing or eliminating overtime payments, and to adapt working time more closely to the requirements of production processes and to fluctuations in demand. Employers, not surprisingly, support it, while unions tend to be opposed.

Reducing wages also cuts labour costs, and is correspondingly supported by employers and opposed by unions. The main radical policies in this

Table 10.1 Radical unemployment policies in Western Europe, 1990–1995

Strategy	Measure	Country
Deregulation	Relaxation of hiring and firing regulations	Italy, Spain
	More flexible working time	Germany
	Reduced wages	(France), Britain, Spain, (Norway)
	Lower statutory charges on labour	EU, France, Britain, Spain
Concertation	Europe-wide concertation	(EU)
	National concertation	Italy, (Spain), Norway
	Local concertation	EU, Germany
Work-sharing	National/industry level	(EU), Germany, (France), (Spain), (Norway)
	Part-time work	Germany, France, Italy, Britain, Spain
	Short-time working	Germany, Italy, Switzerland
	Solidarity contracts	Germany, France, Italy
	Paid leave arrangements	Denmark, Norway
	Overtime restrictions	(France), Spain
Other	Public investment	EU, (Denmark)
	Employer subsidies	Germany, Italy, Britain, Spain
	Reductions in unemployment benefit	(France), Spain, (Denmark)
	Contract labour	Germany
	Employment companies	Germany, (France)
	New areas of work/personal services	EU, France
	Social plans	France
	Job quotas	(France)
	Levy on intensified productivity	(France)
	Foreign worker policy	Switzerland
	Repatriation of immigrants	(France)
	Public sector solution	(Norway)
	Institutional reform	(Germany), Italy, Spain
	Citizens' Income	(Denmark)

Note: Proposals only in parentheses. List is indicative rather than exhaustive. Some policies are not new, just unusual.

regard were the abolition of wages councils and their power to determine minimum levels of pay in Britain, and the introduction of lower apprenticeship wages in Spain.

The rationale of cutting statutory charges on labour is that this enables employers to hire more people by reducing unit labour costs. For this reason employers are generally in favour, while unions this time are relatively unperturbed, since the cost falls upon government. This policy,

focusing on low-paid workers in particular, is now an important component of the EU's economic strategy, but since no agreement has been
reached on the establishment of European-wide taxes to make up the
foregone revenue, implementation has been left to the discretion of
national governments who, in the context of large existing budget deficits,
have not all been quick to act. Nevertheless, social security contributions
have been cut for low-paid workers in France, apprentices in Spain, and
new employees from the ranks of the long-term unemployed in Britain.

Concertation

Concertation in this context means cooperation between government,
employers and trade unions at EU, national and/or local levels in designing
strategies to reduce unemployment. This is not new as such at the macro-
level, being well-established in Denmark and Norway, for example, and,
in a weak consultative form, at the EU level in the form of the Economic
and Social Council, Standing Committee on Employment, and Social
Dialogue, but during the early 1990s there were a number of new moves
in this direction.

At the EU level, the European Commission and European Parliament,
along with certain member states such as Belgium, proposed a Europe-
wide Social Pact in order to coordinate action to combat unemployment,
but the opposition of employers and of some member states ensured that
this idea made no progress whatsoever. Furthermore, it is far from clear
that either trade unions or employers have the institutional capability at
the European level to serve as reliable interlocutors for the Commission
and/or Council.

At the national level there were major tripartite agreements in Italy
and Norway in 1993, both of which included agreements on action to
reduce unemployment, but in Spain efforts to revive the national concertation of the 1980s failed.

The main new policies relating to local concertation were the European
Commission's initiative to create jobs in new areas of work, based on local
networks, and a number of recent initiatives in Germany, especially in the
East.

A major factor impeding the development of concertation as a strategy
to control unemployment is its fragility: in depending upon the cooperation of governments, business and trade unions it is vulnerable to any of
these participants withdrawing or adopting intransigent positions that are
unacceptable to other parties.

Work-sharing

Although most forms of work-sharing fall outside current economic orthodoxy, working time per employee has nevertheless been falling steadily

over time. Between 1983 and 1992 average working hours per week in the European Union fell by 4 per cent, or between 1 and 2 hours per week, due mainly to the shift in employment from agriculture and industry to services (CEC 1994a:104). Norway provides an especially graphic illustration of this tendency: in 1994 the total number of hours worked was virtually the same as in 1972, but 20 per cent more people were employed (see chapter 8).

Five main categories of work-sharing policies can be distinguished: reductions in working time at national or industry level, part-time work, reductions in working time at firm level, paid leave arrangements, and overtime restrictions.

Since 1992 there has been little progress in the area of working time reductions at national or industry level. At the EU level, Ecofin firmly rejected the Commission's proposal for governments to provide incentives and flanking measures to encourage employers and employees to agree on working time reduction. In Germany, a phased reduction of working hours in the metal industry, based on an agreement some years ago, is still taking place, but there are few signs of further progress in this direction. In France, Spain and Norway a number of proposals for a shorter working week have been discussed, but none have been implemented.

The idea of part-time work is hardly radical in itself, but in Germany and Spain, where part-time work has not been common, moves to encourage it do represent a definite break with the past. In Germany there have been a number of recent proposals to extend this form of work, for example via 'working corridors' in which hours vary, rolling four-day weeks in which five employees share four jobs, and flexible working time over a lifetime. The 1993 reform package in Spain encouraged part-time work by reducing employers' social contributions (and thus employees' social protection) and by making it possible to conclude part-time contracts on a fixed-term or indefinite basis. In Britain, where the incidence of part-time work is much higher, the recent non-government Borrie Commission proposed to encourage it further by introducing a part-time benefit, and in France and Italy previous moves to encourage part-time work were extended.

Reductions in working time at firm level can be divided into two types: short-time working, and solidarity contracts.

In short-time working, involuntary reductions in working hours are treated by the state as partial unemployment, so that the employees affected are compensated via partial unemployment benefits. The advantages of short-time work are that the employee keeps his or her job, skills and work habits are retained, the employer saves the costs of dismissal and (possible) rehiring, and state authorities spend less money than if the person affected was completely unemployed. Short-time working is a radical policy only in the sense that it is outside the West European mainstream, as in both the countries in which it is significant, Switzerland and

Germany, it has been established for many years. It is particularly important in Switzerland, where short-time work is calculated to have kept unemployment 0.3 percentage points lower than it would otherwise have been (for 1975, the peak year for short-term work, the reduction was approximately 0.8 percentage points). In Italy the long-standing Cig scheme can be considered to be a functional equivalent of short-time work.

Solidarity agreements are collective agreements that provide for temporary shorter working time for existing employees, in order either to save jobs (the great majority) or to create new ones. In Italy (FIAT) and France, such agreements are encouraged by legislation providing financial incentives for such schemes to be introduced; for instance schemes allowing older workers to take early retirement provided their places are filled by young unemployed workers (France). Only in Germany (VW and the metal industry) was temporary work-sharing implemented without the benefit of such legislation. To some extent temporary work-sharing in Norway can also be classified in this category, although this took place in the public sector rather than the private sector (Oslo City Council).

Work-sharing can also take the form of paid leave arrangements, which enable employees to take leave for defined purposes, for which they are paid by the government, in order to open up temporary jobs for the unemployed. Although there is an education leave scheme in place in Norway for municipal employees, large-scale paid leave arrangements are restricted to Denmark, where they take three forms: education leave, childminding leave, and sabbatical leave. Employees have a right to childminding leave, but must secure the employer's agreement to take education or sabbatical leave. Payments for childminding and sabbatical leave are 70 per cent of unemployment benefit, which means that if the employer hires an unemployed person to take the employee's place, the government generally saves money. Substitution rates are about 50 per cent for education and childminding leave, and 100 per cent (mandatory) for sabbatical leave. All three forms of leave have proved popular, and unemployment is estimated to have been reduced by over 1 per cent of the workforce as a consequence.

Finally, in 1993 the Spanish government moved to make overtime less attractive to employees by removing the legal obligation on employers to pay premium rates, on the rationale that this might open up new jobs for the unemployed. Proposals to restrict overtime in France, however, have not been implemented.

This exhausts the main recent initiatives in regard to work-sharing, but it should be noted that in countries such as France the debate, encouraged by authors such as Guy Aznar (1993), has gone further to encompass a wide variety of possibilities. However, to date these have remained very much on the drawing board.

Radical unemployment policies outside the categories of deregulation, concertation and work-sharing can be divided into old policies transplanted to new countries (public investment at the EU level, employer subsidies in Germany, Britain and Spain; contract labour in Germany, and cuts in unemployment benefit in Spain); old policies that are unusual when compared with other countries (foreign worker policy in Switzerland); populist reactions to high unemployment (repatriation of immigrants in France); discarded policies revisited (public sector solution in Norway); and real innovations (institutional reform in Germany and Italy, citizens' income in Denmark, employment and training companies in Germany, new areas of work at the EU level and in France, and social plans and job quotas in France).

POLITICAL DYNAMICS

The national case studies reveal two types of unemployment policy arena: collective bargaining, involving employers and trade unions at the national, regional, sectoral or firm level, with occasional government participation; and regulation, mainly at the national level, involving the legislature for laws, authorised ministers and officials for regulations and the framing of bills, and employers and unions in either a consultative or deliberative capacity. The other main state institutions involved in unemployment policymaking are labour ministries and related agencies, social insurance agencies, finance ministries, and regional and local government. The unemployed themselves are not represented.

Given this, the policy analysis literature suggests a rather large number of factors that, singly or in combination, might influence the political fate of radical unemployment policies.

Consistency with individual self-interest is one factor. There are also institutional factors such as organisational self-interest, for example the interest of governments in re-election; organisational norms, such as the attachment of finance ministries to rigorous financial control; the nature of the organisation of the labour market, for instance whether union movements are institutionally divided; the nature of relations between labour market actors, for example whether they are conflictual or cooperative; institutional capability, for example the capacity of trade union confederations to deliver the cooperation of their constituents; and the relative power of institutions on the labour market, demonstrated by the balance of power between employers and trade unions.[1] Incrementalists argue that the nature of the policies already in place will limit the search for new policies to those that are fairly similar (Lindblom 1959, 1979). Other possible influences include policy style (Richardson 1982), and, related to this, the degree of openness of the policymaking process (Kitschelt 1986). The informal organisation of policymaking may also be important, for example the structure of epistemic communities (Haas 1992) or advocacy coalitions (Sabatier 1987).

Economic reality also plays a role. When unemployment is high, radical policies may become more acceptable as *status quo* policies are seen to fail, especially if fiscal problems result. Other economic factors, such as the degree of openness to the rest of the world, may constrain the choice of alternative policies (Katzenstein 1985).

On the level of ideas, beliefs about the nature of causal relationships in the economy are obviously relevant: if policymakers do not believe that a policy will work, they are less likely to adopt it, other things being equal. Also relevant are differences in the value placed on various economic means and ends, which may stem from ideological differences, such as the arguably greater concern of the left about unemployment (Hibbs 1977), or general national cultural characteristics, such as attitudes to state intervention in collective bargaining (Castles 1993).

Finally, the fate of radical unemployment policies is likely to depend at least in part on the precise details of their design, such as cost.

Although it is impossible systematically to test all these possibilities, due to lack of relevant data in some cases and lack of cross-national variation in others, comparison of the findings of the case studies, plus utilisation of causal sequences identified in them, do enable two major types of theoretical explanations to be considered as a start. These theories are examined not only with a view to testing how far they can explain the different fates of various types of radical unemployment policy – bearing in mind the possibility of overdetermination – but also with the intention of identifying what other types of factors might serve to fill gaps left by any explanatory failures. This by no means yields a complete picture of the political dynamics of radical unemployment policies, but it does enable a provisional outline to be sketched.

The explanations to be considered are, first, institutional self-interest, especially the interests of employers and trade unions; and, second, economic beliefs and values, with particular reference to ideological differences between left and right.

Institutional self-interest

Although ultimately decisions about policy are attributable to the acts of specific individuals, and so may be influenced by individual idiosyncracies, in general over time these idiosyncracies arguably cancel each other out, so that decisions can be explained in terms of institutional preferences, as if the institution itself were a conscious actor. Thus the idea here is that institutional policy actors have certain perceived interests, such as survival and power. If a radical unemployment policy furthers these interests, the institution concerned will tend to support it; if, on the other hand, it threatens these interests in some way, the institution will tend to oppose it. This type of explanation is used extensively in the case studies, in particular in relation to the interests and relative power of state organisations, employers and trade unions. In this section I investigate it further by using a comparative research design to examine the extent to which the nature of radical unemployment policies adopted can be explained by the different interests and relative power of employers and trade unions.

To survive and prosper in the market, private employers need to make profits, and for this maximum control over labour costs and working practices is desirable in order to maximise competitiveness. This means that employers would be expected to support unemployment policies that reduce labour costs or increase their power in the workplace, but to resist unemployment policies that raise labour costs or interfere with their control of the workplace.

For their part, the survival and power of trade unions – or, rather, of their leaders – depends largely upon (a) the continued support of their members, and (b) maximising the number of members. The first factor implies that the incentive for union leaders is to put the interests of present members first; the second implies an interest in attracting new members either among current employees or among new employees. These concerns logically give union leaders an interest in reducing unemployment insofar as it threatens employed members. In addition, higher levels of employment yield the possibility of new members. If there is a clash between the interests of union members and the unemployed, however, union leaders insofar as they are self-interested must prefer the interests of present members, because it is they who vote in union elections. This means that unions would be expected to support radical unemployment policies only as long as as they do not threaten members' pay or working conditions.

After a systematic comparative analysis of deregulation, part-time work, and firm-level work-sharing in the form of solidarity agreements, the section concludes with some more tentative observations on other ways in which institutional self-interest animates the political dynamics of radical unemployment policies.

Deregulation

The observed support of employers for those forms of deregulation identified earlier as unemployment policies, namely relaxing regulations concerning dismissals and the organisation of working time, and/or reducing statutory charges on labour, can be explained by the reduced labour costs and/or greater power over employment conditions that these measures involve. Conversely, it is not surprising that unions oppose measures that make it easier for employers to dismiss union members, or which eliminate overtime payments and/or oblige employees to work unsocial hours.

This implies that deregulatory moves will be most prevalent where unions are weakest. Figure 10.1 tests this proposition by setting out high and low deregulation countries according to how strong the union movement was during the early 1990s. As union power cannot be measured directly, union participation in economic policymaking is used as a proxy,

Deregulation initiative?	Yes	Germany France Britain Spain	Italy
	No		Denmark Norway Switzerland
		Low	High

Union participation in economic policymaking

Figure 10.1 Deregulation initiatives and union strength

on the grounds that this is more closely correlated with the political power of trade unions than other possible proxies, such as union density. Union participation in economic policymaking is quantified on the basis that it is greater when unions are consulted than when they are ignored, and greater still when agreements are reached that involve government commitments to follow particular union-preferred economic policies. In addition, within each of these categories of agreement and consultation, participation is considered to be greater when there are consultations/ agreements on a wide range of economic issues than when the subject matter is restricted. Resultant ten-point Union Participation Index scores have been worked out for all the countries covered by the present study with the exception of Spain (Compston 1994, 1995a, 1995b). The scores used are national averages for the years 1990–93 inclusive, and suggest that Norway (9), Switzerland (8), Italy (7) and Denmark (6) have more politically powerful union movements than Germany (5), France (3) and Britain (1). On the basis of chapter 6 in this book, Spain is also considered to be a country with a politically weak union movement.

It can be seen that the evidence presented in Figure 10.1 supports the view that deregulation is strongest where unions are weakest. Only Italy is an exception to the pattern.

Part-time work

Self-interest can explain why part-time work is the only form of shorter working time generally supported by employers, as it generally means lower labour costs and increased flexibility in the deployment of employees. Trade unions, on the other hand, tend to oppose expansion of part-time work because they see it as a second-rate alternative to full-time

Intiatives to encourage part-time work?	Yes	Germany France Britain Spain	Italy
	No		Denmark Norway Switzerland

Low   High

Union participation in economic policymaking

Figure 10.2 Part-time work initiatives and union strength

work due to its lower status, lower pay, often inferior working conditions, and, in many cases, weaker legal and social protection. In other words, the political logic of part-time work is the same as for deregulation, which tended to take place in the same countries, although moves to encourage part-time work are not necessarily deregulatory in nature.

The view that initiatives to extend part-time work will therefore be correlated with union weakness is supported by the almost perfect fit revealed in Figure 10.2.

Solidarity agreements

Temporary shorter working time in the form of solidarity agreements is generally considered to be a second-best solution by employers and unions alike, but acceptable as a compromise when (a) the alternative is dismissals, (b) union resistance to dismissals is strong, and (c) in most cases, governments step in to help. The sequence of events in the case of solidarity agreements (Germany, France and Italy) is generally this: (1) a firm gets into trouble and proposes dismissals; (2) the relevant union objects; (3) work-sharing is proposed as an alternative to dismissals, generally by the union; and (4) agreement is reached due either to explicit government intervention or to the firm judging that the costs of dismissals (such as redundancy pay and industrial action by the remaining employees) are higher than the costs of work-sharing. (Norway is not included here because its functional equivalent to solidarity agreements occurs in the public sector.)

In short, employer and union acceptance of temporary work-sharing can be explained in terms of self-interest as a means of enabling each side to avoid an even greater evil than they consider work-sharing to be: dismissals in the case of unions; industrial strife and/or greater financial

Solidarity agreements?	Yes	Germany France	Italy
	No	Britain Spain	Denmark Norway Switzerland
		Low	High

Union participation in economic policymaking

Figure 10.3 Private sector solidarity agreements and union strength

costs in the case of employers. Self-interest also explains why government intervention facilitates agreements on shorter working time, as such intervention alters the balance of costs and benefits to employers and unions by means of financial incentives such as wage subsidies and tax breaks. Finally, self-interest explains why agreements that save jobs are far more numerous than those that create jobs: employees of the company are represented in negotiations with management, but potential new employees are not.

Given that both employers and unions see work-sharing at the firm level as a second-best solution, we would not expect any marked correlation between union strength and firm-level work-sharing. The evidence in Figure 10.3 supports this view.

So why are there solidarity agreements in some countries but not others? Given that these agreements are the result of compromise, one discriminating factor might be how easy or difficult it is for employers and unions to reach compromises in collective bargaining in general. One indicator of this is industrial action. Accordingly, one might expect that solidarity agreements would be more prevalent in countries with low industrial conflict. In order to test this proposition, the eight countries were grouped into three categories on the basis of (a) working days lost and (b) the number of workers involved in industrial action, adjusted by population (ILO 1994). Figure 10.4 sets out the results of cross-tabulating this with the existence of solidarity agreements.

Clearly propensity to compromise as indicated by industrial action does not explain the existence or non-existence of solidarity agreements.

However there is another way to approach this, namely to use the existence of Catholic-based trades unions as an indicator of propensity to compromise, on the rationale that Catholic social doctrine, as distinct from the socialist ideology of many other trade unions, favours class harmony rather than class conflict. Given this, we would expect that solidarity agreements would be more prevalent in countries that have significant

Solidarity agreements?	Yes		Germany France	Italy
	No	Switzerland	Britain Denmark Norway	Spain
		Low	Medium	High

Industrial conflict 1988–93

Figure 10.4 Solidarity agreements and industrial action

separate Catholic-based union confederations, namely France (CFDT), Italy (CISL) and Switzerland (CNG). Figure 10.5 provides considerable support for this proposition.

Other modalities of self-interest

Although lack of information prevents systematic comparative analysis of other hypotheses based on self-interest, a number of observations can nevertheless be made.

The first is a negative point: interpreting the lack of successful moves to cut the working week without loss of pay in terms of a perceived decline in union strength may be a mistake, as the indicator of union strength, the Union Participation Index, was not in general lower in the early 1990s than in the 1980s, when a number of such working week reductions did take place in countries such as Germany, Denmark and Norway (Compston 1994, 1995a, 1995b).

On the other hand, the Danish case study suggests that the success of paid leave arrangements can be largely explained by the imperatives of individual and institutional self-interest: employees benefit from the opportunity to take paid leave for education, childminding or other defined purposes; employer opposition to education and sabbatical leave is defused by their being able to choose whether to allow employees to go on leave; and the popularity of the paid leave arrangements means perceived electoral advantages for political parties that support them.

From the point of view of electoral self-interest more generally, high or rising unemployment might be expected to stimulate governments to try new policies, as existing policies are seen to fail, but unemployment is not the only determinant of electoral success, and measures to reduce unemployment may conflict with the achievement of other electorally-important objectives, such as price stability. For this reason it is not surprising that

Solidarity agreements?	Yes	Germany	France Italy
	No	Britain Spain Denmark Norway	Switzerland
		No	Yes

Separate Catholic-based confederation?

Figure 10.5 Solidarity agreements and Catholic trade union confederations

the case studies do not reveal any clear and simple relationship between levels of unemployment and the extent of policy innovation; certainly high unemployment alone is no guarantee of policy innovation, as the Spanish example demonstrates. On the other hand, in some circumstances radical unemployment policies can be used by political parties in electoral warfare. In Denmark, for example, paid leave arrangements were successfully promoted as 'the big reform' by the Social Democrats during the 1994 election campaign.

There is also some evidence that financial self-interest can influence attitudes to radical unemployment policies. In Germany, for example, the support of local government for labour promotion and training companies appears to have been at least partly motivated by the knowledge that after a company is terminated at the end of its natural life, participants who are still unable to get a job become eligible for unemployment benefits paid by the Federal Labour Office, rather than falling back on social assistance, which has to be paid by local government. Bureaucratic self-interest in the form of a concern for institutional autonomy may also affect institutional reactions to radical unemployment policies: the lack of enthusiasm of the German Federal Labour Office for labour promotion and training companies appears to stem at least partly from the fact that they infringe its autonomy by bringing other policy actors into programme formulation and administration.

For the present, these suggestions must remain tentative, as it has not been possible to subject them to systematic comparative analysis. The main findings of the comparative analysis of the role of self-interest in explaining the political dynamics of radical unemployment policies are that initiatives on deregulation and part-time work are associated with union weakness, while firm-level solidarity agreements are associated with the existence of separate Catholic-based trade union confederations.

Economic beliefs and values

As well as being influenced by self-interest, there can be little doubt that policymakers' responses to radical unemployment policies are also influenced by their factual beliefs about the way the economy works and the relative value they place on different policy objectives. However it is not clear to what extent these beliefs are important. Perceived economic efficacy is not necessarily an essential precondition for a policy to be accepted, because there is always the possibility that the policy will be adopted for other reasons. Policymakers might judge education leave as being ineffective in reducing unemployment, for example, but still adopt it as a training measure, because it was a campaign promise, or simply because they want to be seen to be doing something. Conversely, economically rational policies may be blocked, for example by vested interests, ideological concerns or electoral expediency.

It would take us too far afield to examine all the intellectual arguments relating to the efficacy in relation to unemployment of all the radical unemployment policies identified by the case studies, but it seems clear that although all have some economic plausibility – this being a criterion of selection – the degree of economic respectability of these policies varies. For instance, there appears to be wide although not universal agreement among economists that deregulation, including the increased use of part-time workers, is compatible with good economic management, and that resistance to deregulation is in many cases attributable to the vested interests of employees rather than to economic counter-arguments. Concertation, on the other hand, has significantly less support, although this varies by country: in Norway, for instance, it is considered economically efficient, but in Britain it is seen as misguided. Support among economists for work-sharing (apart from part-time work) appears to be weaker still.

The economic rationale for work-sharing is that if there is not enough work to go around, then unemployment will be lower if the available work is shared out among more people. This is an immediately appealing idea in its logic and simplicity, but professional economists are often unimpressed.

First, it is argued that cutting working time without also cutting wages means higher costs for employers and therefore reduced competitiveness and, ultimately, higher unemployment again – a vicious circle. For this reason economists tend to agree that if working time is to be cut, wages should be cut too.

Even if cuts in working hours are accompanied by proportionate wage cuts, however, employers' labour costs may still rise. The Confederation of British Industry, for example, argues that more people doing the same work means increased costs for recruitment and training, and would require additional equipment to produce the same output (*Financial Times* 19 November 1993:2). However there are countervailing tendencies as well: average productivity per hour tends to be higher for employees who work shorter hours, which implies improved competitiveness, and the problem of less efficient equipment utilisation can be solved by introducing more flexible working hours in order to extend equipment operating times (CEC 1994b:7; Bosch 1994:21, 12–19; CEC 1995:119–120).

A further economic objection is that the cost to the state of any measures to encourage work-sharing by offsetting the impact of concomitant wage cuts on living standards, such as wage subsidies or tax breaks, would increase budget deficits at a time when they are already high.

There is also the problem that it might not be possible to find enough skilled new employees to do the work no longer being done by those going on shorter time, which would mean that shorter hours would lead to production cuts and/or higher wages for workers in short supply (CEC 1993:9). However this argument does not preclude moves to encourage agreements on shorter hours in sectors where labour shortages are not a problem, or in the area of unskilled or semi-skilled work, and furthermore leaves open the possibility that work-sharing could be extended if the provision of training was improved.

This labour shortage objection is related to a more general economic argument centred on the idea that there is a certain rate of unemployment below which inflation tends to accelerate: the so-called Non-Accelerating Inflation Rate of Unemployment (NAIRU) (see, for example, Layard *et al.* 1991:502–8). This means that if the present rate of unemployment is at or below the NAIRU, job-sharing through shorter hours would be counter-productive because any resulting short-term reduction in unemployment would lead to higher inflation and thence to reduced competitiveness and/or restrictive economic measures, which would push unemployment back up to, or past, the NAIRU. The only difference would be that production would now be lower, because those still in work would be working shorter hours. Work-sharing, according to this perspective, is pointless, since it is the number of people doing the work, not the amount of work itself, that is the critical factor in determining the rate of unemployment.

Finally, there is the view that work-sharing does not really reduce unemployment at all but merely spreads it around. This is the reverse side of the rationale that work-sharing spreads employment more widely. According to this perspective, only increasing the total volume of work counts as real progress in reducing unemployment. Work-sharing can only complicate matters by threatening competitiveness, living standards and economic management in general, and should be rejected as a counsel of despair.

Given these different evaluations of the main types of radical unemployment policies, one would expect that deregulation, including part-time work, would be more successful in gaining official acceptance than concertation or work-sharing. However our findings do not provide any clearcut confirmation of this view: although there appear to have been relatively few initiatives relating to concertation, work-sharing schemes appear to have been about as successful in gaining official acceptance in our eight countries as moves to extend deregulation (see Table 10.1).

On the other hand, the case studies indicate that forms of work-sharing in which competitiveness considerations are taken into account, such as firm-level work-sharing (Germany, France, Italy and Switzerland) and paid leave arrangements (Denmark and, to a much lesser extent, Norway), are more acceptable than moves to cut working time without cutting wages, which were proposed but rejected not only at the national level (France, Spain, Norway) but also at the EU level. Only working time reductions already agreed continued to be implemented (Germany).

But economic arguments are not just about facts, they are also about values: the fact that a given policy would harm competitiveness may be a knock-down argument to a businessman, for example, but constitute just one consideration among others for a trade unionist. For this reason we would expect that the reception of radical unemployment policies would be influenced by differences in economic values. The most obvious source of these is the ideological divide between left and right. The possibility that the reception of radical unemployment policies is affected by whether the government is dominated by the left or by the right is now considered in relation to deregulation, work-sharing in general, part-time work, and work-sharing at the firm level.

Deregulation

Given the value placed by the right on economic freedom, moves to fight unemployment by deregulatory means would be expected to be more common in countries governed by the right (conservative, liberal and Christian democratic parties) than in those governed by the left (socialist, social democratic and labour parties). This view receives a certain amount of support from Figure 10.6, although these results are far from conclusive and do not explain the acceptance/rejection of deregulation as well as union strength does (see Figure 10.1).

Work-sharing in general

One of the main political values associated with the left is solidarity, the idea that people should stick together and help one another. This implies that left parties should be more supportive of work-sharing in general than right parties, although support for part-time work might be expected to be somewhat inhibited by the links of leftist parties with trade unions.

However the evidence from the case studies is mixed: while left parties were generally more favourable towards work-sharing in France and at the EU level, for example, they opposed work-sharing in Spain and

Deregulatory initiative?	Yes	Spain	Germany France from 1993 Britain Italy
	No	France to 1993 Denmark from 1993 Norway	Denmark to 1993 Switzerland

| | Left | Right |

Dominance in government

Figure 10.6 Deregulation and left/right governments

Norway, and right parties in France showed considerable interest in the idea at times. Furthermore, in Denmark the paid leave arrangements introduced by the Social Democratic government were developed and piloted by the previous conservative-led government. In short, there is no clear left/right divide on work-sharing in general.

Part-time work

Here one might expect that the right would be more favourable than the left, since part-time work does not increase employers' wage costs but employees are often disadvantaged by lower wages, less job security and poorer working conditions. However although Figure 10.7 suggests that

Part-time work initiative?	Yes	Spain	Germany France from 1993 Britain Italy
	No	France to 1993 Denmark from 1993 Norway	Denmark to 1993 Switzerland

| | Left | Right |

Dominance in government

Figure 10.7 Part-time work initiatives and left/right governments

Firm-level work-sharing	High	Norway	Germany France from 1993 Italy Switzerland
	Low	France to 1993 Spain Denmark from 1993	Britain Denmark to 1993

Left   Right

Dominance in government

Figure 10.8 Firm-level work-sharing and left/right governments

initiatives to extend part-time work are more common under right governments, this evidence is far from conclusive, and again union strength seems to be a more powerful explanatory factor (see Figure 10.2).

Work-sharing at firm level

One might expect that the value of solidarity associated with left parties would lead left governments to be more supportive than right governments of work-sharing at the firm level, defined as including both private sector solidarity agreements (Germany, France, Italy), their equivalent in the public sector (Norway), and short-time working (Germany, Switzerland). However Figure 10.8 suggests the opposite: work-sharing at firm level was more common under governments of the right. Restricting attention to private sector solidarity agreements, which would shift Norway and Switzerland vertically, does not change the overall picture.

However the findings in relation to self-interest suggest that there is also another possibility. Although private sector solidarity agreements were not found to be associated with union strength, there was a correlation with the existence of significant separate Catholic-based union confederations, the apparent explanation being that Catholic social ideology is more conducive to cooperation with employers than the more robust class conflict view often taken by socialist trade unions.

On this basis, we might expect that Christian democrat-dominated governments would favour firm-level work-sharing more than other forms of government. However the evidence from the case studies does not really support this view, and adding left governments to Christian democratic governments, on the grounds that both value solidarity, does not alter the picture (not tabulated).

		Yes	France Italy	Germany
Solidarity *agreements?*		No	Spain	Britain Denmark Norway Switzerland

	Yes	No

Predominantly Catholic population?

Figure 10.9 Solidarity agreements and Catholicism

A further possibility is that the critical factor is the general ideological ambience of Catholicism, rather than Catholic governments as such. To test this idea, Figure 10.9 cross-tabulates countries inside and outside the 'Catholic family of nations', as Castles (1994) puts it, against private sector solidarity agreements.

This reveals a similar association between solidarity agreements and Catholicism as that already identified between solidarity agreements and the existence of a significant separate Catholic trade union movement, the only difference being that Germany and Spain are exceptions, rather than Germany and Switzerland.

The political dynamics of radical unemployment policies

Before reviewing the results of the above analysis of the role of self-interest and economic beliefs and values, there are a couple of other possible explanations of the acceptance/rejection of radical unemployment policies that should be mentioned.

First, there is some evidence that work-sharing schemes may be more attractive to employees, and therefore to the government and other institutions, if they are perceived to be fair. In France, for example, a feeling that sacrifices are shared unequally appears to have eroded willingness to accept a wage cut in exchange for a general reduction in working hours, while in Denmark popular support for paid leave arrangements appears to have been linked to a view that the available work ought to be shared with the unemployed.

Second, the German case suggests that institutional flux is important in facilitating the acceptance of new policies: the experience of adapting West German political, bureaucratic and labour market institutions to the new eastern Länder suggests that when these institutions and/or the relations between them change, unemployment policies and programmes change too.

For the moment, further analysis must wait. Comparative analysis has already produced some interesting findings even though they are not conclusive, if only because the possibility of over-determination cannot be excluded at this stage.

First, the pattern of acceptance/rejection of deregulatory moves and initiatives to extend part-time work can be explained reasonably well in terms of the conflict of interests between employers and trade unions: employers were in favour, unions were opposed, and both types of policy innovation were more politically successful in countries in which trade unions were relatively weak. Only Italy was an exception.

Second, union strength was irrelevant to the extension of private sector solidarity agreements, in accordance with the prediction that this would be so because both sides of industry considered these to be a second-best solution to employment problems.

Third, the use of deregulation as an unemployment policy was somewhat more common under right governments than under left governments, although this correlation is fairly weak.

Fourth, contrary to expectations, the ideological divide between left and right did not appear to be related in any systematic way to attitudes to work-sharing in general, part-time work or work-sharing at firm level.

Finally, extension of solidarity agreements was associated with Catholicism, both in general and in the form of separate Catholic trade union confederations. Christian democratic governments, however, were irrelevant.

Given the short period under study and the small number of countries covered, it is important not to place too much reliance on our results just yet: they need to be extended to a larger number of countries over a longer period and to be supplemented with tests of other theoretical perspectives before anything like a definitive picture of the politics of radical unemployment policies can emerge. Nevertheless, the findings set out above do suggest that employer and union self-interest is more important in explaining the political dynamics of deregulation and work-sharing than ideological differences between left and right, and that the ideology that does seem to matter, at least in regard to solidarity agreements, is social Catholicism.

CONCLUSIONS

This study, the first of its type, is exploratory rather than definitive. Nevertheless, a number of tentative conclusions can be drawn concerning the conditions that facilitate official acceptance of work-sharing policies, its main policy focus. More specifically, there are four main conditions under which work-sharing, apart from part-time work, would become more likely to be accepted and/or extended: government activism; economic incentives; multiple purposes; and good fiscal fit.

Government activism

Our study found that, in general, reliance on collective bargaining alone produced only scattered instances of work-sharing. When governments take action, however, more gets done. For example, government intervention facilitates collective agreements on reduced working time, and in Denmark the initiative for paid leave arrangements came from the government and was supported both by legislation and an extensive public relations campaign. Only part-time work, which in most cases is imposed by employers, seems to be expanding as a 'natural' consequence of the market system. This implies that if work-sharing in forms other than part-time work is to become widespread, an active role for government is essential.

Economic incentives

As noted earlier, the principal source of contention between employees and employers in regard to work-sharing is whether any cut in working hours will be accompanied by a proportionate cut in wages: employers favour wage cuts, in order to avoid raising hourly labour costs and thus reducing competitiveness, but employees resist them, because they wish to maintain existing living standards. The result of this difference of opinion is generally a stand-off. If the state steps in to at least partly finance a solution by providing economic incentives to employers and/or employees, however, agreements become much easier to reach. Such incentives can be provided in a number of ways.

First, wage subsidies can be introduced to ensure that employees' living standards are largely or wholly maintained when wages as well as hours are cut. This is what happened at FIAT in Italy, for example, and it was critical in securing agreement. Similarly, partial unemployment benefits are paid by the state to workers on short time in Germany and Switzerland, and to those taking paid leave in Denmark.

A second possibility is for the government to cut employers' non-wage labour costs, for example their social security contributions. This means that employers can cut their total labour cost per employee when hours are cut, while at the same time ensuring that the employee receives much the same wages by giving him or her a greater share of the proportionately smaller gross wage. Cutting statutory charges on labour is official EU policy for the low-paid, but could equally well be used for employees on shorter hours. Furthermore, it could be financed by raising statutory charges on employers whose employees work comparatively long hours.

A third possibility is to cut the taxes and/or social security charges of employees. This would also mean that even if gross wages were lower, take-home pay could remain much the same. This was a feature of the Karlsen plan in Norway, at least for the low-paid.

Finally, employers can be persuaded to agree to shorter working time by making the alternative of dismissals costly by instituting – or retaining – high redundancy payments. This appears to have been one of the main reasons for the interest shown in work-sharing by the management of Volkswagen, for example.

Tailoring programmes to fulfil multiple purposes

Work-sharing schemes may be made more attractive to employees and employers if they also serve purposes apart from the solidaristic one of creating (or saving) jobs, as this increases the size of the support constituency for the proposal both within policymaking institutions and among employers and employees. The Danish paid leave arrangements furnish the best examples of such schemes: as well as reducing unemployment, education leave helps the employer by training his or her workforce, and helps the employee by improving chances of promotion and/or personal satisfaction, while the attraction of childminding leave for parents is obvious and sabbatical leave enables employees to have time off for purposes defined by themselves.

Another possibility is to incorporate into work-sharing schemes more flexible working hours, as recommended by Karlsen in Norway and Aznar in France. In this way employer opposition can be at least partly disarmed, although at the cost of some loss of attractiveness for employees.

Good fiscal fit

The major problem for the state in providing incentives for employees and/or employers to accept work-sharing is, of course, cost: wage subsidies cost money, and cuts in taxes and contributions reduce revenue. Therefore if the provision of financial incentives to employees and/or employers is to be fiscally sustainable, it needs to be at least partly financed by consequent savings elsewhere. The extent to which this is possible depends upon the nature of the fiscal interaction between the work-sharing scheme and other labour market and welfare state programmes: the fiscal fit.

If work-sharing really results in a reduction in unemployment, the cost of subsidising it should be at least partly offset by not having to pay out so much in unemployment benefits. For example, the acceptance of the Danish paid leave arrangements appears to be at least partly due to the fact that they are largely self-financing, as (a) the proportion of employees taking leave who are replaced by people previously unemployed is quite high – 100 per cent for sabbatical leave (for which a replacement is mandatory), and between 50 per cent and 60 per cent for education leave and childminding leave – and (b) only 80 per cent of unemployment benefit was paid to those taking childminding and sabbatical leave (1994 figures). Similarly, in Switzerland the payment of partial unemployment benefit to workers on short time is considered to be cost-effective compared to the alternative of dismissals and the consequent need to pay full unemployment benefit.

But fiscal fit is not just a question of how much schemes cost, all things taken into account, but is also a function of who pays. More specifically, if those with the power to introduce work-sharing do not have to pay for it, or do not have to pay much, they are more likely to adopt it. This implies that work-sharing programmes should be designed in such a way as to ensure that the most important institutions gain a fiscal benefit, or at least do not lose out too heavily. One way to do this is to provide for costs to be transferred onto institutions that cannot block the introduction of the scheme in question, such as semi-independent social security agencies, or levels of government other than the one with the formal power to introduce it.

Logically, the degree of fiscal fit of a policy is a function not only of its design, but also of the nature and power dynamics of the existing system of fiscal transfers in which the policy is, or would be, embedded: the welfare state. Because there are substantial differences between the structures of different national welfare states, policies with a good fiscal fit in one country may perform poorly in this respect in another: they need to be tailored for specific welfare states. For instance, policies designed to offset the effect on living standards of wage cuts due to cuts in working time via the payment of partial unemployment benefit are better accommodated by welfare states in which unemployment benefit levels are high, such as Denmark, than by welfare states in which benefit levels are low, such as Britain, since an adequate level of payment for recipients will save the state more money – or lose it less money – in the former case. This means that reform of other welfare state programmes may need to accompany the adoption of work-sharing policies.

The issue of fiscal fit is, from a political point of view, one of the most important issues that needs to be faced by policy entrepreneurs in designing work-sharing schemes. Both the white art of designing in offsetting savings elsewhere in the welfare state, and the black art of transferring costs onto politically weak institutions, need to be practised if one is serious about operating successfully in what the hard men of politics refer to as 'the real world'. A systematic investigation of the issue of fiscal fit is therefore an important item on the agenda of future research in this area.

We began this study with the premiss that present unemployment policies have failed, and that they need to be supplemented or replaced by new policies, unorthodox policies, radical policies. A number of such policies have been identified for a range of West European countries, and a start has been made in elucidating their political dynamics, using both historical and comparative methodologies. More needs to be done, but for work-sharing enough has been discovered to conclude, in summary, that the most politically feasible work-sharing schemes have three main features. First, they meet other objectives as well as unemployment reduction. Second, they enable employers to retain competitiveness, and employees to maintain living standards, via state provision of economic incentives. Finally, they have a good fiscal fit with the rest of the welfare state, in that their design involves obvious offsetting savings elsewhere and/or a transfer of costs onto politically weak institutions.

NOTE

1   For reviews of recent literature on policymaking theory see, for example, Burch and Wood (1983), chapter 1; Krasner 1984; Koeble 1995; Pontusson 1995.

REFERENCES

Aznar, Guy (1993) *Travailler moins pour travailler tous* (Paris, Syros).

Castles, F.G., (1993) (ed.) *Families of Nations: Patterns of Public Policy in Western Democracies* (Aldershot: Dartmouth).

—— (1994), 'On religion and public policy: does catholicism make a difference?', *European Journal of Political Research* 25(1).

Bosch, Gerhard (1994) *Flexibility and Work Organisation: Report of Expert Working Group* (Brussels, DGV).

Burch, Malcolm, and Wood, Bruce (1983) *Public Policy in Britain* (Oxford: Martin Robertson).

CEC (Commission of the European Communities)(1993), 'Growth, Competitiveness, Employment: The Challenges and Ways Forward into the 21st Century', *Bulletin of the European Communities*, Supplement 6/93.

—— (1994a) *Employment in Europe 1994* (Brussels, DGV).

—— (1994b) *Seminar of Social Partners on Competitiveness, Productivity and Employment, Brussels, 12–13 April 1994: Note from the Commission Services*, 2/230/94 (Brussels, DGII).

—— (1995) 'Competitiveness, Productivity and Employment', *European Economy*, 59.

Compston, Hugh (1994) 'Union participation in economic policy-making in Austria, Switzerland, the Netherlands, Belgium and Ireland, 1970–1992', *West European Politics*, 17(1).

—— (1995a) 'Union participation in economic policy-making in Scandinavia, 1970–1992', *West European Politics*, 18(1).

—— (1995b) 'Union participation in economic policy-making in France, Italy, Germany and Britain, 1970–1993', *West European Politics*, 18(2).

Financial Times.

Haas, Peter M. (1992) 'Introduction: epistemic communities and international policy coordination', *International Organization*, 46(1).

Hibbs, D. (1977) 'Political parties and macroeconomic policy', *American Political Science Review*, 71.

International Labour Organisation (1994) *Yearbook of Labour Statistics* (Geneva: ILO).

Katzenstein, Peter (1985) *Small States in World Markets* (New York: Cornell University Press).

Kitschelt, Herbert P. (1986) 'Political opportunity structures and political protest: anti-nuclear movements in four democracies', *British Journal of Political Studies*, 16.

Koeble, Thomas A. (1995) 'The new institutionalism in political science and sociology', *Comparative Politics*, 27(2).

Krasner, Stephen D. (1984) 'Approaches to the state: alternative conceptions and historical dynamics', *Comparative Politics*, 16.

Layard, Richard, Nickell, Stephen and Jackman, Richard (1991) *Unemployment: Macroeconomic Performance and the Labour Market* (Oxford: Oxford University Press).

Lindblom, C. (1959) 'The science of "muddling through"', *Public Administration Review*, 19.

—— (1979) 'Still muddling, not yet through', *Public Administration Review*, 39.

Pontusson, Jonas (1995) 'From comparative public policy to political economy: putting political institutions in their place and taking interests seriously', *Comparative Political Studies*, 28(1).

Richardson, J. (1982) (ed.) *Policy Styles in Western Europe* (London: Allen and Unwin).

Sabatier, Paul A. (1987) 'Knowledge, policy-oriented learning, and policy change: an advocacy coalition framework', *Knowledge: Creation, Diffusion, Utilization*, 8(4).

Visser, Jelle (1991) 'Trends in trade union membership', *OECD Employment Outlook*, (July).

Index

ABM *see* job creation, Germany
Abreu, O. 111, 117
Adamy, W. 24
Agence pour l'Emploi des Cadres
    (APEC, France) 48
Allais, Maurice 53
Alvarez Aledo, C. 117
ANBA 23
Arbeit und Recht 29
Arthur, B.W. 80
Artus, P. 57
Associations for Employment in
    Industry and Commerce
    (ASSEDIC, France) 49
Atkinson, A.B. 137
Aubry, M. 49, 57
Aznar, G. 57-8, 59, 60–1, 63, 66, 76,
    193

Bach, H.-U. 26
Bagguley, P. 95
Balladur, E. 56, 57
Bandemer, S. von 42
Banham, J. 95
Basedow, J. 35
Bastian, Jens 12
Beharell, A. 91
Bentivoglio, M. 72, 76
Bentolila, S. 115, 117, 118
Berlusconi, S. 68, 75
Blaas, W. 172, 174–6
Blancke, Susanne 21–46
Blank, Kermit 168–87
Blyton, P. 106, 115
Boissard, D. 47, 57
Bon, Michel 49, 54
Borrie Commission on Social Justice
    (Britain) 99
Bosch, G. 14, 18, 31, 32, 33, 34

Britain 87–102; deregulation of
    employment law 91, 96;
    employers' incentives 91–2, 99;
    institutional framework 95; local
    interventionism 92–3; mainstream
    unemployment policies 89; part-
    time workers' assistance 93;
    policy constraints 97; radical
    measures, piloting 99–100;
    training policy 95–7; unemploy-
    ment as political issue 94–5;
    unemployment benefits, replaced
    90; unemployment rates in 88;
    work experience schemes 95–6;
    work-sharing 97–9; Workstart
    Scheme 92
Brittan, S. 131
Bruche, G. 38
Brunhes, Bernard 59, 60, 65
Bulletin of the European
    Communities 7
Bulletin of the European Union 11
Burchell, B. 98
Bushell, R. 119

CASA (Denmark) 138
Cassa Integrazione Guadagni
    (Cig, Italy) 70, 72, 73, 74, 76, 79,
    82
Castles, F.G. 195
Catholicism and solidarity agreements
    207
Central Bureau of Statistics (Norway)
    146–7, 149, 154, 159, 164
Central Federation of Swiss
    Employers' Organisations (ZSA)
    170
Chirac, Jacques 48, 51, 53, 55, 56, 65,
    66

Christian People's Party (CVP,
    Switzerland) 171, 183
Ciampi, C. 75, 79
citizen's income, Denmark 126, 130–1;
    moral aspects 138–40; origins
    136–8; outlook for 143–4;
    political settings 138–40
City Challenge Grant scheme
    (Britain) 92
Clarke, Kenneth 12
CNG (trade union, Switzerland) 171,
    185, 200
Cohen, Leonard 44
collective bargaining: France 63;
    Germany 24, 39–41; Italy 75
Commission for Social Justice 99
Commission of the European
    Communities (CEC) 7, 192, 203;
    and France 50; and investment in
    infrastructure 7, 8–9; and new
    areas of work 10; working time
    reductions 11–14
Community Programme (Britain) 95
Companies for Labour Promotion,
    Employment and Structural
    Development (ABS, Germany)
    32, 35
company lay-offs, France 56–7
Compston, Hugh 1–20, 184, 188–213
concertation: Germany 31–2, 190; Italy
    76–7, 190; Norway 151–2, 190,
    191; in Western Europe 190, 191,
    202
Confederación Española de la
    Pequeña y Mediana Empresa
    (CEYPME) 105
Confederación Española de
    Organizaciones Empresariales
    (CEOE) 105, 106, 114, 116
Confederación Sindical de Comisiones
    Obreras (CCOO, Spain) 105, 114,
    115, 116
Confédération Française
    Démocratique du Travail
    (CFDT) 55, 60, 63, 64, 200
Confédération Générale du Travail
    (CGT, France) 59–60, 64
Confederation of British Industry
    (CBI) 14, 95, 202
Confindustria (Italy) 73
Conseil National du Patronat Français
    (CNPF) 55, 57, 58, 64
contract labour: Germany 33–4; Spain
    107–8

Contract Labour Act (Germany) 33
Coriat, B. 53
Costa, C. 111, 117
Crewe, I. 87
Cripps, F. 98
Csonka, A. 132n, 142
Cuevas, J.M. 112, 116

D'Aloia, G. 77
Dansk Arbejdsgiverforening
    (Denmark) 140
Danthine, J.P. 172, 174
de la Hoz, J.M. 105, 115
Delors, Jacques 13, 15
demand management strategies,
    Germany 24
Denmark
    citizen's income 126, 130–1; moral
        aspects 138–40; origins 136–8;
        outlook for 143–4; political
        settings 138–40
    expenditure on labour market
        policy 125
    paid leave arrangements 126,
        127–30, 131–6, 193, 200–1; costs
        and benefits 132; employees'
        barriers 140–1; employers'
        attitudes 133; employers' barriers
        141–2; at individual level 132–3;
        job rotation in 128, 130; and
        labour market 133–4; in long run
        142–3; number granted 129;
        outlook for 140; and public
        sector 134–5; at societal level 135
    self-employment in 124
    unemployment rates in 124
    vocational training 124–5
    work-sharing 126
    working time reduction 126
Department of Employment (Britain)
    89, 96
Deregulation and Contracting Out
    Act (Britain, 1994) 91
deregulation of employment: beliefs
    and values in 204, 205; Britain
    91, 96, 197; Germany 28–9, 197;
    Italy 73–5, 197; and political bias
    of government 205; self-interest
    in 196–7; Spain 106–9, 197;
    Western Europe 189–91
Det Okonomiske Rad (Denmark)
    140
Die Volkwirtschaft 176
Dini, L. 75

dismissals regulations, Spain 108–9
distributive policies, Germany 36–7; in
    East Germany 41–2; local
    cooperation 42–3, 201
Dolado, J.J. 103, 110, 115, 117, 118,
    119, 120
Drèze, J. 65, 120
Driver, C. 94, 98

early retirement: France 57–8;
    Germany 23, 24; Italy 71, 74, 80;
    Spain 110–11
Ecofin 8, 12, 13, 17, 192
Economic and Social Agreement
    (Spain) 114
economic beliefs and values in
    unemployment policy 202–7
    on deregulation 204, 205
    part-time employment 205
    work-sharing 204–6; at firm level
    206–7
Edinburgh Growth Initiative (1992) 4,
    8
Elster, J. 44
employees, working time reductions
    14
employers: incentives, Britain
    91–2, 99; and working time
    reductions 11
Employers' Association (NHO,
    Norway) 146–7, 151, 155, 157,
    159, 164–6
Employment Initiative Contract,
    France 51, 52
Employment News 90, 91, 93
Employment Promotion Programmes
    (Spain) 112–13
Employment Protection Acts (Britain,
    1975, 1980) 91
Employment Training Scheme
    (Britain) 95
Engelen-Kefer, U. 35
Engineering Employers Federation
    (Britain) 92
Esping-Andersen, G. 139
Estivill, J. 105, 115
European 9, 12
European Council 8, 9, 10, 13, 15
European Council Resolution 21 3
European Economy 68
European Industrial Relations Review
    (EIRR) (Spain) 109, 110, 111,
    112, 116, 118
European Parliament 9, 11

European Trade Union Confederation
    (ETUC) 11, 16
European Trade Union Institute
    (ETUI) 11
European Union 6–20; radical
    unemployment policies of 8–13
Evans, B. 96
External Services for Work and
    Employment (SETE, France) 48

Farnham, D. 89, 96
Federal Labour Office (BA, Germany)
    23–4, 26, 27, 31, 201
Federal Ministry of Labour
    (Germany) 23
Federal Office for Industry,
    Commerce and Labour
    (Switzerland) 179
Federal Organisation of Employer
    Associations (Germany) 28
Federation of German Trade Unions
    29
Federation of Swiss Industry (Vorort)
    170
female employment: Norway 157;
    Switzerland 174–5
Ferrera, M. 69
Fiat 78–80, 82, 193
Fina, L. 114, 115
Financial Times 9, 11, 12, 13, 14, 92,
    93, 202
financing unemployment policies,
    Germany 37–9
Flechsenhar, H.R. 178
Flynn, Commissioner P. 11, 13
Force Ouvrière (France) 64
foreign workers in Switzerland 174–5,
    176–7, 181
Forsyth, M. 91
Foundation for Vocational Training
    (FORCEM, Spain) 112
France 47–67; collective bargaining 63;
    company lay-offs 56–7; early
    retirement 57–8; immigrants,
    repatriation 53–4; institutional
    framework 48–9; job creation 55,
    56; part-time employment 59, 63;
    personal services 55–6; recent
    developments 50–2; shift working
    63; solidarity agreements 57–8,
    193, 198–9; subsidies in 51; trade
    unions in 63–4; unemployment
    benefits 49–50; unemployment
    rates in 51; vocational training in

52–3; work-sharing 59–62;
workfare 54–5; working time
reduction in 50, 59–62, 63
Franco, Francisco 107, 113, 115
Frankl, B. 136
Franks, J.R. 117
Freddi, G. 81

Gandois, Jean 57
García Perea, P. 109, 119
Gattaz, Yvon 56
GEPI (special fund, Italy) 71
German reunification 41–2
Germany
    collective bargaining 24, 39–41
    distributive policies 36–7; in East
        Germany 41–2; local cooperation
        42–3, 201
    institutional reform 34–6
    job creation policies 22, 24, 29, 30,
        35, 38
    part-time employment 29, 192
    redistributive policies 36–7; collec-
        tive bargaining 39–41; financing
        37–9
    regulative policies: in East
        Germany 41–2; financing,
        shunting yard 37–9
    self-regulative policies 39–41;
        collective bargaining 39–41; local
        cooperation 42–3, 201
    short-time employment 193
    solidarity agreements 26–8, 198–9
    unemployment rates in 22–3
    working time flexibility 28–9
    working time reduction 25–9, 192;
        flexibility of 28–9, 189; industry-
        wide 25–6; part-time employment
        29; temporary 26–8
Gillespie, R. 115, 116
Giraud, Michel 59
Giugni, Gino 79
Glynn, S. 87, 94
Godet, Michel 54
Gómez, R. 109, 119
González, Felipe 118
Gorz, André 55, 59, 60, 66
Goul Andersen, J. 137–8, 143
Granados Cabezas, V. 113
Granovetter, M. 70
Grant, W. 94
Graziano, L. 69
Grieve-Smith, J. 100
Grossen, G. 172

Grubb, D. 111
Gualmini, Elisabetta 68–86
Guardian 9, 11, 12, 13, 15

Haas, P.M. 73, 84, 194
Hall, P. 80, 182
Handelsblatt 28
Hansard 90, 91, 96
Haskell, J. 96
Heath, Edward 87
Heinrich Landert Corporation 180–1
Henley, A. 96
Héritier, Pierre 55
Hibbs, D. 195
Hohn, H.W. 39
Holland, Stuart 13

Il Sole 24 ore 73
Immergut, E. 183
immigrants repatriation, France 53–4
Independent 9, 12
Industrial Training Boards (Britain) 89
inflation: Spain 114; and working time
    reductions 14–15
infrastructure, investment in 8–9
Institute for Applied Social Science
    (FAFO, Norway) 156, 159, 163
Institute of Economic Affairs
    (Britain) 96
institutional self-interest 195–201; in
    deregulation 196–7; in part-time
    employment 197–8; in solidarity
    agreements 198–200
International Labour Organisation
    199
investment in infrastructure 8–9
Italy 68–86; collective bargaining 75;
    deregulation of employment
    conditions 73–5; early retirement
    71, 74, 80; hiring procedures
    reform 74; industrial labour
    relations 81–2; innovation,
    obstacles to 82; institutional
    reforms 75–6; mainstream labour
    policies 71; part-time employ-
    ment 72; qualification pro-
    grammes 75–6; solidarity
    agreements 76, 77–8, 80, 82, 193,
    198–9; state intervention 81;
    subsidies 72–3, 80; unemployment
    rates in 69; vocational training
    72, 75; working time reduction
    76–7
iwd 28, 29

Jeanneney, Jean-Marcel 65
Jelved, Marianne 137
Jimeno, J.F. 103, 110, 117, 119, 120
job creation: France 55, 56; Germany
    22, 24, 29, 30, 35, 38; Italy 74;
    and working time reductions 15
Job Release Scheme (Britain) 94
job rotation in paid leave
    arrangements, Denmark 128, 130
jobseekers allowance, Britain 90
Jordan, B. 130
Jospin, Lionel 56, 65
Juppé, Alain 51, 53, 66

Karlsen, T.K. 146–67
Katzenstein, P.J. 170–1, 172, 195
Keller, B. 39, 40
King, D. 89, 97, 101
Kitschelt, H.P. 194
Knuth, M. 31, 32, 33
Kommission für Konjunkturfrage 185
Korpi, W. 182
Krone, S. 33, 43

La Palombara, J. 69
Labbé, Daniel 64
labour charges, cuts in 9
labour costs
    Germany: shunting yard logic 37–9;
        subsidies for 30–1, 41
    Spain 106–7
    unit costs 14
    and working time reductions 15–16
labour market expenditure, Denmark
    125
labour market institutions, Switzerland
    170–2
Labour Party (Norway) 148
Labour Promotion Act (Germany,
    1969) 24, 29–30, 32–4
labour promotion and training in
    Germany 31–3
labour shortages 14
labour supply as policy instrument,
    Switzerland 174–6
Lambelet, J.C. 172, 174
Lange, P. 81
Laroque, M. 49
Law on Equal Wages (Norway) 147
Lawlor, T. 115
Layard, R. 14, 98–9, 203
Le Figaro 54
Le Monde 50, 55, 56, 63, 64
Le Nouvel Economiste 56, 62

Le Pen, Jean-Marie 47, 53
Libération 60
Lindblom, C. 194
Lipietz, Alain 60, 62
LO (Denmark) 140
Local Enterprise Companies
    (Scotland) 89
Loftager, Jørn 123–45
Lowi, T. 36
Lucio, M.M. 105, 106, 115
Lupton, C. 89, 96

MacDonald, D. 160
Madsen, P. Kongshøj 123–45
Magno, M. 77
Malinvaud, E. 65
Manpower Services Commission
    (Britain) 89, 95
March, J.G. 21, 70
Martí, F. 110
Martin, C. 96
Martín, Jesús M. 110
Meinhardt, V. 27
Milner, Susan 47–67
Minimum Income (RMI, France) 50,
    54
Ministries of Labour: Denmark 125;
    France 48, 56, 63; Italy 76, 79
Ministry for Employment and
    Municipal Affairs (Norway)
    156
Ministry of Finance and Customs
    (Norway) 148, 151, 157
Mitterand, François 56, 59
Moncloa Pacts (Spain) 114
monetarist policies, Germany 24
Moore, C. 93
Mouriaux, René 47–67

Nath, S. 94
National Agency for Adult
    Vocational Training (AFPA,
    France) 48–9
National Bureau of Statistics
    (Norway) 159
National Employment Agency
    (ANPE, France) 48–9, 54
National Employment Agency
    (Norway) 146, 150, 151, 153–4
National Institute for Social Insurance
    (Italy) 71
National Labour Market Board
    (Denmark) 125
Nergård, K. 164

Non-Accelerating Inflation Rate of
Unemployment (NAIRU) 14–15,
203
North, D.C. 80
Norway 146–67
austerity policies 151–2
female employment 157
oil, dependence on 149
part-time employment 154
public sector employment 154,
155–6, 161
recent economic developments 149
regulatory regime 148–9
6-hour working day 156–7, 161–2
Solidarity 2000 151
trade union membership 163–4
unemployment, development of
150–1
unemployment benefits 152, 153
unemployment policies: active
152–4; passive 152
unemployment rates in 147
vocational training 152, 153
work sharing 157–60, 161–2, 193
Norwegian Institute for Municipal and
Regional Development Research
155
NOU (Norway) 151

Observatoire Français de la
Conjoncture Économique
(OFCE) 56, 60
Okonomiministeriet (Denmark) 137
Olesen, Aase 138
Olgaard, A. 131
Olsen, J.P. 21, 70
Organization for Economic
Cooperation and Development
(OECD) 170, 181, 182
overtime restrictions, Spain 111–12,
193

Page, E. 100
paid leave arrangements, Denmark
126, 127–30, 131–6, 193, 200–1;
costs and benefits 132; employees' barriers 140–1; employers'
attitudes 133; employers' barriers
141–2; at individual level 132–3;
job rotation in 128, 130; and
labour market 133–4; in long run
142–3; number granted 129;
outlook for 140; and public
sector 134–5; at societal level 135

Panduro, B. 137
partial retirement, France 58
part-time employment 192; beliefs and
values in 205; Britain 93; France
59, 63; Germany 29; Italy 72;
Norway 154; and political bias of
government 205; self-interest in
197–8; Spain 111
Party of European Socialists 11, 16
Pedersen, P.J. 138
Pérez-Díaz, V.M. 70, 114
personal services, France 55–6
Philpott, J. 98
Plan for Economic Convergence
(Spain) 109
Polanyi, K. 68
Prodi, Romano 83
Propuesta Sindical Prioritaria (Spain)
116
Public Employment Office (Spain) 112
public sector employment, Norway
154, 155–6, 161
Puig, J.E. 112

radical unemployment policy: defined
3–4; in European Union 8–13,
189–94; political dynamics of
207–8; *see also* individual policies
in each country
Ramaux, C. 64
Raoult, Eric 54
Rapporto 72, 75
Rasmussen, Poul 135
redistributive policies, Germany 36–7;
collective bargaining 39–41;
financing 37–9
redundancies, Spain 108–9
Regalia, I. 70–1, 73, 81
Regini, M. 73, 81
Regonini, G. 73
regulative policies, Germany: in East
Germany 41–2; financing,
shunting yard 37–9
regulatory regime, Norway 148–9
Reissert, B. 38
Reyneri, E. 82
Rhodes, Martin 72, 103–22
Richardson, J. 93, 194
Rigaudiat, J. 18
Rigby, M. 115
Rodriquez, J.C. 70
Rojo Torrecilla, E. 104
Rokkan, S. 165
Rosdücher, J. 27

Rose, R. 73, 100
Rueff, J. 47

Sabatier, P.A. 194
Saint-Paul, G. 118
Salaverria, J.M. 119
Salisbury, R.H. 36
Sanz, J.J. 112
Schaad, J. 180
Schellenbauer, P. 180
Schmid, H. 173
Schmidt, G. 24, 38
Schmidt, M.G. 172–4, 179, 181
Schreiner, O. 29
Schweizerische Bankgesellschaft
    170
Scottish Development Agency 93
Sebastián, C. 120
secondary labour markets in Germany
    29–34; contract labour 33–4;
    labour cost subsidies 30–1; labour
    promotion and training 31–3
Séguin, Phillippe 55–6, 65, 66
Seifert, H. 26, 27
self-employment, Denmark 124
self-regulative policies, Germany:
    collective bargaining 39–41; local
    cooperation 42–3, 201
shift working, France 63
short-time employment 192–3;
    Germany 22, 24; Switzerland
    177–81; Western Europe 192
Snower, D. 100, 120
social closure logic of collective
    bargaining, Germany 39–41
Social Democratic Party (SP,
    Switzerland) 171, 183, 184–5
social pact, Europe-wide 10
social plan, France 57
Solchaga, C. 109, 117
Solidaristic and Flexible part-time
    work (SOFLEX, Switzerland)
    180–1
Solidarity 2000 (Norway) 151
solidarity agreements: Catholicism and
    207; France 57–8, 198; Germany
    26–8, 198–9; Italy 76, 77–8, 80,
    82, 198; self-interest in 198–200;
    Western Europe 193
Soskice, D. 70
Spain 103–22; contract labour 107–8;
    deregulation of employment
    106–9; dismissals regulations
    108–9; early retirement 110–11;

employment policy decentralisa-
    tion 112–13; incentives of
    unemployed 109–10; institutional
    reform 112–13; labour costs
    106–7; overtime restrictions
    111–12, 193; part-time employ-
    ment 111, 192; redundancies
    108–9; shorter standard working
    hours 112; unemployment rates
    in 104; working time reduction
    110–12
Spitznagel, E. 26
START Contract Labour Co.
    (Germany) 33–4
Steinmo, S. 70
Stöbe, S. 42
Stokke, T. 163
Streeck, W. 70
subsidies: in France 51; in Germany
    30–1, 41; in Italy 72–3, 80
Swiss Trade Union Federation (SGB)
    171, 185–6
Switzerland 168–87; female employ-
    ment 174–5; foreign workers in
    174–5, 176–7, 181; labour market
    institutions 170–2; labour supply
    as policy instrument 174–6;
    policy innovation 182–4;
    short-time employment 177–81,
    192–3; trade unions 170–1;
    unemployment insurance 173–4,
    181; unemployment policy 172–3;
    unemployment rates 169

Taddéi, Dominique 59, 63, 65
Temporary Short-time Working
    Compensation Scheme (Britain)
    97
Thatcher, Margaret 88
The Times 96
Toharia, L. 107, 110, 117
Tonge, Jonathan 87–102
Trade Union and Employment Rights
    Act (Britain, 1993) 91
Trade Union Confederation
    (LO, Norway) 146–51, 155, 157,
    160, 162–3, 165–6
trade unions: and deregulation
    initiatives 197; France 58, 63;
    membership, Norway 163–4; and
    part-time work 198; Spain
    115–17; Switzerland 170–1; on
    work-sharing, Britain 98; and
    working time reductions 11

Trades Union Congress (Britain) 95, 97
Training and Enterprise Councils (TECs, Britain) 89, 92, 93, 95–7, 99–100, 101
Training Commission (Britain) 89, 93, 95
Training for Work programme (Britain) 97
training *see* vocational training
transaction cost theory of employment policy 36–7
Trans-European Network 8
Treu, T. 75, 77
Tsakalotos, E. 96

unemployment benefits: Britain, replaced 90; France 49–50; Germany 30–1; Norway 152, 153
unemployment insurance: Germany 23; Switzerland 173–4, 181
unemployment rates: Britain 88; Denmark 124; France 51; Germany 22–3; Italy 69; Norway 147; Spain 104; Switzerland 169
Union for Employment in Industry and Commerce (UNEDIC, France) 49–50, 58, 64
Unión General de Trabajadores (UGT, Spain) 105, 115, 116
Union Participation Index 197, 200

Viby Mogensen, G. 137–8
Vittori, J.–M. 47, 57
vocational training: policy, Britain 95–7; Denmark 124–5; France 52–3; Germany 24, 31–3; Italy 72, 75; Norway 152, 153
Volkswagen Company 26–7, 193
VSA (trade union, Switzerland) 171

Wagner, A. 33
Walter, T. 130, 131
Walwei, U. 35
Ward, T. 98
Webb, S. 131
Weick, K.E. 83
Weinkopf, C. 33, 43
Wells, J. 100
Wells, W. 111
Widmaier, Ulrich 21–46
Wiesenthal, H. 40
Williamson, O.E. 36
work, new areas of 10
work-sharing 11, 13, 17
    beliefs and values in 204–5; at firm level 206–7
    Britain 97–9
    Denmark 126
    France 59–62
    Norway 157–60, 161–2
    and political bias of government 206
    rejection of 14–17
    in Western Europe 190, 191–4
Workers' Statute: Italy 75, 79; Spain 105, 107–8
workfare, France 54–5
working time flexibility 190; in Germany 28–9
working time reduction 10–13
    Denmark 126
    France 50, 59–62, 63
    Germany 25–9, 192; flexibility of 28–9, 189; industry-wide 25–6; part-time employment 29; temporary 26–8
    Italy 76–7
    rejection of 14–17
    Spain 110–12
Western Europe 192
Workstart Scheme, Britain 92

Youth Guarantee (Norway) 152–3